Anonymous

The Record of the Royal Society of London, 1897

Anonymous

The Record of the Royal Society of London, 1897

ISBN/EAN: 9783337070328

Printed in Europe, USA, Canada, Australia, Japan

Cover: Foto ©ninafisch / pixelio.de

More available books at **www.hansebooks.com**

THE RECORD

OF THE

ROYAL SOCIETY OF LONDON.

1897.

LONDON:
HARRISON AND SONS, ST. MARTIN'S LANE,
Printers in Ordinary to Her Majesty.
1897.

No. 1.

LONDON:
HARRISON AND SONS, PRINTERS IN ORDINARY TO HER MAJESTY,
ST. MARTIN'S LANE.

PREFACE.

The present volume may be regarded as the complement of the 'Year-book' published a few months ago. The information contained in the 'Year-book' is liable to change, and it is proposed to issue a fresh edition of this every year as soon after the Anniversary Meeting as possible. The present volume, which we have called 'The Record,' contains information, largely historical, such as will not need more than slight additions from time to time; it is proposed to issue a new edition of this every few years, according as it may be found desirable.

We very gladly take this opportunity of acknowledging the very great assistance given to us in the preparation both of this volume and of the 'Year-book' by Mr. H. Rix, the late Assistant-Secretary of the Society.

M. Foster,
A. W. Rücker, } *Secs. R.S.*

CONTENTS.

	PAGE
Some Account of the Foundation and Early History of the Royal Society	1
Charta Prima, Præsidi, Concilio, et Sodalibus Regalis Societatis Londini, à Rege Carolo Secundo concessa	19
First Charter, granted to the President, Council, and Fellows of the Royal Society of London, by King Charles the Second	31
Charta Secunda, Iisdem ab Eodem concessa	44
Second Charter, granted to the same by the same	58
Charta Tertia, Iisdem ab Eodem concessa	73
Third Charter, granted to the same by the same	85
A License for Purchasing in Mortmain to the yearly value of One Thousand Pounds, granted by King George the First	97
A Note on the History of the Statutes of the Society—	
The First Statutes	100
The Statutes from 1663 to 1752	100
The Statutes from 1752 to 1776	105
The Statutes from 1776 to 1847	111
The Changes from 1847 to 1888	113
Benefactors of the Society	115
The Trusts of the Royal Society	120
Institutions upon which the Royal Society is represented	135
Other Public Functions performed by the Royal Society	136
Description of the Kew Observatory	137
The Botanic Gardens, Chelsea, formerly known as "The Physick Garden"	153
The Lawes Agricultural Trust	155
History of the Government Grant for Scientific Investigations—	
I. "Government Grant" of £1000 a year	158
II. "Government Fund" of £4000 a year and "Government Grant" of £1000 a year	159
III. "Government Grant" of £4000 a year	161
The Publications of the Royal Society	164
The 'Philosophical Transactions'	164
The 'Proceedings of the Royal Society'	165
Catalogue of Scientific Papers	166

CONTENTS.

	PAGE
The Library	168
Instruments and Historical Relics in the Possession of the Royal Society	171
List of Portraits and Busts in the Apartments of the Society	175
Catalogue of the Medals in the Possession of the Society	183
Presidents of the Royal Society	205
Treasurers of the Royal Society	211
Secretaries of the Royal Society	211
Foreign Secretaries of the Royal Society	213
Names of Persons to whom the Medals of the Royal Society have been awarded—	
Copley Medal	214
Rumford Medal	216
Royal Medal	216
Davy Medal	218
Darwin Medal	218

LIST OF ILLUSTRATIONS.

	PAGE
Plate 1. Portraits of Lord Brouncker, P.R.S., Sir Joseph Williamson, P.R.S., Sir Christopher Wren, P.R.S., and Sir John Hoskins, P.R.S. .... to face p.	10
Plate 2. Portraits of Samuel Pepys, P.R.S., the Earl of Carbery, P.R.S., Henry Oldenburg, Sec. R.S., and the Hon. Robert Boyle, F.R.S. .... to face p.	18
Arms of the Royal Society..	14
Seal of the Royal Society..	99
The Rumford Medal	122
The Copley Medal..	124
The Davy Medal..	127
The Darwin Medal	130
The Buchanan Medal	132
The Royal Medal..	133
View of Kew Observatory in 1891..	138
Kew Observatory. Plan 1..	140
,, Plan 2..	145
Sir Isaac Newton's Reflecting Telescope	172

RECORD

OF

THE ROYAL SOCIETY.

SOME ACCOUNT OF THE FOUNDATION AND EARLY HISTORY OF THE ROYAL SOCIETY.

The "first ground and foundation of the Royal Society" is given by Wallis* as follows:—

"About the year 1645, while I lived in London (at a time when, by our civil wars, academical studies were much interrupted in both our Universities), beside the conversation of divers eminent divines, as to matters theological, I had the opportunity of being acquainted with divers worthy persons, inquisitive into natural philosophy, and other parts of human learning; and particularly of what hath been called the *New Philosophy* or *Experimental Philosophy*. We did by agreements, divers of us, meet weekly in London on a certain day [and hour, under a certain penalty, and a weekly contribution for the charge of experiments, with certain rules agreed upon amongst us],† to treat and discourse of such affairs; of which number were *Dr. John Wilkins* (afterwards *Bishop of Chester* [then chaplain to the Prince Elector Palatine, in London]), *Dr. Jonathan Goddard, Dr. George Ent, Dr. Glisson, Dr. Merret* (Drs. in Physick), *Mr. Samuel Foster*, then Professor of Astronomy at Gresham College, *Mr. Theodore Haak*‡ (a German of the Palatinate, and then resident in London, who, I think, gave the first occasion, and first suggested those meetings), and many others.

"These meetings we held sometimes at *Dr. Goddard's* lodgings in *Wood Street* (or some convenient place near), on occasion of his keep-

* Dr. John Wallis, mathematician, b. 1616, d. 1703. The passage quoted is from his letter to Dr. Thomas Smith, dated January 29, 1696-7, published in Thomas Hearne's Appendix to his preface to 'Peter Langtoft's Chronicle,' vol. 1, p. 161, edit. London, 1725.

† The passages in square brackets are taken from Wallis's 'A Defence of the Royal Society,' 1678.

‡ Misprinted *Hank*.

B

ing an operator in his house for grinding glasses for telescopes and microscopes; sometimes at a convenient place [The Bull Head] in *Cheapside*, and [in term-time] at Gresham College [at Mr. Foster's lecture (then Astronomer Professor there), and, after the lecture ended, repaired, sometimes to Mr. Foster's lodgings, sometimes to some other place not far distant].

"Our business was (precluding matters of theology and state affairs) to discourse and consider of *Philosophical Enquiries*, and such as related thereunto: as *Physick, Anatomy, Geometry, Astronomy, Navigation, Staticks, Magneticks, Chymicks, Mechanicks*, and natural *Experiments*; with the state of these studies, as then cultivated at home and abroad. We then discoursed of the *circulation of the blood, the valves in the veins, the venæ lacteæ, the lymphatick vessels, the Copernican hypothesis, the nature of comets and new stars, the satellites of Jupiter, the oval shape (as it then appeared) of Saturn, the spots in the sun, and its turning on its own axis, the inequalities and selenography of the Moon, the several phases of Venus and Mercury, the improvement of telescopes, and grinding of glasses for that purpose, the weight of air, the possibility or impossibility of vacuities and Nature's abhorrence thereof, the Torricellian experiment in quicksilver*, the *descent of heavy bodies*, and the degrees of *acceleration therein*; and divers other things of like nature. Some of which were then but new discoveries, and others not so generally known and embraced as now they are, with other things appertaining to what hath been called *The New Philosophy*, which from the times of *Galileo* at *Florence*, and *Sir Francis Bacon (Lord Verulam)* in England, hath been much cultivated in *Italy, France, Germany*, and other parts abroad, as well as with us in *England*.

"About the year 1648, 1649, some of our company being removed to Oxford (first *Dr. Wilkins*, then I, and soon after Dr. Goddard) our company divided. Those in London continued to meet there as before (and we with them, when we had occasion to be there), and those of us at Oxford, with *Dr. Ward* (since *Bishop of Salisbury*), *Dr. Ralph Bathurst* (now *President of Trinity College in Oxford*), *Dr. Petty* (since Sir William Petty), *Dr. Willis* (then an eminent physician in *Oxford*), and divers others, continued such meetings in Oxford, and brought these studies into fashion there; meeting first at Dr. Petty's lodgings (in an apothecarie's house), because of the convenience of inspecting drugs, and the like, as there was occasion; and after his remove to Ireland (though not so constantly) at the lodgings of *Dr. Wilkins*, then Warden of Wadham College, and after his removal to *Trinity College in Cambridge*, at the lodgings of the *Honourable Mr. Robert Boyle*, then resident for divers years in Oxford."

It is to this private Society, meeting partly in London, partly at Oxford, that Boyle most probably refers when, in his letters to Mons. Marcombes (October 22, 1646), to Francis Tallents (February 20,

1646–47), and to Samuel Hartlib (May 8, 1647), he speaks of "The Invisible College."*

The Oxford Society became in 1651 the Philosophical Society of Oxford, of which meetings continued to be held at irregular intervals until 1690 when they ceased. The London Society continued to meet until about the year 1658, "usually at Gresham College, at the Wednesday's and Thursday's lectures of Dr. Wren and Mr. Rook, where there joined with them several eminent persons of their common acquaintance: The *Lord Viscount Brouncker*, the now *Lord Brereton, Sir Paul Neil, Mr. John Evelyn, Mr. Henshaw, Mr. Slingsby, Dr. Timothy Clarke, Dr. Ent, Mr. Ball, Mr. Hill, Dr. Crone*, and diverse other gentlemen, whose inclinations lay the same way. This custom was observed once, if not twice, a week in term-time; till they were scattered by the miserable distractions of that fatal year; till the continuance of their meetings there might have made them run the hazard of the fate of *Archimedes:* for then the place of their meeting was made a *quarter for soldiers*."†

In 1660 the meetings at Gresham College were revived, and on the 28th November in that year the first Journal-book of the Society was opened with the following entry :—

"Memorandum that Novemb. 28, 1660, These persons following, according to the usuall custom of most of them, mett together at Gresham Colledge to heare Mr. Wren's lecture, viz. The Lord Brouncker, Mr. Boyle, Mr. Bruce, Sir Robert Moray, Sir Paul Neile, Dr. Wilkins, Dr. Goddard, Dr. Petty, Mr. Ball, Mr. Rooke, Mr. Wren, Mr. Hill. And after the lecture was ended, they did, according to the usual manner, withdrawe for mutuall converse. Where amongst other matters that were discoursed of, something was offered about a designe of founding a Colledge for the promoting of Physico-Mathematicall Experimentall Learning. And because they had these frequent occasions of meeting with one another, it was proposed that some course might be thought of, to improve this meeting to a more regular way of debating things, and according to the manner in other countryes, where there were voluntary associations of men in academies, for the advancement of various parts of learning, so they might doe something answerable here for the promoting of experimentall philosophy.

"In order to which, it was agreed that this Company would continue their weekly meeting on Wednesday, at 3 of the clock in the tearme time, at Mr. Rooke's chamber at Gresham Colledge; in the vacation, at Mr. Ball's chamber in the Temple. And towards the defraying of occasionall expenses, every one should, at his first ad-

* Sprat's 'Life of the Honourable Robert Boyle,' prefixed to Boyle's 'Works,' folio, London, 1744, pp. 17, 20, 24.

† Sprat's 'History of the Royal Society' (1734), p. 57.

mission, pay downe ten shillings, and besides engage to pay one shilling weekly, whether present or absent, whilest he shall please to keep his relation to this Company. At this Meeting Dr. Wilkins was appointed to the chaire, Mr. Ball to be Treasurer, and Mr. Croone, though absent, was named for Register.

"And to the end that they might the better be enabled to make a conjecture of how many the elected number of this Society should consist, therefore it was desired that a list might be taken of the names of such persons as were known to those present, whom they judged willing and fit to joyne with them in their designe, who, if they should desire it, might be admitted before any other."*

Upon which this following Catalogue was offered:

Lord Hatton.	Mr. Povey.	Dr. Coxe.
Mr. Robert Boyle.	Mr. Wilde.	Dr. Merrett.
Mr. Jones.	Dr. Baines.	Dr. Whistler.
Mr. Coventry.	Dr. Wren.	Dr. Clarke.
Mr. Brereton.	Mr. Smith.	Dr. Bathurst.
Sir Kenelme Digby.	Mr. Ashmole.	Dr. Cowley.†
Sir Ant. Morgan.	Mr. Newburg.	Dr. Willis.
Mr. John Vaughan.	Dr. Ward.	Dr. Henshaw.
Mr. Evelyn.	Dr. Wallis.	Dr. Ffinch.
Mr. Rawlins.	Dr. Glisson.	Mr. Austen.
Mr. Matthew Wren.	Dr. Bates.	Mr. Oldenburg.
Mr. Slingsby.	Dr. Ent.	Mr. Pett.
Mr. Henshaw.	Dr. Scarburgh.	Mr. Croone.
Mr. Denham.	Dr. Phrasier.	

On the following Wednesday, being the 5th December, a Meeting was held, of which the following is recorded in the Journal-book:—

"Sir Robert Moray brought in word from the court, that the King had been acquainted with the designe of this Meeting. And he did well approve of it, and would be ready to give encouragement to it."

"It was ordered that Mr. Wren be desired to prepare against the next meeting for the Pendulum Experiment.

"That Mr. Croone be desired to looke out for some discreet person skilled in short-hand writing, to be an amanuensis.

"It was then agreed that the number be not increased, but by consent of the Society who have already subscribed their names: till such time as the orders for the constitution be settled.

"That any three or more of this company (whose occasions will permit them,) are desired to meete as a Committee, at 3 of the

---

* 'Journal-book,' vol. 1, p. 1.
† He had been created M.D. at Oxford, Dec. 2, 1657. Wood, 'Fas. Oxon.'

clock on Fryday, to consult about such orders in reference to the constitution, as they shall think fitt to offer to the whole company, and so to adjourne *de die in diem.*"

Under the above date of the 5th Dec. 1660, the first page of the Journal-book contains the following obligation:—

"Wee whose names are underwritten, doe consent and agree that wee will meet together weekely (if not hindered by necessary occasions), to consult and debate concerning the promoting of experimentall learning. And that each of us will allowe one shilling weekely, towards the defraying of occasionall charges. Provided that if any one or more of us shall thinke fitt at any time to withdrawe, he or they shall, after notice thereof given to the Company at a meeting, be freed from this obligation for the future."

To this are attached the signatures of all those persons comprised in the Catalogue of names prepared at the meeting on the 28th of November, as also of seventy-three others, who were subsequently elected into the Society, as may be seen in the Journal-book.

On the 12th December another Meeting was held. The following is the entry in the Journal-book :—

"It was referred to my Lord Brouncker, Sir Robert Moray, Sir Paul Neil, Mr. Matthew Wren, Dr. Goddard, and Mr. Christopher Wren, to consult about a convenient place for the weekly meeting of the Society.

"It was then voted that no person shall be admitted into the Society without scrutiny, excepting only such as are of the degree of Barons or above.

"Sir Kenelme Digby, Mr. Austen, and Dr. Bates, were then by vote chosen into the Society.

"That the stated number of this Society be five and fifty. That twenty-one of the stated number of this Society be the *quorum* for Elections.

"That any person of the degree of Baron or above may be admitted as supernumerarys, if they shall desire it, and will conforme themselves to such orders as are or shall be established.

"Whereas it was suggested at the Committee that the Colledge of Physitians would afford convenient accommodation for the meeting of this Society; uppon supposition that it be graunted and accepted of, it was thought reasonable, that any of the Followes of the said Colledge, if they shall desire it, be likewise admitted as Supernumerarys, they submitting to the Lawes of the Society, both as to the pay at their admission, and the weekly allowance; as likewise the particular works or tasks that may be allotted to them.

"That the Publick Professors of Mathematicks, Physick, and Naturall Philosophy, of both Universitys, have the same priviledge with the Colledge of Physitians, they paying as others at their admission, and contributing their weekely allowance and assistance, when their occasions do permitt them to be in London.

"That the *quorum* of this Society be nine for all matters excepting the Businesse of Elections.

"*Concerning the Manner of Elections.*

"That no man shall be elected the same day he is proposed. That at the least twenty-one shall be present at each election.

"That the Amanuensis doe provide severall little scroles of paper of an equall length and breadth, in number double to the Society present. One halfe of them shall be marked with a crosse, and being roled up shall be lay'd in a heap on the table, the other halfe shall be marked with cyphers, and being roled up shall be lay'd in another heap. Every person coming in his order shall take from each heap a role, and throwe which he please privately into an urne, and the other into a boxe. Then the Director, and two others of the Society, openly numbering the crossed roles in the urn, shall accordingly pronounce the election.

"That if two-thirds of the present number do consent uppon any scrutiny, that election to be good, and not otherwise.

"*Concerning the Officers and Servants of the Society.*

"The standing Officers of this Society to be three, that is to say, a President or Director, a Treasurer, and a Register. The President to be chosen monthly.

"The Treasurer to continue one yeare, as also the Register.

"That there be likewise two servants belonging to this Society, an Amanuensis, and an Operator.

"That the Treasurer doe every quarter give in an account of the Stock in his hand, and all disbursements made to the President or Director, and any three others to be appointed by the Society: who are to report it to the Society.

"That any bill of charges brought in by the Amanuensis and Operator, and subscribed by the President and Register for any experiment made, and subscribed by the Curators of the experiment, or the major part of them, be a sufficient warrant to the Treasurer for the payment of that sum.

"That the Register provide three bookes, one for the statutes and names of the Society, another for experiments and the result of debates: and a third for occasionall orders.

"That the salary of the Amanuensis be 40*l*. per annum, and his pay for particular business at the ordinary rate, either by the sheet or otherwise, as the President and Register can best agree with him.

"That the salary of the Operator be foure pounds by the yeare, and for any other service, as the Curators who employ him shall judge reasonable.

"That at every meeting, three or more of the Society be desired that they would please to be reporters for that meeting, to sitt at table with the Register and take notes of all that shall be materially offered to the Society and debated in it, who together may form a report against the next meeting to be filed by the Register.

"When the admission-money comes to 20*l*., then to stop."

At a subsequent meeting, held December 19, 1660, it was "ordered that the next meeting should be at Gresham Colledge, and so from weeke to weeke till further order," the suggestion that the Society should meet at the College of Physicians being given up.

On the 6th March, 1660-61, Sir Robert Moray (one of the Privy Council and of great influence with the King) was chosen President, and on April 10th was re-elected "for an other month."

It would appear that some time previous to 16th October, 1661, the Society had petitioned His Majesty to incorporate them, for on that day "Sir Robert Moray acquainted the Society that hee and Sr. Paul Neile kiss'd the King's hands in the Company's Name, and is intreated by them to return most humble thancks to His Majesty for the Reference he was pleased to graunt of their Petition : and to this favour and honour hee was pleased to offer of him selfe to bee enter'd one of the Society."

The Charter of Incorporation (see p. 19) passed the Great Seal on the 15th July, 1662. This is, therefore, the date of the beginning of the Royal Society. The Charter was read before the Society on the 13th August of the same year, and on the 29th the President, Council, and Fellows went to Whitehall and returned their thanks to His Majesty.

The first Charter, however, did not give the Fellows all the privileges which they desired, and, representations having been made, a second Charter (see p. 44), supplying the desired privileges, and retaining all the clauses of incorporation contained in the first Charter, passed the Great Seal on the 22nd of April, 1663, and was read before the Society on the 13th May following. In 1669 a third Charter (see p. 73) was given, but this does little more than grant to the Society lands in Chelsea (the Chelsea College), and while confirming the powers given by the second Charter makes some slight changes. It is practically the second Charter which ensures the Society its privileges, and by which the Society has since been, and continues to be, governed.

The list* of the President and Council, named by the second Charter, and of the Fellows nominated by them, is as follows :—

* Reprinted from Thomson's 'History of the Royal Society.'

THE FIRST PRESIDENT AND COUNCIL OF THE ROYAL SOCIETY, NAMED BY HIS MAJESTY'S CHARTER, DATED 22ND APRIL, 1663.

BORN.	DIED.	
1620	April 5, 1684	William Lord Viscount Brouncker, President.
	July 4, 1673	Sir Robert Moray, Kt.
Feb. 25, 1627	Dec. 31, 1691	Robert Boyle, Esq.
	1697	William Brereton, Esq.—afterwards Lord Brereton.
July 11, 1603	June 11, 1665	Sir Kenelme Digby, Kt.
		Sir Gilbert Talbot, Kt.
		Sir Paule Neile, Kt.
		Henry Slingesby, Esq.—expelled June 24, 1675.
May 16, 1623	Dec. 16, 1687	Sir William Petty, Kt.
		Timothy Clarke, M.D.
1614	Nov. 19, 1672	John Wilkins, D.D.—afterwards Bishop of Chester.
1604	Oct. 13, 1689	George Ent, M.D.—afterwards Sir George Ent, Kt.
		William Erskine, Esq.
1617	Mar. 24, 1675	Jonathan Goddard, M.D., Prof. Med. Gresh.
		William Balle, Esq., Treasurer.
Aug. 20, 1629	June 11, 1672	Matthew Wren, Esq.
Oct. 31, 1620	Feb. 27, 1706	John Evelyn, Esq.
1617	1699	Thomas Henshaw, Esq.
1602	1666	Dudley Palmer, Esq.
		Abraham Hill, Esq.
	Sept. 1677	Henry Oldenburg, Esq., Secretary.

Which Council did, at a Meeting held May 20, 1663, by virtue of the power given them by the charter for two months, declare the following Persons Members of the Society.

BORN.	DIED.	
	1690	James Lord Annesley—afterwards Earl of Anglesey.
		John Alleyn, Esq.
May 23, 1617	May 18, 1692	Elias Ashmole, Esq.
		John Austen, Esq.
Nov. 3, 1625	1697	John Aubrey, Esq.
1620	1687	George Duke of Buckingham.
	Oct. 10, 1698	George Lord Berkeley—afterwards Earl of Berkeley.
	Oct. 20, 1685	Robert Lord Bruce—afterwards Earl of Aylesbury.
		Richard Boyle, Esq.
1622	Sept. 5, 1681	Thomas Bayne, M.D.—afterwards Kt.
Oct. 1630	May 4, 1677	Isaac Barrow, B.D.—afterwards D.D.
		Peter Balle, M.D.
		John Brook, Esq.—afterwards Sir John Brook, Bart.
		David Bruce, M.D.—expelled Nov. 18, 1675.
1608	April 19, 1669	George Bate, M.D.

Foundation and Early History. 9

BORN.	DIED.	
Jan. 25, 1640	Aug. 18, 1707	William Lord Cavendish—afterwards Duke of Devonshire.
1619	1707	Walter Charleton, M.D.
	Nov. 11, 1671	Edward Cotton, D.D., Archdeacon of Cornwall.
	1690	Daniel Colwall, Esq.
		John Clayton, Esq.—afterwards Sir John Clayton, Kt.
		Thomas Coxe, M.D.
	Oct. 12, 1684	William Croone, M.D.
	1676	John Earl of Crawford and Lindsay.
	1680	Henry Marquis of Dorchester.
1617	Nov. 23, 1684	William Earl of Devonshire.
1615	Mar. 28, 1669	Sir John Denham, Knight of the Bath.
1631	1701	Mr. John Dryden, the poet.
1618	Jan. 6, 1689	Seth Lord Bishop of Exeter—afterwards of Salisbury.
	1673	Andrew Ellis, Esq.
		Sir Francis Feane, Knight of the Bath.
1621	Sept. 5, 1680	Sir John Finch, Kt.
		Mons. Le Febure.
	Oct. 14, 1677	Francis Glisson, M.D.
1620	April 18, 1674	John Graunt, Esq.
	1670	Christopher Lord Hatton.
		Charles Howard, Esq.
		William Hoare, M.D.
	1673	Sir Robert Harley, Kt.
		Nathaniel Henshaw, M.D.
		James Hayes, Esq.—afterwards Kt.
1615	Jan. 24, 1697	William Holder, D.D.
	1690	Theodore Haake, Esq.
		William Hammond, Esq.
		John Hoskyns, Esq.—afterwards Bart.
July 18, 1635	Mar. 3, 1702	Robert Hooke, M.A.—afterwards LL.D.
		Richard Jones, Esq.—afterwards Earl of Ranelaugh.
	1680	Alexander Earl of Kincardin.
	1678	Sir Andrew King, Kt.
		John Lord Lucas.
		James Long, Esq.—afterwards Bart.
		Anthony Lowther, Esq.
	1695	John Lord Viscount Massarene.
		Sir Anthony Morgan, Kt.
1614	1695	Christopher Merret, M.D.
	Dec. 15, 1681	James Earl of Northampton.
		Sir Thomas Nott, Kt.—expelled Nov. 18, 1675.
Dec. 7, 1637	Aug. 25, 1670	William Neile, Esq.
1622	Oct. 31, 1679	Jaspar Needham, M.D.
		Sir William Persall, Kt.
		Sir Richard Powle, Knight of the Bath.

BORN.	DIED.	
	1682	Sir Robert Paston, Knight of the Bath—afterwards Earl of Yarmouth.
		Sir Peter Pett, Kt.—expelled Nov. 18, 1675.
	June 1714	Walter Pope, M.D.
Mar. 1, 1610	Dec. 12, 1685	John Pell, D.D.
		Peter Pett, Esq.
		Henry Powle, Esq.
		Thomas Povey, Esq.
		Henry Proby, Esq.
	Dec. 24, 1686	Philip Packer, Esq.
		William Quatremaine, M.D.
July 27, 1625	May 28, 1672	Edward Earl of Sandwich.
		Sir James Shaen, Kt.
	1618	July 26, 1693	Charles Scarburgh, M.D.—afterwards Sir C. Scarburgh, Kt.
	April 12, 1678	Thomas Stanley, Esq.
		George Smyth, M.D.
		Alex. Stanhope, Esq.—withdrawn Mar. 8, 1681.
	1636	Sept. 11, 1702	Robert Southwell, Esq.—afterwards Sir Robert Southwell, Kt.
		William Schroter, Esq.
	1636	May 20, 1718	Thomas Sprat, M.A.—afterwards D.D. and Bishop of Rochester.
		Christopher Terne, M.D.
		Samuel Tuke, Esq.—afterwards Kt.
		Cornelius Vermuyden, Esq.—afterwards Kt.
	Dec. 29, 1707	Sir Cyril Wyche, Kt.
		Sir Peter Wyche, Kt.
	1616	1703	John Wallis, D.D.
	1606	Oct. 31, 1687	Edmund Waller, Esq.
	1631	Sept. 3, 1701	Joseph Williamson, Esq.—afterwards Kt.
	1636	July 3, 1672	Francis Willughby, Esq.
		William Winde, Esq.
		John Winthrop, Esq.
		Thomas Wren, M.D.
Oct. 20, 1632	Feb. 25, 1723	Christopher Wren, LL.D.—afterwards Kt.
		Edmund Wylde, Esq.
	May 11, 1684	Daniel Whistler, M.D.
	Dec. 15, 1679	Sir Edward Bysshe, Kt.
	1615	Dec. 4, 1679	Sir John Birkenhead, Kt.
April 14, 1629	1695	Mons. Christian Huygens, of Zulichem.
Sept. 17, 1615	April 9, 1670	Mons. Samuel Sorbiere.

The second Charter, confirmed on this point by the third, provides for a Council of twenty-one (the President or his Deputy being always one), of whom ten are to be changed each year on St. Andrew's Day. The election of the Council, the President, the Treasurer, and the two Secretaries is placed in the hands of the President, Council,

and Fellows, as is also the reception and admission of members. But, otherwise, "the making of laws, statutes, and ordinances, and the transaction of all matters relating to management of the Society and its affairs" is entrusted to the President and Council alone. Hence by the Charter, the Bye Laws, or Statutes, as they are called, by which the Society is governed, are made and changed by the President and Council alone, the Fellows at large having no voice in the matter. At p. 100 will be found a Note on the Statutes, which gives a brief history of the successive changes in the internal administration by the President and Council from the foundation of the Society to recent times; it is unnecessary to repeat these here.

Attention, however, may be called to the fact that, as is stated in that Note, the printing of the 'Philosophical Transactions,' which was begun in 1665, the first number appearing on Monday, March 6, 1664-5, was at first "the single act of the respective Secretaries" (being, in fact, in the first instance a speculation on the part of Henry Oldenburg), though a certain supervision was exercised by the President and Council. This system was continued through 46 volumes consisting of 496 numbers. With the 47th volume, published in 1753 (the publication in numbers was thenceforward discontinued) the publication was placed by new Statutes directly in the hands of the President and Council, a Committee of Papers being established.

In addition to the 'Philosophical Transactions,' the Society, having powers by their Charter to appoint a printer and engraver, published or sanctioned the publication of separate works on Natural Knowledge. Among the works which received their imprimatur are the following:—

- Hooke, Robert, 'Micrographia: or some Physiological Descriptions of Minute Bodies made by Magnifying Glasses.' Folio. *London* 1665.
- Graunt, John, 'Natural and political Observations . . . made upon the Bills of Mortality, with reference to the Government, Religion, Trade, Growth, Air, Diseases, and the several changes of the City [of London].' (3rd edition, enlarged.) 8vo. *London* 1665.
- Sprat, Thomas, 'The History of the Royal Society of London for the improving of Natural Knowledge.' 4to. *London* 1667.
- Malpighi, Marcello, 'Dissertatio epistolica de Bombyce; Societati Regiæ Londini dicata.' 4to. *Londini* 1669.
- Holder, William, 'Elements of Speech; with an Appendix, concerning persons Deaf and Dumb.' 8vo. *London* 1669.
- Evelyn, John, 'Sylva, or a Discourse of Forest Trees.' Folio. *London* 1670.
- Horrocks, Jeremiah, 'Opera posthuma.' 4to. *Londini* 1673.
- Malpighi, Marcello, 'Anatome Plantarum,' Folio. *Londini* 1675.

Willughby, Francis, 'Ornithologiæ libri tres; totum opus recognovit, digessit, supplevit Joannes Raius.' Folio. *Londini* 1676.

Evelyn John, 'A Philosophical Discourse of Earth, relating to the Culture and Improvement of it for Vegetation. . . .' 8vo. *London* 1676.

'Philosophical Collections' [by Robert Hooke].* 4to. *London* 1679-82.

'Lectiones Cutlerianæ, or a Collection of Lectures: Physical, Mechanical, Geographical, and Astronomical. . . .' 4to. *London* 1679.

Also several separate Tracts, by Robert Hooke. 4to. 1679-82.

Papin, Denis, 'A New Digester, or Engine for softning Bones.' 4to. *London* 1681.

Grew, Nehemiah, 'Musœum Regalis Societatis: or a Catalogue and Description of the Natural and Artificial Rarities belonging to the Society, and preserved at Gresham Colledge.' Folio. *London* 1681.

Grew, Nehemiah, 'The Anatomy of Plants. With an Idea of a Philosophical History of Plants, and several other Lectures read before the Royal Society.' Folio. *London* 1682.

Ray, John, 'Historia Plantarum, species hactenus editas aliasque insuper multas noviter inventas et descriptas complectens . . . .' Folio. *Londini* 1686-88.

Flamsteed, John, 'Tide-table for 1687.'

Papin, Denis, 'A continuation of the New Digester of Bones; together with some improvements and new uses of the air-pump.' 4to. *London* 1687.

Newton, Isaac, 'Philosophiæ† Naturalis Principia Muthematica.' Autore Is. Newton. Imprimatur: S. Pepys, Reg. Soc. Præses. Julii 5, 1686. 4to. *Londini* 1687.

Malpighi, Marcello, 'Opera Posthuma.' Folio. *Londini* 1697.

'Commercium Epistolicum D. Johannis Collins, et aliorum de Analysi promota: jussu Societatis Regiæ in lucem editum.' 4to. *Londini* 1712.

---

* " Ordered and desired—That Mr. Hooke may publish (as he hath now declared he is ready to doe) a sheet or two every fortnight of such Phylosophicall matters as he shall meet with from his Correspond^{ts}, not making use of any thing conteind in the Register Books without the leave of the Councel and Author."—*Council Minutes*, July 3, 1679.

† " Ordered—That Mr. Newton's book be printed forthwith in a quarto of a fair letter."—*Journal-book*, May 19, 1686.

" Ordered that Mr. Newton's book be printed, and that E. Halley shall undertake the business of looking after it, and printing it at his own charge, which he engaged to do."—*Council Minutes*, June 2, 1686.

" Ordered that the President be desired to licence Mr. Newton's book entituled 'Philosophiæ naturalis principia mathematica,' and dedicated to the Society."—*Council Minutes*, June 30, 1686.

As has been shown above, the Society, at and before its incorporation, held its meetings at Gresham College. After June 28, 1665, the meetings were for a while discontinued, on account of the plague, and the seventh and eighth numbers of the 'Philosophical Transactions' were printed at Oxford. On March 14, 1665-6, the meetings were resumed at Gresham College, but in September of the same year the Great Fire in London again interrupted them. The meetings due on September 5 and 12 were not held, and though the Society seems to have met on September 19 and some following weeks at Dr. Pope's lodging, or in other rooms in Gresham College, it left the College, which, on account of the fire, was much occupied by merchants, and in January 9, 1666-7, met at Arundel House, in the Strand, originally the Bishop of Bath's Palace, at the site now occupied by Arundel and Norfolk Street; here rooms had been placed at the disposal of the Society by Mr. Henry Howard.

At Arundel House the meetings continued to be held regularly, with an interruption from May to October, 1667, caused by the arrest and detention in the Tower, on suspicion of treasonable practices, of Henry Oldenburg, one of the secretaries, until December, 1673, when the Society once more returned to Gresham College, though for some little time the meetings appear to have been occasionally held at Arundel House.

Under the presidency of Isaac Newton, an anxiety that the Society should possess a house of its own became very marked, and in 1710 a house in Crane Court, in Fleet Street, having been purchased on borrowed money, the Society met there on November 8.

Here they continued for the greater part of the century, indeed until November 30, 1780, when, Sir Joseph Banks being president, they took possession of rooms in Somerset House, which had been placed at their disposal by the Government.

The Society remained in Somerset House until 1857. In that year the apartments were required for Government offices, and the Society was temporarily transferred to that part of Burlington House which is now occupied by the offices of the Royal Academy of Arts. The new wings and the gateway were subsequently added, and in 1873 the Society took up its permanent quarters in the east wing, which it still occupies.

The second Charter gave the President, Council, and Fellows the same right " to demand and receive the bodies of executed criminals, and to anatomize them as the College of Physicians, and the Company of Surgeons of London use or enjoy." On January 20, 1663-4, at a meeting of the Council, " The general and particular Warrants to demand Bodies for dissection, drawn up by Sr Anthony Morgan, were read and approved." The original copy of this general Warrant, signed by Lord Brouncker, is preserved in the Archives of the Society.

The privilege appears to have been exercised for a time with considerable vigour, Dr. Charleton being appointed, by a Resolution of April 20th in the same year, "to have the care of Dissecting Bodies for one year." But although there are several entries in the Council Minutes relating to Anatomical Experiments, and in June, 1668, Henry Howard, afterwards sixth Duke of Norfolk, gave the Society a room in Arundel House for that purpose, no clear reference

ARMS OF THE ROYAL SOCIETY.

to the privilege in question has been found later than the Minute of August 29, 1666, when it was ordered "That an Amanuensis should make a Copy of the Warrant for demanding a Body for dissection, to be performed in Gresham College by some of the Fellows of the Society at their own charges." Ultimately it fell wholly into abeyance.

The second Charter also granted the Society the use of arms, and in August, 1663, Charles II presented the Society with the mace, which is still in their possession, the warrant for which is dated May 23, 1663.*

After the Incorporation, the now Royal Society conducted its meetings very much as they had been conducted while it was yet a private Society. What was the character of the meetings at that time may be learnt from the following record of the fourth meeting after the one at which the charter was read, copied from the Journal-book:—

September 10*th*, 1662.

"Mersennus, his account of the tenacity of cylindricall bodies was read by Mr. Croone, to whome the prosecution of that matter by consulting Galilæo, was referred when the translation of that Italian treatise wherein he handleth of this subject shall bee printed.

"It was order'd, that, at the next meeting Experiments should bee made with wires of severall matters of ye same size, silver, copper, iron, &c., to see what weight will breake them; the curator is Mr. Croone.

"The reading of the french manuscript brought in by Sr. Robert Moray about taking heights and distances by catoptricks was differred till the description of the instrument should come.

"Dr. Goddard made an experiment concerning the force that presseth the aire into lesse dimensions; and it was found, that twelve ounces did contract $\frac{1}{24}$ part of Aire. The quantity of Air is wanting.

"My Lord Brouncker was desired to send his Glass to Dr. Goddard, to make further experiments about the force of pressing aire into less dimensions.

"Dr. Wren was put in mind to prosecute Mr. Rook's observations concerning the motions of the satellites of Jupiter.

"Dr. Charleton read an Essay of his, concerning the velocity of sounds, direct and reflexe, and was desired to prosecute this matter; and to bring his discourse again next day to bee enter'd.

"Dr. Goddard made the Experiment to show how much aire a man's lungs may hold, by sucking up water into a separating glasse after the lungs have been well emptied of Aire. Severall persons of the Society trying it, some sucked up in one suction about three pintes of water, one six, another eight pintes and three quarters, &c. Here was observed the variety of whistles or toues, which ye water made at the severall hights, in falling out of the glasse again.

"Mr. Evelyn's experiment was brought in of Animal engrafting, and in particular of making a Cock spur grow on a Cock's head.

"It was discoursed whether there bee any such thing as sexes in

---

* The legend that this mace of the Society was the "bauble" turned out of the House of Commons by Oliver Cromwell has been exposed by Weld, 'Hist. Roy. Soc.,' vol. 1, p. 132, &c.

trees and other plants; some instances were brought of Palme trees, plum trees, hollies, Ash trees, Quinces, pionies, &c., wherein a difference was said to be found, either in their bearing of fruit or in their hardnesse and softness, or in their medicall operations: some said that the difference which is in trees as to fertility or sterility may be made by ingrafting.

"Mention was made by Sr. Rob. Moray of a French Gentleman who having been some while since in England, and present at a meeting of the Society, discoursed that the nature of all trees was to run altogether to wood, which was changed by a certaine way of cutting them, whereby they were made against their nature to beare fruit, and that according as this cutting was done with more, or lesse, skill the more or less fruitfull the tree would bee.

"A proposition was offered by Sr. Robert Moray about the planting of Timber in England and the preserving of what is now growing.

"Mr. Boyle shew'd a Puppey in a certaine liquour, wherein it had been preserved during all the hott months of the Summer, though in a broken and unsealed glasse.

"Sir James Shaen proposed a Candidate by Sr. Rob. Moray."

It is evident that one most important feature of a meeting was the performing of experiments before the members. In the warrant issued in 1663, ordering the mace to be made for the Royal Society, the Society is spoken of as "for the improving of Natural Knowledge by experiments." The experiment was performed for and by itself, and not merely, as now, in illustration of a "paper communicated." Papers were read then as now; but the reading of such papers formed only a part, and by no means a great part, of the business of the meeting. Much time was spent in discussing the bearings of such experiments as were shown, and in devising other experiments to be shown at some subsequent meeting, or in instituting investigations to be carried out in divers places and under various circumstances. And from the very first much of the energy of the Society was spent in foreign correspondence, in giving information or advice upon inquiries reaching them, in seeking news, or in instigating researches in foreign places. The Letter-books of the Society contain very many letters between the Society and various learned bodies and individuals abroad; the first Letter-book begins with one dated 22nd July, 1661 (that is, before the incorporation of the Society), and addressed by the then President, Sir Robert Moray, to one Monsieur de Monmort, requesting the interchange of scientific communications. Monsieur de Monmort appears to have been the patron of science at whose house in Paris there assembled that small body of savants who later, in 1666, were incorporated as the "Académie des Sciences."

The importance of the experiments carried out at the meetings is shown by the Society early availing itself of the power granted to it by the Charter of "appointing two or more curators of experiments," and appointing to this office Robert Hooke, who had been the assistant to Boyle, admitting him at the same time as a Fellow of the Society.

He was elected Curator to the Society on January 11, 1664-65, "for perpetuity, with a salary of £30 a year, *pro tempore*," apartments being assigned to him for residence. He held the appointment concurrently with the secretaryship, to which he was elected in 1677.

In 1684 Papin was chosen joint Curator with Hooke, and continued so until 1687, when he became Professor at Marburg. Both Hooke and Papin were very active in providing experiments to be shown at the meetings.

There appear to have been additional Curators for special departments, besides the general Curatorship of Robert Hooke. Thus, in November, 1667, Dr. Lower was appointed " Curator in Anatomical Experiments." In April, 1672, Dr. Grew was appointed "to be a Curator to the Royal Society for the Anatomy of Plants for a year, upon subscriptions amounting to £50, to be made by such members of the Society as should be willing to contribute thereto," and in December of that year the Council promised to "recommend him to the Society, to continue him another year, if the subscribers would please to continue their contributions." Whether he was actually continued does not appear. It will also be noticed that in the account of the meeting of September 10, 1662, given above, Mr. Croone is named as the Curator of a special series of experiments.

On February 27, 1683-84, "Mr. Hally was desired to bring in experiments at the meetings of the Society in the manner of a Curator, and he should be considered for it as others had been. He was desired to proceed first upon magnetism, which he promised to doe."

On May 27, 1685, Mr. Molt was "imployed in making the chymical operations," and in 1707 Dr. Douglas and Mr. Hawksbee were similarly employed to prepare experiments, and were paid for so doing, but do not appear to have borne the title of Curator. Dr. Desaguliers, however, seems to have borne the title. He was elected a Fellow on July 15, 1714, and was excused his fees, on account of his usefulness in the Curatorship.

Some of the experiments were instituted at the instigation of King Charles II; and in the early days the Society seems often to have prepared experiments at its meeting, hoping, but in many instances in vain, that the King would do them the honour to witness them.

In order to carry out their inquiries and investigations more efficiently, the Society not only appointed special committees to make inquiries concerning and to report on particular questions, as, for instance, when Sir John Lawson desired that a Committee might be appointed "to examine Mr. Greatrix's Diving-instrument, or to direct a good way for staying under water for a considerable time, to lay the foundation of the mole at Tangier" (Council Minutes, January 13, 1663), but also instituted permanent Committees, each to take charge of some special branch of Natural Knowledge. Thus, in the first year after the second Charter, on March 30th, 1664, the following eight Committees were appointed:—

"1. Mechanical. To consider of and improve all Mechanical Inventions. [69 names.]
2. Astronomical and Optical. [15 names.]
3. Anatomical. All the Physitians of the Society, Mr. Boyle, Dr. Wilkins, Mr. Hook.
4. Chymical. Duke of Buckingham, Mr. Boyle, Sr. Kenelme Digby, Mr. Charles Howard, Mr. Henshaw, Mr. Le Feburc, Sr. Robert Paston, All the Physitians of the Society.
5. Georgical. [32 names.]
6. For Histories of Trades. [35 names.]
7. For Collecting all the Phænomena of Nature hitherto observed, and all Experiments made and recorded. [21 names.]
8. For Correspondence. [20 names.]"*

As will be seen from the Note on the Statutes, the time of the weekly meetings of the Society was fixed, at first in 1663, to be on Wednesday at 2 P.M., but the hour was soon, in July of the same year, changed to 3 P.M. In 1776 the time of the meeting is fixed as Thursday at 6 P.M., but between this and the above date were changes from Wednesday to Thursday and back again, and from 3 P.M. to 4 P.M., and again to 6 P.M. Since 1710 the meetings have been on Thursdays, the hour being changed in 1780 from 6 to 8 P.M., about 1831 to 8.30 P.M., and in 1880 to 4 30 P.M.

** The portraits of the six early Presidents given in Plates 1 and 2 are from negatives kindly lent by the Editor of the 'Leisure Hour.' A nearly complete series of portraits of the Presidents, mostly from pictures in the possession of the Society, is given in the July number of that periodical for 1896. The portraits of Boyle and Oldenburg are from photographs made for this 'Record' from paintings in the apartments of the Society.

* MS. Journal-book, vol. 2, fol. 61.

Plate 2.

Pepys.   Vaughan
         (Earl of Carbery)

Brouncker   Ro: Boy.

CHARTA PRIMA,*

Praesidi, Concilio, et Sodalibus REGALIS SOCIE-
TATIS Londini, à Rege CAROLO SECUNDO
concessa, A.D. MDCLXII.

CAROLUS SECUNDUS, Dei gratia Angliae Scotiae Franciae
et Hiberniae Rex, Fidei Defensor, etc., omnibus, ad quos
praesentes Literae pervenerint, salutem.

Diu multùmque apud nos statuimus, ut imperii fines, sic
etiam artes atque scientias ipsas promovere. Favemus
itaque omnibus disciplinis; particulari autem gratia indulgemus philosophicis studiis, praesertim iis, quae solidis
experimentis conantur aut novam extundere philosophiam,
aut expolire veterem. Ut igitur inclarescant apud nostros
hujusmodi studia, quae nusquam terrarum adhuc satis
emicuerunt, utque nos tandem universus literarum orbis
non solùm fidei defensorem, sed etiam veritatis omnimodae
et cultorem ubique et patronum, semper agnoscat:

Sciatis, quòd nos de gratia nostra speciali ac ex certa
scientia et mero motu nostris ordinavimus constituimus
concessimus et declaravimus, ac per praesentes pro nobis
heredibus et successoribus nostris ordinamus constituimus concedimus et declaramus, quòd de caetero in perpetuum erit Societas, de Praesidente† Concilio et Soda-
libus consistens, quae vocabitur et nuncupabitur Regalis *Incorporation, and Corporate Name.*
Societas; Et eandem Societatem, per nomen Praesidis
Concilii et Sodalium Regalis Societatis, unum corpus
corporatum et politicum in re facto et nomine realiter et
ad plenum, pro nobis heredibus et successoribus nostris,
facimus ordinamus creamus et constituimus per praesentes, et quòd per idem nomen habeant successionem perpetuam; Et quòd ipsi et eorum successores (quorum studia
applicanda sunt ad rerum naturalium artiumque utilium

---

* The Latin text of the Charters here given has been printed from
the transcript in Weld's 'History of the Royal Society,' after careful
collation with the enrolments at the Public Record Office, by Mr.
R. E. G. Kirk, Record Agent. Several corrections have been made,
but for convenience' sake Weld's extensions of the abbreviations used
in the original have been retained.

† *Sic.*

scientias experimentorum fide ulteriùs promovendas), per idem nomen Praesidis Concilii et Sodalium Regalis Societatis praedictae, sint et erunt perpetuis futuris temporibus personae habiles et in lege capaces ad habendum perquirendum percipiendum et possidendum terras et tenementa prata pascua pasturas libertates privilegia franchesias jurisdictiones et hereditamenta quaecunque sibi et successoribus suis in feodo et perpetuitate, vel pro termino vitae vitarum vel annorum, seu aliter quocunque modo, ac etiam bona et catalla, ac omnes alias res, cujuscunque fuerint generis naturae speciei sive qualitatis; Necnon ad dandum concedendum dimittendum et assignandum eadem terras tenementa et hereditamenta, bona et catalla, et omnia facta et res necessarias faciendum et exequendum de et concernentia eisdem,* per nomen praedictum; Et quòd per nomen Praesidis Concilii et Sodalium Regalis Societatis praedictae placitare et implacitari, respondere et responderi, defendere et defendi de caetero in perpetuum valeant et possint, in quibuscunque Curiis placeis et locis, et coram quibuscunque Judicibus et Justiciariis et aliis personis et officiariis nostris heredum et successorum nostrorum, in omnibus et singulis actionibus placitis sectis querelis causis materiis rebus et demandis quibuscunque, cujuscunque sint aut erunt generis naturae vel speciei, eisdem modo et forma, prout aliqui ligei nostri intra hoc Regnum nostrum Angliae, personae habiles et in lege capaces, aut ut aliquod corpus corporatum vel politicum intra hoc Regnum nostrum Angliae, habere perquirere recipere possidere, dare et concedere, placitare et implacitari, respondere et responderi, defendere vel defendi valeant et possint, valeat et possit; Et quòd iidem Praeses Concilium et Sodales Regalis Societatis praedictae et successores sui habeant in perpetuum Commune Sigillum, pro causis et negotiis suis et successorum suorum quibuscunque agendis deserviturum; et quòd benè liceat et licebit eisdem Praesidi Concilio et Sodalibus Regalis Societatis praedictae, et successoribus suis pro tempore existentibus, Sigillum illud de tempore in tempus frangere mutare et de novo facere, prout eis meliùs fore videbitur expediri.

Et, quòd intentio nostra regia meliorem sortiatur effectum, ac pro bono regimine et gubernatione praedictae Regalis Societatis de tempore in tempus, volumus, ac per praesentes pro nobis heredibus et successoribus nostris

* *Sic.*

concedimus eisdem Praesidi Concilio et Sodalibus Societatis Regalis praedictae et successoribus suis, quòd de caetero in perpetuum Concilium praedictum erit et consistet ex viginti et una personis (quarum Praesidem semper unum esse volumus); Et quòd omnes et singulae aliae personae quae intra unum mensem proximùm sequentem post datum praesentium per Praesidem et Concilium, et in omni tempore sequenti per Praesidem Concilium et Sodales, in eandem Societatem accipientur et admittentur ut Membra Regalis Societatis praedictae, et in Registro per ipsos conservando annotatae fuerint, erunt vocabuntur et nuncupabuntur Sodales Regalis Societatis praedictae: quos, quantò eminentiùs omnis generis doctrinae bonarumque literarum studio clarescant, quantò ardentiùs hujusce Societatis honorem studia et emolumentum* promoveri cupiant, quantò vitae integritate morumque probitate ac pietate emineant, et fidelitate animique erga nos Coronam et dignitatem nostram sincero affectu polleant, eò magis idoneos et dignos, qui in Sodalium ejusdem Societatis numerum adsciscantur, omnino censeri volumus.

The Council to consist of 21 (of whom the President to be always one).

The Fellows to be chosen in the first month, by the President and Council; after that month, by the President, Council, and Fellows.

Et, pro meliori executione voluntatis at concessionis nostrae in hac parte, assignavimus nominavimus constituimus et fecimus, ac per praesentes pro nobis heredibus et successoribus nostris assignamus nominamus constituimus et facimus, praedilectum et fidelem nobis Willielmum, Vicecomitem Brouncker, Cancellarium praecharissimae consorti nostrae Reginae Catherinae, fore et esse primum et modernum Praesidem Regalis Societatis praedictae; volentes quòd praedictus Willielmus, Vicecomes Brouncker, in officio Praesidis Regalis Societatis praedictae à datu praesentium usque ad festum Sancti Andreae proximùm sequens post datum praesentium continuabit, et quousque unus alius de Concilio Regalis Societatis praedictae pro tempore existente ad officium illud debito modo electus praefectus et juratus fuerit, juxta ordinationem et provisionem in his praesentibus inferiùs expressam et declaratam (si praedictus Willielmus, Vicecomes Brouncker, tam diu vixerit); sacramento corporali in omnibus et per omnia officium illud tangentia benè et fideliter exequendum, secundùm veram intentionem harum praesentium, coram praedilecto et perquam fideli Consanguineo et Consiliario nostro Edwardo, Comite Clarendon, Cancellario nostro Angliae, priùs praestito: cui quidem Edwardo, Comiti Clarendon, Cancellario nostro praedicto, sacra-

William, Viscount Brouncker, to be the first President;

to hold till St. Andrew's Day next (if he shall so long live), and till another out of the Council be chosen and sworn;

but first to be sworn in before the Lord Chancellor.

---

* Or *emolumenta.*

mentum praedictum administrare plenam potestatem et authoritatem damus et concedimus, in hacc verba sequentia, viz.: *I, William, Viscount Brouncker, doe promise to deale faithfullie and honestlie in all things belonging to the trust committed to mee as President of this Royall Societie, during my employment in that capacitie. So helpe me God!* Assignavimus etiam constituimus et focimus, ac per praesentes pro nobis heredibus et successoribus nostris facimus, dilectos nobis et fideles Robertum Moray, Militem, unum à Secretioribus nostris Conciliis in Regno nostro Scotiae, Robertum Boyle, Armigerum, Willielmum Brereton, Armigerum, filium primogenitum Baronis de Brereton, Kenelm. Digby, Militem, praecharissimae matri nostrae Mariae Reginae Cancellarium, Paulum Neile, Militem, unum Generosorum Camerae privatae nostrae, Henricum Slingesby, Armigerum, alium Generosorum praedictae privatae Camerae nostrae, Willielmum Petty, Militem, Johannem Wallis, in Theologia Doctorem, Timotheum Clarke, in Medicinis Doctorem et unum Medicorum nostrorum, Johannem Wilkins, in Theologia Doctorem, Georgium Ent, in Medicinis Doctorem, Willielmum Aerskine, unum a Poculis nostris, Jonathan. Goddard, in Medicinis Doctorem et Professorem Collegii de Gresham, Christopherum Wren, in Medicinis Doctorem, Saville Astronomiae Professorem in Academia nostra Oxoniensi, Willielmum Balle, Armigerum, Matthaeum Wren, Armigerum, Johannem Evelyn, Armigerum, Thomam Henshawe, Armigerum, Dudley Palmer, de Greys Inn in comitatu nostro Middlesexiae, Armigerum, et Henricum Oldenburg, Armigerum, unà cum Praeside praedicto, fore et esse primos et modernos viginti et unum de Concilio Regalis Societatis praedictae; continuandos in eisdem officiis à datu praesentium usque ad praedictum festum Sancti Andreae Apostoli proximùm sequens, et deinde, quousque aliae idoneae personae et habiles et sufficientes in officia praedicta electae praefectae et juratae fuerint (si tam diu vixerint, aut pro aliqua justa et rationabili causa non amotae* fuerint); sacramentis corporalibus coram Praeside praedictae Regalis Societatis, ad officia sua benè et fideliter in omnibus et per omnia officia illa tangentia exequenda, priùs praestandis, secundùm formam et effectum praedicti sacramenti, mutatis mutandis, Praesidi Regalis Societatis praedictae per Cancellarium nostrum Angliae administrandi (cui quidem Praesidi pro tempore existenti

* *Sic.*

sacramenta praedicta administrare plenam potestatem et authoritatem pro nobis heredibus et successoribus nostris damus et concedimus per praesentes) : Et quòd eaedem personae sic, ut praefertur, ad Concilium praedictae Regalis Societatis electae praefectae et juratae, et in posterum eligendae praeficiendae et jurandae de tempore in tempus, eruut et existent auxiliantes consulentes et assistentes in omnibus materiis rebus et negotiis meliorem regulationem gubernationem et directionem praedictae Regalis Societatis, et cujuslibet Membri ejusdem, tangentibus seu concernentibus.

Et ulteriùs volumus, ac per praesentes pro nobis heredibus et successoribus nostris concedimus praefatis Praesidi Concilio et Sodalibus Regalis Societatis praedictae et successoribus suis, quòd Praeses Concilium et Sodales Regalis Societatis praedictae pro tempore existentes (quorum Praesidem pro tempore existentem unum esse volumus) de tempore in tempus perpetuis futuris temporibus potestatem et authoritatem habeant et habebunt nominandi et eligendi, et quòd eligere et nominare possint et valeant, quolibet anno in praedicto festo Sancti Andreae, unum de Concilio praedictae Regalis Societatis pro tempore existente, qui sit et erit Praeses Regalis Societatis praedictae usque ad festum Sancti Andreae Apostoli exinde proximùm sequens (si tam diu vixerit, aut interim pro aliqua justa et rationabili causa non amotus fuerit), et exinde, quousque unus alius in officium Praesidis Regalis Societatis praedictae electus praefectus et nominatus fuerit; quòdque ille, postquam sic, ut praefertur, electus et nominatus fuerit in officium Praesidis Regalis Societatis praedictae, antequam ad officium illud admittatur, sacramentum corporale coram Concilio ejusdem Regalis Societatis, aut aliquibus septem vel pluribus eorum, ad officium illud rectè benè et fideliter in omnibus officium illud tangentibus exequendum praestabit, secundùm formam et effectum praedicti sacramenti, mutatis mutandis ; (cui quidem Concilio, aut aliquibus septem vel pluribus eorum, sacramentum praedictum administrare pro nobis heredibus et successoribus nostris plenam potestatem et authoritatem de tempore in tempus, quotiescunque necessarium fuerit, damus et concedimus per praesentes;) et quòd post hujusmodi sacramentum sic, ut praefertur, praestitum, officium Praesidis Regalis Societatis praedictae usque ad festum Sancti Andreae Apostoli exinde proximùm sequens exequi valeat et possit : Et si

The President, Council, and Fellows (of whom the President to be one), to elect, annually, on St. Andrew's Day, one out of the Council to be President; who is to hold, if not dead nor amoved, till the next St. Andrew's Day, and till another shall be chosen; having first taken the Oath before the Council or seven or more of them.

On the Death or Amotion of a President, the Coun-

<small>cil and Fellows, or any seven or more of them, are to elect another, out of the Council; who is to hold, during the residue of the year (being first sworn), and until another be chosen and sworn.</small>

contigerit Praesidem Regalis Societatis praedictae pro tempore existentem, aliquo tempore quamdiu fuerit in officio Praesidis ejusdem Regalis Societatis, obire vel ab officio suo amoveri, quòd tunc et toties benè liceat et licebit Concilio et Sodalibus praedictae Regalis Societatis, vel aliquibus septem vel pluribus eorum (quorum Praesidem* Concilii praedicti ad talem electionem semper unum esse volumus), alium de praedicto numero Concilii praedicti in Praesidem Regalis Societatis praedictae eligere et praeficere; et quòd ille sic electus et praefectus officium illud habeat et exerceat durante residuo ejusdem anni, et quousque alius ad officium illud debito modo electus et juratus fuerit, sacramento corporali in forma ultimè specificata priùs praestando; et sic toties quoties casus sic acciderit.

<small>If any of the Council die, or be amoved, or retire (and power of amotion is hereby given to the President and Council or major part of them, whereof the President to be one); the President, Council, and Fellows, or the major part of them (the President to be one), may supply the vacancy out of the Fellows; and the elected shall hold (being first sworn) till the next St. Andrew's Day, and till another Election.</small>

Et ulteriùs volumus, quòd quandocunque contigerit aliquem vel aliquos de Concilio Regalis Societatis praedictae pro tempore existentem mori, vel ab officio illo amoveri, vel decedere, (quos quidem de Concilio Regalis Societatis praedictae et eorum quemlibet pro malè se gerendis aut aliqua alia rationabili causa amobiles esse volumus, ad beneplacitum Praesidis et caeterorum de Concilio praedicto superviventium et in officio illo remanentium, vel majoris partis eorundem, quorum Praesidem pro tempore existentem unum esse volumus,) quòd tunc et toties benè liceat et licebit praefatis Praesidi Concilio et Sodalibus Regalis Societatis praedictae, vel majori parti eorundem (quorum Praesidem Regalis Societatis praedictae pro tempore existentem unum esse volumus), unum alium vel plures alios de Sodalibus Regalis Societatis praedictae, loco sive locis ipsius vel ipsorum sic mortuorum decedentium vel amotorum, ad supplendum praedictum numerum viginti et unius personarum de Concilio Regalis Societatis praedictae, nominare eligere et praeficere; et quòd ille sive illi sic in officio illo electi et praefecti idem officium habeat et habeant usque ad festum Sancti Andreae Apostoli tunc proximùm sequens, et exinde, quousque unus alius vel plures alii electus praefectus et nominatus fuerit, electi praefecti et nominati fuerint; sacramento corporali ad officium illud in omnibus et per omnia officium illud tangentia coram Praeside et Concilio Regalis Societatis praedictae, vel aliquibus septem vel pluribus eorum pro tempore existentibus, benè et fide-

---

* *Sic.* The deceased or removed President could not take part in the election of his successor. *Cf.* the second Charter.

liter exequendum, secundùm veram intentionem praesentium, priùs praestando.

Et ulteriùs volumus, ac per praesentes pro nobis heredibus et successoribus nostris concedimus praefatis Praesidi Concilio et Sodalibus praedictae Regalis Societatis et successoribus suis, quòd ipsi et successores sui quolibet anno, in praedicto festo Sancti Andreae Apostoli, plenam potestatem et authoritatem habeant et habebunt eligendi nominandi praeficiendi et mutandi decem de Sodalibus Regalis Societatis praedictae, ad supplendum loca et officia decem praedicti numeri viginti et unius de Concilio Regalis Societatis praedictae; quoniam regiam voluntatem nostram esse declaramus, et per praesentes pro nobis heredibus et successoribus nostris concedimus, quòd decem de Concilio praedicto, et non ampliùs, per Praesidem Concilium et Sodales Regalis Societatis praedictae annuatim mutati et amoti fuerint. *On every St. Andrew's Day, Ten (and no more) of the Council are to be changed.*

Volumus etiam, et pro nobis heredibus et successoribus nostris concedimus praefatis Praesidi Concilio et Sodalibus praedictae Regalis Societatis et successoribus suis, quòd si contigerit Praesidem ejusdem Regalis Societatis pro tempore existentem aegritudine vel infirmitate detineri, vel in servitio nostro heredum vel successorum nostrorum versari, vel aliter esse occupatum, ita quòd necessariis negotiis ejusdem Regalis Societatis officium Praesidis tangentibus attendere non poterit; quòd tunc et toties benè liceat et licebit eidem Praesidi sic detento versato vel occupato unum de Concilio praedictae Regalis Societatis pro tempore existente, fore et esse Deputatum ejusdem Praesidis, nominare et appunctuare; qui quidem Deputatus, in officio Deputati Praesidis praedicti sic faciendus et constituendus, sit et erit Deputatus ejusdem Praesidis, de tempore in tempus, toties quoties praedictus Praeses sic abesse contigerit, durante toto tempore, quo praedictus Praeses in officio Praesidis continuaverit; nisi interim praedictus Praeses Regalis Societatis praedictae pro tempore existens unum alium de praedicto Concilio ejus Deputatum fecerit et constituerit; Et quòd quilibet hujusmodi Deputatus praedicti Praesidis, sic ut praefertur fiendus* et constituendus, omnia et singula, quae ad officium Praesidis praedictae Regalis Societatis pertinent seu pertinere debent, vel per praedictum Praesidem virtute harum Literarum nostrarum Patentium limitata et appunctuata fore* facienda et exequenda, de

The President may appoint one out of the Council to be his Deputy:

who may act as such during his absence; unless he appoint some other out of the Council to be so.

Such Deputy may, in the President's absence, do all acts that he himself could do if present.

* *Sic.*

tempore in tempus, toties quoties praedictus Praeses sic abesse contigerit, durante tali tempore, quo Deputatus praedicti Praesidis continuaverit, facere et exequi valeat et possit, vigore harum Literarum nostrarum Patentium, adeò plenè liberè et integrè, ac in tam amplis modo et forma, prout Praeses praedictus, si praesens esset, illa facere et exequi valeret et posset; sacramento corporali super sancta Dei Evangelia in forma et effectu ultimè specificatis per hujusmodi Deputatum ad omnia et singula, quae ad officium Praesidis pertinent, benè et fideliter exequenda, coram praefato Concilio praedictae Regalis Societatis, vel aliquibus septem vel pluribus eorum, priùs praestando; et sic toties quoties casus sic acciderit: cui quidem Concilio vel aliquibus septem vel pluribus eorum pro tempore existentibus, sacramentum praedictum administrare potestatem et authoritatem, quoties casus sic acciderit, damus et concedimus per praesentes, absque aliquo brevi commissione sive ulteriori warranto in ea parte à nobis heredibus vel successoribus nostris procurando seu obtinendo.

But he must first be sworn before the Council, or seven or more of them.

Et ulteriùs volumus, ac per praesentes pro nobis heredibus et successoribus nostris concedimus praefatis Praesidi Concilio et Sodalibus Regalis Societatis praedictae et successoribus suis, quòd ipsi et successores sui de caetero in perpetuum habeant et habebunt unum Thesaurarium, duos Secretarios, unum Clericum, et duos Servientes ad Clavas, qui de tempore in tempus super Praesidem attendant; quòdque praedicti Thesaurarius Secretarii Clericus et Servientes ad Clavas eligendi et nominandi, antequam ad officia sua separalia et respectiva exequenda admittantur, sacramenta sua corporalia in forma et effectu ultimè specificatis, coram Praeside et Concilio ejusdem Regalis Societatis, aut aliquibus septem vel pluribus eorum, [ad] officia sua separalia et respectiva in omnibus illa tangentibus rectè benè et fideliter exequenda praestabunt; et quòd post hujusmodi sacramenta sic, ut praefertur, praestita, officia sua respectiva, exerceant et utantur; quibus quidem Praesidi et Concilio, aut aliquibus septem vel pluribus eorum, sacramenta praedicta de tempore in tempus administrare praedictis separalibus et respectivis officiariis et successoribus suis plenam potestatem et authoritatem damus et concedimus per praesentes: Et assignavimus nominavimus elegimus creavimus constituimus et fecimus, ac per praesentes pro nobis heredibus et successoribus nostris assignamus nominamus eligimus

The President, Council, and Fellows may have one Treasurer, two Secretaries, a Clerk, and two Serjeants at Mace:

who are all to be sworn before the President and Council, or any seven or more of them.

William Balle appointed Treasurer, John Wilkins and Henry Oldenburg Secretaries.

creamus constituimus et facimus, dilectos subditos nostros Willielmum Balle, Armigerum, fore et esse primum et modernum Thesaurarium; et praedictum* Johannem Wilkins et Henricum Oldenburg fore et esse primos et modernos Secretarios praedictae Regalis Societatis; continuandos in eisdem officiis usque ad praedictum festum Sancti Andreae Apostoli proximùm sequens post datum praesentium: Quòdque de tempore in tempus et ad omnia tempora, in praedicto festo Sancti Andreae Apostoli (si non fuerit dies Dominicus, et si fuerit dies Dominicus, tunc die proximè sequenti), Praeses Concilium et Sodales praedictae Regalis Societatis pro tempore existentes, aut major pars eorundem (quorum Praesidem pro tempore existentem unum esse volumus), alios probos et discretos viros, de tempore in tempus, in Thesaurarium, Secretarios, Clericum, et Servientes ad Clavas praedictae Regalis Societatis eligere nominare et praeficere valeant et possint; quòdque illi, qui in separalia et respectiva officia praedicta sic, ut praefertur, electi praefecti et jurati fuerint, officia illa respectiva exercere et gaudere possint et valeant usque ad praedictum festum Sancti Andreae extunc proximùm sequens, sacramentis suis praedictis sic, ut praefertur, priùs praestandis; et sic toties quoties casus sic acciderit: Et si contigerit aliquem vel aliquos officiariorum praedictorum ejusdem Regalis Societatis obire, vel ab officiis suis respectivis amoveri, quòd tunc et toties benè liceat et licebit Praesidi Concilio et Sodalibus praedictae Regalis Societatis, vel majori parti eorundem (quorum Praesidem pro tempore existentem unum esse volumus), alium vel alios in officium sive officia illarum personarum sic defunctarum sive amotarum eligere et praeficere; et quòd ille sive illi sic electus et praefectus electi et praefecti officia praedicta respectiva habeat et exerceat habeant et exerceant durante residuo ejusdem anni, et quousque alius sive alii ad officia illa respectiva debito modo electus et juratus fuerit, electi et jurati fuerint; et sic toties quoties casus sic acciderit.

Et insuper volumus, ac de gratia nostra speciali ac ex certa scientia et mero motu nostris concedimus praefatis Praesidi Concilio et Sodalibus Regalis Societatis praedictae et successoribus suis, quòd Praeses et Concilium praedictae Regalis Societatis pro tempore existentes, et major pars eorundum (quorum Praesidem pro tempore existentem unum esse volumus), pariter congregare et assemblare

* *Sic.*

And on every St. Andrew's day yearly (unless it be Sunday), the President, Council, and Fellows, or the major part of them (of whom the President to be one), are to elect others in the Offices of Treasurer, Secretaries, Clerk, and Serjeants at Mace: who, after being sworn, are to officiate till the next St. Andrew's Day.

And if any of them die or be amoved, the like election to be made of others to supply their places, for the residue of the year, and till others shall be duly elected and sworn.

The President and Council, and the major part of them (of whom the President to be one), may meet in a College or *other public Place or Hall in London, or within ten miles of it; and make Laws, Statutes, and Ordinances, and do all other things relating to the affairs of the Society.*

possint et valeant in collegio sive alio publico loco sive aula intra Civitatem nostram London, vel in aliquo alio loco conveniente intra decem milliaria ejusdem Civitatis nostrae ; et quòd ipsi sic congregati et assemblati habebunt et habeant plenam authoritatem potestatem et facultatem de tempore in tempus condendi constituendi ordinandi faciendi et stabiliendi hujusmodi leges statuta jura ordinationes et constitutiones, quae eis, aut eorum majori parti, bona salubria utilia honesta et necessaria juxta eorum sanas discretiones fore videbuntur, et omnia quaecunque alia negotiis et rebus Regalis Societatis praedictae spectantia* agendi et faciendi : quae omnia et singula leges statuta jura ordinationes et constitutiones sic ut praefertur facienda volumus, et per praesentes pro nobis heredibus et successoribus nostris firmiter injungendo praecipimus et mandamus, quòd de tempore in tempus inviolabiliter observata fuerint, secundùm tenorem et effectum eorundem ; ita tamen, quòd praedicta leges statuta jura ordinationes et constitutiones sic ut praefertur facienda, et eorum quaelibet, sint rationabilia, et non sint repugnantia nec contraria legibus consuetudinibus juribus sive statutis hujus Regni nostri Angliae.

Power is given to the Council and Fellows to appoint one or more Printer or Printers, and one or more Engraver or Engravers; and to authorise them by writing under the Common Seal, and signed by the President, to print such things (touching or concerning the Society) as shall be given them in charge by the President and Council, or any seven or more of them (of whom the President to be one).

Et ulteriùs de ampliori gratia nostra speciali ac ex certa scientia et mero motu nostris dedimus et concessimus, ac per praesentes pro nobis heredibus et successoribus nostris damus et concedimus, praefatis Concilio et Sodalibus praedictae Regalis Societatis et successoribus suis, plenam potestatem et authoritatem de tempore in tempus eligendi nominandi et constituendi unum vel plures Typographos sive Impressores, et Chalcographos seu Sculptores ; et ipsi vel ipsis per scriptum Communi Sigillo praedictae Regalis Societatis sigillatum, et manu Praesidis pro tempore existentis signatum, facultatem concedendi, ut imprimant talia res materias et negotia praedictam [Regalem]† Societatem tangentia vel concernentia, qualia praedictis Typographo vel Impressori, Chalcographo vel Sculptori, vel Typographis vel Impressoribus, Chalcographis vel Sculptoribus, de tempore in tempus per Praesidem et Concilium praedictae Regalis Societatis, vel aliquos septem vel plures eorum (quorum Praesidem pro tempore existentem unum esse volumus), commissa fuerint ; sacramentis suis

They must be first sworn before the President and

corporalibus, antequam ad officia sua exercenda admittantur, coram Praeside et Concilio pro tempore existen-

---

* *Sic.*
† From the Patent Roll.

tibus, vel aliquibus septem vel pluribus eorum, in forma et effectu ultimè specificatis, priùs praestandis: quibus quidem Praesidi et Concilio, vel aliquibus septem vel pluribus eorum, sacramenta praedicta administrare plenam potestatem et authoritatem damus et concedimus per praesentes. *Council, or any seven or more of them.*

Et ulteriùs, quòd praedicti Praeses Concilium et Sodales praedictae Regalis Societatis in philosophicis suis studiis meliorem sortiantur effectum, de ampliori gratia nostra speciali ac ex certa scientia et mere motu nostris dedimus et concessimus, ac per praesentes pro nobis heredibus et successoribus nostris damus et concedimus, praedictis Praesidi Concilio et Sodalibus praedictae Regalis Societatis et successoribus suis, quòd ipsi et successores sui de tempore in tempus habeant et habebunt plenam potestatem et authoritatem de tempore in tempus, et ad talia tempestiva tempora, secundùm eorum discretionem, requirere capere et recipere cadavera talium personarum, quae mortem manu carnificis passae fuerunt, et ea anatomizare, in tam amplis modo et forma, et ad omnes intentiones et proposita, prout Collegium Medicorum et Corporatio Chirurgorum Civitatis nostrae London eisdem cadaveribus usi vel gavisi fuerunt, aut uti vel gaudere valeant et possint. *The same Right to demand, receive, and anatomize the Bodies of executed Criminals, is given to this Society, as the College of Physicians and the Corporation of Surgeons of London have or use.*

Et ulteriùs, pro melioratione experimentorum artium et scientiarum praedictae Regalis Societatis, de abundantiori gratia nostra speciali ac ex certa scientia et mero motu nostris dedimus et concessimus, ac per praesentes pro nobis heredibus et successoribus nostris damus et concedimus, praefatis Praesidi Concilio et Sodalibus praedictae Regalis Societatis et successoribus suis, quòd ipsi et successores sui de tempore in tempus habeant et habebunt plenam potestatem et authoritatem, per literas vel epistolas, sub manu praedicti Praesidis in praesentia Concilii, vel aliquorum septem vel plurium eorum, et in nomine Regalis Societatis, ac Communi Sigillo suo praedicto sigillatas, mutuis intelligentiis fruentur* et notitiis cum omnibus et omnimodis personis peregrinis et alienis, utrum privatis vel collegiatis, corporatis vel politicis, absque aliqua molestatione interruptione vel inquietatione quacunque: Proviso tamen, quòd haec indulgentia nostra sic ut praefertur concessa ad ulteriorem non extendatur usum, quàm particulare beneficium et interesse praedictae Regalis Societatis in materiis seu rebus philosophicis mathematicis aut mechanicis. *Licence to hold a Literary Correspondence, on Philosophical, Mathematical, or Mechanical Subjects, with all sorts of Foreigners; by Letters sealed with the Common Seal of the Society, and signed by the President in the presence of the Council or any seven or more of them.*

* *Sic*, for *fruendi.*

Licence to build a College or Colleges in London, or within ten Miles of London.

Et ulteriùs dedimus et concessimus, ac per praesentes pro nobis heredibus et successoribus nostris damus et concedimus, praefatis Praesidi Concilio et Sodalibus Regalis Societatis praedictae et successoribus suis plenam potestatem et authoritatem erigendi aedificandi et extruendi, aut erigi aedificari et extrui faciendi vel causandi, intra Civitatem nostram London, vel decem milliaria ejusdem, unum vel plura Collegium vel Collegia cujuscunque modi vel qualitatis, pro habitatione assemblatione et congregatione praedictorum Praesidis Concilii et Sodalium praedictae Regalis Societatis et successorum suorum, negotia sua et alias res eandem Regalem Societatem concernentia ad ordinandum et disponendum.

If any Abuses or Differences arise, they shall be reformed and settled by the Lord Chancellor Clarendon alone, while living; afterwards by the Archbishop of Canterbury, the Lord Chancellor, or Keeper, the Lord Treasurer, the Bishop of London, the Lord Privy Seal, and the two Secretaries of State for the time being, or four or more of them.

Et ulteriùs volumus, ac per praesentes pro nobis heredibus et successoribus nostris ordinamus constituimus et appunctuamus, quòd si aliqui abusus vel discrepantiae in posterum orientur et accident de gubernatione aut aliis rebus vel negotiis praedictae Regalis Societatis, unde ejusdem constitutioni stabilimini et studiorum progressui vel rebus et negotiis aliqua inferatur injuria vel impedimentum ; quòd tunc et toties per praesentes pro nobis heredibus et successoribus nostris [ordinamus]* authorizamus nominamus assignamus et constituimus praefatum praedilectum et perquam fidelem Consanguineum et Conciliarium nostrum Edwardum, Comitem Clarendon, Cancellarium nostrum Regni nostri Angliae, per seipsum durante vita sua, et post ejus mortem tunc Archiepiscopum Cantuariensem, Cancellarium vel Custodem Magni Sigilli Angliae, Thesaurarium Angliae, Episcopum Londinensem, Custodem Privati Sigilli, et duos Principales Secretarios, pro tempore existentes, aut aliquos quatuor vel plures eorum, easdem discrepantias et abusus reconciliare componere et reducere.

General Clauses.

Et ulteriùs volumus, ac per praesentes pro nobis heredibus et successoribus nostris firmiter injungendo praecipimus et mandamus omnibus et singulis Justiciariis Majoribus Aldermannis Vicecomitibus Ballivis Constabulariis et aliis officiariis ministris et subditis nostris heredum et successorum nostrorum quibuscunque, quòd de tempore in tempus sint auxiliantes et assistentes praedictis Praesidi Concilio et Sodalibus Regalis Societatis praedictae et successoribus suis in omnibus et per omnia, secundùm veram intentionem harum Literarum nostrarum Patentium.

* From the Patent Roll.

Eò quòd expressa mentio de vero valore annuo vel de certitudine praemissorum sive eorum alicujus, aut de aliis donis sive concessionibus per nos seu per aliquem progenitorum sive praedecessorum nostrorum praefatis Praesidi Concilio et Sodalibus Regalis Societatis ante haec tempora factis, in praesentibus minimè facta existit; aut aliquo statuto actu ordinatione provisione proclamatione sive restrictione in contrarium inde antehac habito facto edito ordinato sive proviso, aut aliqua alia re causa vel materia quacunque, in aliquo non obstante.

In cujus rei testimonium has Literas nostras fieri fecimus Patentes. TESTE Me ipso, apud Westmonasterium, quinto decimo die Julii, anno regni nostri decimo quarto.

Per ipsum Regem.
HOWARD.*

FIRST CHARTER,

Granted to the President, Council, and Fellows of the Royal Society of London, by King Charles the Second, A.D. 1662.

Charles the Second, by the grace of God King of England, Scotland, France, and Ireland, Defender of the Faith, &c., to all to whom these present Letters shall come, greeting.

We have long and fully resolved with Ourself to extend not only the boundaries of the Empire, but also the very arts and sciences. Therefore we look with favour upon all forms of learning, but with particular grace we encourage philosophical studies, especially those

---

* This document, with those of a similar nature, subsequently granted to the Society, are preserved in a strong box in the apartments of the Royal Society. The first Charter is on four skins of vellum; it was drawn by Sir Robert Sawyer, then Attorney-General, and is remarkable for its clearness and legal terseness. The first skin contains some remarkably handsome ornamented capitals and flowers, with a finely executed Portrait of Charles II. in Indian ink within the initial letter C. The Great Seal of the Kingdom in green wax is appended to the Charter.

which by actual experiments attempt either to shape out a new philosophy or to perfect the old. In order, therefore, that such studies, which have not hitherto been sufficiently brilliant in any part of the world, may shine conspicuously amongst our people, and that at length the whole world of letters may always recognise us not only as the Defender of the Faith, but also as the universal lover and patron of every kind of truth:

Know ye that we, of our special grace and of our certain knowledge and mere motion, have ordained, established, granted, and declared, and by these presents for us, our heirs, and successors do ordain, establish, grant, and declare, that from henceforth for ever there shall be a Society, consisting of a President, Council, and Fellows, which shall be called and named The Royal Society; And for us, our heirs, and successors we do make, ordain, create, and constitute by these presents the same Society, by the name of The President, Council, and Fellows of the Royal Society, one body corporate and politic in fact, deed, and name, really and fully, and that by the same name they may have perpetual succession; and that they and their successors (whose studies are to be applied to further promoting by the authority of experiments the sciences of natural things and of useful arts), by the same name of The President, Council, and Fellows of the Royal Society aforesaid, may and shall be in all future times persons able and capable in law to have, acquire, receive, and possess lands and tenements, meadows, feedings, pastures, liberties, privileges, franchises, jurisdictions, and hereditaments whatsoever, to themselves and their successors in fee and perpetuity, or for term of life, lives, or years, or otherwise in whatsoever manner, and also goods and chattels, and all other things, of whatsoever kind, nature, sort, or quality they may be; and also to give, grant, demise, and assign the same lands, tenements, and hereditaments, goods and chattels, and to do and execute all acts and things necessary of and concerning the same, by the name aforesaid; And that by the name of The President, Council, and Fellows of the Royal Society aforesaid they may henceforth for ever be able and have power to plead and be impleaded, to answer and be answered, to defend and be defended, in whatsoever Courts and places, and before whatsoever Judges and Justices and other persons and officers of us, our heirs, and successors, in all and singular actions,

Incorporation, and Corporate Name.

Capacity to purchase,

and to grant;

to sue and be sued;

pleas, suits, plaints, causes, matters, things, and demands whatsoever, of whatsoever kind, nature, or sort they may or shall be, in the same manner and form as any of our lieges within this our Realm of England, being persons able and capable in law, or as any body corporate or politic within this our Realm of England, may be able and have power to have, acquire, receive, possess, give, and grant, to plead and be impleaded, to answer and be answered, to defend or be defended; And that the same President, Council, and Fellows of the Royal Society aforesaid, and their successors, may have for ever a Common Seal, to serve for transacting the causes and affairs whatsoever of them and their successors; and that it may and shall be good and lawful to the same President, Council, and Fellows of the Royal Society aforesaid, and to their successors for the time being, to break, change, and make anew that Seal from time to time, according as it shall seem most expedient to them. *and to have a Common Seal, alterable at pleasure.*

And that our royal intention may obtain the better effect, and for the good rule and government of the aforesaid Royal Society from time to time, we will, and by these presents for us, our heirs, and successors do grant to the same President, Council, and Fellows of the Royal Society aforesaid, and to their successors, that henceforth for ever the Council aforesaid shall be and consist of twenty-one persons (of whom we will the President to be always one); And that all and singular other persons who within one month next following after the date of these presents shall be received and admitted by the President and Council, and in all time following by the President, Council, and Fellows, into the same Society, as Members of the Royal Society aforesaid, and shall have been noted in the Register by them to be kept, shall be and shall be called and named Fellows of the Royal Society aforesaid: whom, the more eminently they are distinguished for the study of every kind of learning and good letters, the more ardently they desire to promote the honour, studies, and advantage of this Society, the more they are noted for integrity of life, uprightness of character, and piety, and excel in fidelity and affection of mind towards us, our Crown, and dignity, the more we wish them to be especially deemed fitting and worthy of being admitted into the number of the Fellows of the same Society. *The Council to consist of 21 (of whom the President to be always one). The Fellows to be chosen in the first month, by the President and Council; after that month, by the President, Council, and Fellows.*

And for the better execution of our will and grant

in this behalf, we have assigned, nominated, constituted, and made, and by these presents for us, our heirs, and successors do assign, nominate, constitute, and make, our very well-beloved and trusty William, Viscount Brouncker, Chancellor to our very dear consort, Queen Catherine, to be and become the first and present President of the Royal Society aforesaid; willing that the aforesaid Wil- *[margin: William, Viscount Brouncker, to be the first President;]* liam, Viscount Brouncker, shall continue in the office of President of the Royal Society aforesaid from the date of these presents until the feast of St. Andrew next following after the date of these presents, and until one *[margin: to hold till St. Andrew's Day next (if he shall so long live), and till another out of the Council be chosen and sworn;]* other of the Council of the Royal Society aforesaid for the time being shall have been elected, appointed, and sworn to that office in due manner, according to the ordinance and provision below in these presents expressed and declared (if the aforesaid William, Viscount Brouncker, shall live so long); having first taken a corporal oath well and faithfully *[margin: but first to be sworn before the Lord Chancellor.]* to execute his office in and by all things touching that office, according to the true intention of these presents, before our very well-beloved and very trusty Cousin and Councillor Edward, Earl of Clarendon, our Chancellor of England: to which same Edward, Earl of Clarendon, our Chancellor aforesaid, we give and grant full power and authority, to administer the oath aforesaid in these words following, that is to say:—

[margin: The President's Oath.] I, William, Viscount Brouncker, do promise to deal faithfully and honestly in all things belonging to the trust committed to me as President of this Royal Society, during my employment in that capacity. So help me God!

We have also assigned, constituted, and made, and by these presents for us, our heirs, and successors do make, our *[margin: The first Council named;]* beloved and trusty Robert Moray, Knight, one of our Privy Council in our Realm of Scotland; Robert Boyle, Esquire; William Brereton, Esquire, eldest son of the Baron de Brereton; Kenelm Digby, Knight, Chancellor to our very dear mother, Queen Maria; Paul Neile, Knight, one of the Gentlemen of our Privy Chamber; Henry Slingesby, Esquire, another of the Gentlemen of our aforesaid Privy Chamber; William Petty, Knight; John Wallis, Doctor in Divinity; Timothy Clarke, Doctor in Medicine and one of our Physicians; John Wilkins, Doctor in Divinity; George Ent, Doctor in Medicine; William Aerskine, one of our Cup-bearers; Jonathan Goddard, Doctor in Medicine and Professor of Gresham College; Christopher Wren, Doctor in Medicine, Saville

Professor of Astronomy in our University of Oxford; William Balle, Esquire; Matthew Wren, Esquire; John Evelyn, Esquire; Thomas Henshawe, Esquire; Dudley Palmer, of Grey's Inn, in our County of Middlesex, Esquire; and Henry Oldenburg, Esquire, together with the President aforesaid, to be and become the first and present twenty-one of the Council of the Royal Society aforesaid; to be continued in the same offices from the date of these presents until the aforesaid feast of Saint Andrew the Apostle next following, and thenceforth until other fitting and able and sufficient persons shall have been elected, appointed, and sworn into the offices aforesaid (if they shall live so long, or shall not have been amoved for any just and reasonable cause); first taking corporal oaths before the President of the aforesaid Royal Society, well and faithfully to execute their offices in and by all things touching those offices, according to the form and effect of the aforesaid oath, *mutatis mutandis*, to be administered to the President of the Royal Society aforesaid by our Chancellor of England; (to which same President for the time being, for us, our heirs, and successors, we give and grant by these presents full power and authority to administer the oaths aforesaid;) And that the same persons, so as it is aforesaid elected, appointed, and sworn, and hereafter to be elected, appointed, and sworn from time to time, to the Council of the aforesaid Royal Society, shall be and become aiding, counselling, and assistant in all matters, business, and affairs touching or concerning the better regulation, government, and direction of the aforesaid Royal Society, and of every Member of the same.
to continue as above, unless amoved for just cause; but first to take, before the President, the like oath as his, mutatis mutandis.

And further we will, and by these presents for us, our heirs, and successors do grant to the aforesaid President, Council, and Fellows of the Royal Society aforesaid, and to their successors, that the President, Council, and Fellows of the Royal Society aforesaid for the time being (of whom we will the President for the time being to be one) may and shall have from time to time in all future times for ever power and authority to nominate and elect, and that they may be able and have power to elect and nominate, every year, on the aforesaid feast of St. Andrew, one of the Council of the aforesaid Royal Society for the time being, who may and shall be President of the Royal Society aforesaid until the feast of St. Andrew the Apostle thereafter next following (if he shall live so long,
The President, Council, and Fellows (of whom the President to be one), to elect, annually, on St. Andrew's Day, one out of the Council to be President: who is to hold, if not dead nor amoved, till the next St. Andrew's Day, and till another, shall be chosen: having first taken the Oath before the Council or seven or more of them.

or shall not be amoved meanwhile for any just and reasonable cause), and thenceforth until another shall have been elected, appointed, and nominated to the office of President of the Royal Society aforesaid; and that he, after that he shall so have been elected and nominated, as it is aforesaid, to the office of President of the Royal Society aforesaid, before he be admitted to that office, shall take a corporal oath before the Council of the same Royal Society, or any seven or more of them, rightly, well, and faithfully to execute that office in all things touching that office, according to the form and effect of the aforesaid oath, *mutatis mutandis* (to which same Council, or to any seven or more of them, we give and grant by these presents for us, our heirs, and successors, full power and authority to administer the aforesaid oath from time to time, as often as it shall be necessary); and that after having so taken such oath, as it is aforesaid, he may be able and have power to execute the office of President of the Royal Society aforesaid until the feast of St. Andrew the Apostle thereafter next following; And if it shall happen that the President of the Royal Society aforesaid for the time being, at any time, so long as he shall be in the office of President of the same Royal Society, shall die or be amoved from his office, that then and so often it may and shall be good and lawful to the Council and Fellows of the aforesaid Royal Society, or to any seven or more of them (of whom we will the President of the Council aforesaid to be always one at such an election),* to elect and appoint another of the aforesaid number of the Council aforesaid as President of the Royal Society aforesaid; and that he so elected and appointed may have and exercise that office during the residue of the same year, and until another shall have been in due manner elected and sworn to that office, first taking a corporal oath in the form last specified; and so as often as the case shall so happen.

<small>On the Death or Amotion of a President, the Council and Fellows, or any seven or more of them, are to elect another, out of the Council: who is to hold, during the residue of the year (being first sworn), and until another be chosen and sworn.</small>

<small>If any of the Council die, or be amoved, or retire (and power of amotion is hereby given to the President and Council or major part of them, whereof the President to be one); the President, Council, and Fellows, or</small>

And further we will, that whenever it shall happen that any one or any of the Council of the Royal Society aforesaid for the time being shall die, or be amoved from that office, or retire (which same [members] of the Council of the Royal Society aforesaid, and every one of them, we will to be amoveable for misbehaviour or any other reasonable cause, at the good pleasure of the Presi-

---

* So in the original; see p. 24.

dent and of the rest of the Council aforesaid surviving and remaining in that office, or of the major part of the same, of whom we will the President for the time being to be one), that then and so often it may and shall be good and lawful to the aforesaid President, Council, and Fellows of the Royal Society aforesaid, or to the major part of the same (of whom we will the President of the Royal Society aforesaid for the time being to be one), to nominate, elect, and appoint one other or several others of the Fellows of the Royal Society aforesaid, in the place or places of him or them so dead, retired, or amoved, to fill up the aforesaid number of twenty-one persons of the Council of the Royal Society aforesaid; and that he or they so elected and appointed in that office may have the same office until the feast of St. Andrew the Apostle then next following, and thenceforth until one other or several others shall have been elected, appointed, and nominated; first taking a corporal oath before the President and Council of the Royal Society aforesaid, or any seven or more of them for the time being, well and faithfully to execute that office in and by all things touching that office, according to the true intention of these presents. *the major part of them (the President to be one), may supply the vacancy out of the Fellows: and the elected shall hold (being first sworn) till the next St. Andrew's Day, and till another Election.*

And further we will, and by these presents for us, our heirs, and successors do grant to the aforesaid President, Council, and Fellows of the aforesaid Royal Society, and to their successors, that they and their successors, every year, on the aforesaid feast of St. Andrew the Apostle, may and shall have full power and authority to elect, nominate, appoint, and change ten of the Fellows of the Royal Society aforesaid, to fill up the places and offices of ten of the aforesaid number of twenty-one of the Council of the Royal Society aforesaid; for we do declare it to be our royal pleasure, and by these presents for us, our heirs, and successors we do grant, that ten of the aforesaid Council, and no more, shall be annually changed and amoved by the President, Council, and Fellows of the Royal Society aforesaid. *On every St. Andrew's Day, Ten (and no more) of the Council are to be changed.*

We will also, and for us, our heirs, and successors do grant to the aforesaid President, Council, and Fellows of the aforesaid Royal Society, and to their successors, that if it shall happen that the President of the same Royal Society for the time being is detained by sickness or infirmity, or is employed in the service of us, our heirs, or successors, or is otherwise occupied, so that he shall not

The President may appoint one out of the Council to be his Deputy;	be able to attend to the necessary affairs of the same Royal Society touching the office of President, that then and so often it may and shall be good and lawful to the same President so detained, employed, or occupied, to
who may act as such during his absence; unless he appoint some other out of the Council to be so.	nominate and appoint one of the Council of the aforesaid Royal Society for the time being to be and become the Deputy of the same President; which same Deputy, so to be made and appointed in the office of Deputy of the President aforesaid, may and shall be the Deputy of the same President from time to time, as often as the aforesaid President shall happen to be so absent, during the whole time in which the aforesaid President shall continue in the office of President; unless in the meanwhile the aforesaid President of the Royal Society aforesaid for the time being shall have made and appointed one other of the aforesaid
Such Deputy may, in the President's absence, do all acts that he himself could do if present.	Council his Deputy; And that every such Deputy of the aforesaid President so to be made and appointed, as it is aforesaid, may be able and have power to do and execute all and singular things which pertain or ought to pertain to the office of President of the aforesaid Royal Society, or which are limited and appointed to be done and executed by the aforesaid President, by virtue of these our Letters Patent, from time to time, as often as the aforesaid President shall so happen to be absent, during such time as he shall continue the Deputy of the aforesaid President, by force of these our Letters Patent, as fully, freely, and wholly, and in as ample manner and
But he must first be sworn before the Council, or seven or more of them.	form, as the aforesaid President, if he were present, would be able and have power and do and execute those things; a corporal oath first to be taken by such Deputy upon the holy Gospels of God, in the form and effect last specified, well and faithfully to execute all and singular things which pertain to the office of President, before the aforesaid Council of the aforesaid Royal Society, or any seven or more of them; and so as often as the case shall so happen: to which same Council, or to any seven or more of them, for the time being, we do give and grant by these presents power and authority to administer the oath aforesaid as often as the case shall so happen, without procuring or obtaining any writ, commission, or further warrant in that behalf from us, our heirs, or successors.
The President, Council, and Fellows, may have one Treasurer, two Secretaries, a	And further we will, and by these presents for us, our heirs, and successors do grant to the aforesaid President, Council, and Fellows of the Royal Society aforesaid, and to their successors, that they and their successors henceforth

for ever may and shall have one Treasurer, two Secretaries, one Clerk, and two Serjeants-at-Mace, who may from time to time attend upon the President; and that the aforesaid Treasurer, Secretaries, Clerk, and Serjeants-at-Mace, to be elected and nominated, before they be admitted to execute their several and respective offices, shall take their corporal oaths in the form and effect last specified, before the President and Council of the same Royal Society, or any seven or more of them, rightly, well, and faithfully to execute their several and respective offices in all things touching the same; and that after having so taken such oaths, as it is aforesaid, they may exercise and use their respective offices; to which same President and Council, or to any seven or more of them, we do give and grant by these presents full power and authority to administer the oaths aforesaid from time to time to the aforesaid several and respective officers and their successors: And we have assigned, nominated, chosen, created, appointed, and made, and by these presents for us, our heirs, and successors do assign, nominate, choose, create, appoint, and make, our beloved subjects William Balle, Esquire, to be and become the first and present Treasurer, and the aforesaid John Wilkins and Henry Oldenburg to be and become the first and present Secretaries, of the aforesaid Royal Society; to be continued in the same offices until the aforesaid feast of St. Andrew the Apostle next following after the date of these presents: And that from time to time and at all times on the aforesaid feast of Saint Andrew the Apostle (unless it shall be Sunday, and if it be Sunday, then on the day next following) the President, Council, and Fellows of the aforesaid Royal Society for the time being, or the major part of the same (of whom we will the President for the time being to be one), may be able and have power to elect, nominate, and appoint other upright and discreet men, from time to time, as Treasurer, Secretaries, Clerk, and Serjeants-at-Mace of the aforesaid Royal Society; and that those who shall so have been elected, appointed, and sworn to the aforesaid several and respective offices, as it is aforesaid, may be able and have power to exercise and enjoy those respective offices until the aforesaid feast of St. Andrew then next following, their aforesaid oaths, as it is aforesaid, first to be taken; and so as often as the case shall so happen: And if it shall happen that any one or any of the officers aforesaid of the same

And if any of them die or be amoved, the like election to be made of others to supply their places, for the residue of the year, and till others shall be duly elected and sworn.

Royal Society shall die, or be amoved from their respective offices, that then and so often it may and shall be good and lawful to the President, Council, and Fellows of the aforesaid Royal Society, or to the major part of the same (of whom we will the President for the time being to be one), to elect and appoint another or others to the office or offices of those persons so deceased or amoved; and that he or they so elected and appointed may have and exercise the respective offices aforesaid during the residue of the same year, and until another or others shall have been in due manner elected and sworn to those respective offices; and so as often as the case shall so happen.

The President and Council, or the major part of them (of whom the President to be one), may meet in a College or other public Place or Hall in London, or within ten miles of it; and make Laws, Statutes, and Ordinances, and do all other things relating to the affairs of the Society.

And moreover we will, and of our special grace and of our certain knowledge and mere motion do grant to the aforesaid President, Council, and Fellows of the Royal Society aforesaid, and to their successors, that the President and Council of the aforesaid Royal Society for the time being, and the major part of the same (of whom we will the President for the time being to be one), may be able and have power to meet together and assemble in a College or other public place or Hall within our City of London, or in any other convenient place within ten miles of our same City; and that they so met together and assembled shall and may have full authority, power, and faculty from time to time to draw up, constitute, ordain, make, and establish such laws, statutes, acts, ordinances, and constitutions as shall seem to them, or to the major part of them, to be good, wholesome, useful, honourable, and necessary, according to their sound discretions, and to do and perform all other things whatsoever belonging to the affairs and matters of the Royal Society aforesaid; all and singular which laws, statutes, acts, ordinances, and constitutions so to be made as it is aforesaid, we will, and by these presents for us, our heirs, and successors, firmly enjoining, do order and command, that they shall be inviolably observed from time to time, according to the tenor and effect of the same: so nevertheless that the aforesaid laws, statutes, acts, ordinances, and constitutions so to be made as it is aforesaid, and every one of them, be reasonable, and not repugnant or contrary to the laws, customs, acts, or statutes of this our Realm of England.

Power is given to the Council and Fellows to appoint one or more Printer or Print-

And further, of our more ample special grace and of our certain knowledge and mere motion, we have given and granted, and by these presents for us, our heirs, and successors do give and grant to the aforesaid Council and Fellows of the aforesaid Royal Society, and to their successors, full power and authority from time to time to elect, nominate, and appoint one or more Typographers or Printers, and Chalcographers or Engravers, and to grant to him or them, by a writing, sealed with the Common Seal of the aforesaid Royal Society, and signed by the hand of the President for the time being, faculty to print such things, matters, and affairs touching or concerning the aforesaid [Royal] Society, as shall have been committed to the aforesaid Typographer or Printer, Chalcographer or Engraver, or Typographers or Printers, Chalcographers or Engravers, from time to time, by the President and Council of the aforesaid Royal Society, or any seven or more of them (of whom we will the President for the time being to be one); their corporal oaths first to be taken, before they be admitted to exercise their offices, before the President and Council for the time being, or any seven or more of them, in the form and effect last specified; to which same President and Council, or to any seven or more of them, we do give and grant by these presents full power and authority to administer the oaths aforesaid.

[margin: ers, and one or more Engraver or Engravers; and to authorise them by writing under the Common Seal, and signed by the President, to print such things (touching or concerning the Society) as shall be given them in charge by the President and Council, or any seven or more of them (of whom the President to be one).]

[margin: They must be first sworn before the President and Council, or any seven or more of them.]

And further, in order that the aforesaid President, Council, and Fellows of the aforesaid Royal Society may obtain the better effect in their philosophical studies, of our more ample special grace and of our certain knowledge and mere motion, we have given and granted, and by these presents for us, our heirs, and successors, do give and grant, to the aforesaid President, Council, and Fellows of the aforesaid Royal Society, and to their successors, that they and their successors from time to time may and shall have full power and authority from time to time, and at such* seasonable times, according to their discretion, to require, take, and receive the bodies of such persons as have suffered death by the hand of the executioner, and to anatomize them, in such ample form and manner, and to all intents and purposes, as the College of Physicians and the Corporation of Surgeons of our City of London have used or enjoyed, or may be able and have power to use or enjoy, the same bodies.

[margin: The same Right to demand, receive, and anatomize the Bodies of executed Criminals, is given to this Society, as the College of Physicians and the Corporation of Surgeons of London have or use.]

And further, for the improvement of the experiments, arts, and sciences of the aforesaid Royal Society, of our more abundant special grace and of our certain know-

* So in the original.

ledge and mere motion, we have given and granted, and by these presents for us, our heirs, and successors do give and grant, to the aforesaid President, Council, and Fellows of the aforesaid Royal Society, and to their successors, that they and their successors from time to time may and shall have full power and authority, by letters or epistles under the hand of the aforesaid President, in the presence of the Council, or of any seven or more of them, and in the name of the Royal Society, and sealed with their Common Seal aforesaid, to enjoy mutual intelligence and knowledge with all and all manner of strangers and foreigners, whether private or collegiate, corporate or politic, without any molestation, interruption, or disturbance whatsoever: Provided nevertheless, that this our indulgence, so granted as it is aforesaid, be not extended to further use than the particular benefit and interest of the aforesaid Royal Society in matters or things philosophical, mathematical, or mechanical.

<small>*Licence to hold a Literary Correspondence, on Philosophical, Mathematical, or Mechanical Subjects, with all sorts of Foreigners; by Letters sealed with the Common Seal of the Society, and signed by the President in the presence of the Council or any seven or more of them.*</small>

And further we have given and granted, and by these presents for us, our heirs, and successors do give and grant to the aforesaid President, Council, and Fellows of the Royal Society aforesaid, and to their successors, full power and authority to erect, build, and construct, or to make or cause to be erected, built, and constructed, within our City of London, or ten miles of the same, one or more College or Colleges, of whatsoever kind or quality, for the habitation, assembly, and meeting of the aforesaid President, Council, and Fellows of the aforesaid Royal Society, and of their successors, for the ordering and arranging of their affairs and other matters concerning the same Royal Society.

<small>*Licence to build a College or Colleges in London, or within ten miles of London.*</small>

And further we will, and by these presents for us, our heirs, and successors do ordain, constitute, and appoint, that if any abuses or differences hereafter shall arise and happen concerning the government or other matters or affairs of the aforesaid Royal Society, whereby any injury or hindrance may be done to the constitution, stability, and progress of the studies, or to the matters and affairs, of the same; that then and so often, by these presents, for us, our heirs, and successors, we do authorise, [ordain,] nominate, assign, and appoint our aforesaid very well-beloved and very trusty Cousin and Councillor Edward, Earl of Clarendon, our Chancellor of our Realm of England, by himself during his life, and, after his death, then the Archbishop of Canterbury, the

<small>*If any Abuses or Differences arise, they shall be reformed and settled by the Lord Chancellor Clarendon alone, while living; afterwards by the Archbishop of Canterbury, the Lord Chancellor, or Keeper, the Lord Treasurer, the Bishop of London, the Lord Privy Seal, and the two Secretaries of State for*</small>

Chancellor or Keeper of the Great Seal of England, the Treasurer of England, the Bishop of London, the Keeper of the Privy Seal, and the two Principal Secretaries for the time being, or any four or more of them, to reconcile, compose, and adjust the same differences and abuses. the time being, or four or more of them.

And further we will, and by these presents, for us, our heirs, and successors, firmly enjoining, do order and command all and singular the Justices, Mayors, Aldermen, Sheriffs, Bailiffs, Constables, and other officers, ministers, and subjects whomsoever of us, our heirs, and successors, that they be from time to time aiding and assistant to the aforesaid President, Council, and Fellows of the Royal Society aforesaid, and to their successors, in and by all things, according to the true intention of these our Letters Patent. General Clauses.

Although express mention of the true yearly value or of the certainty of the premises, or of any of them, or of other gifts or grants before these times made by us or by any of our progenitors or predecessors to the aforesaid President, Council, and Fellows of the Royal Society, is not made in these presents; or any statute, act, ordinance, provision, proclamation, or restriction to the contrary thereof heretofore had, made, enacted, ordained, or provided, or any other thing, cause, or matter whatsoever, in any wise notwithstanding.

In witness whereof we have caused these our Letters to be made Patent. Witness Ourself, at Westminster, the fifteenth day of July, in the fourteenth year of our reign.

By the King himself.
HOWARD.

CHARTA SECUNDA,

Iisdem ab eodem concessa, A.D. MDCLXIII.

CAROLUS SECUNDUS, Dei gratia Angliae Scotiae Franciae et Hiberniae Rex, Fidei Defensor, etc., omnibus ad quos hac Literae nostrae Patentes pervenerint, salutem.

Diu multùmque apud nos statuimus, ut imperii fines, sic etiam artes atque scientias ipsas promovere. Favemus itaque omnibus disciplinis; particulari autem gratia indulgemus philosophicis studiis, praesertim iis, quae solidis experimentis conantur aut novam extundere philosophiam, aut expolire veterem. Ut igitur inclarescant apud nostros hujusmodi studia, quae nusquam terrarum adhuc satis emicuerunt, utque nos tandem universus literarum orbis non solùm fidei defensorem, sed etiam veritatis omnimodae et cultorem ubique et patronum, semper agnoscat:

Incorporation and Corporate Name.

Sciatis, quòd nos de gratia nostra speciali ac ex certa scientia et mero motu nostris ordinavimus constituimus et concessimus, ac per presentes pro nobis heredibus et successoribus nostris ordinamus constituimus et concedimus, quòd de caetero in perpetuum erit Societas, de Praeside Concilio et Sodalibus consistens, qui vocabuntur et nuncupabuntur Praeses Concilium et Sodales Regalis Societatis Londini pro Scientia naturali promovenda (cujus quidem Societatis nos ipsos Fundatorem et Patronum per praesentes declaramus); Et eandem Societatem, per nomen Praesidis Concilii et Sodalium Regalis Societatis Londini pro Scientia naturali promovenda, unum corpus corporatum et politicum in re facto et nomine realiter et ad plenum pro nobis heredibus et successoribus nostris facimus ordinamus creamus et constituimus per praesentes, et quòd per idem nomen habeant successionem perpetuam; Et quòd ipsi et eorum successores (quorum studia ad rerum naturalium artiumque utilium scientias experimentorum fide ulteriùs promovendas, in Dei Creatoris gloriam et generis humani commodum, applicanda sunt), per idem nomen Praesidis Concilii et Sodalium Regalis Societatis Londini pro Scientia naturali promovenda, sint et erunt perpetuis futuris temporibus personae habiles et in lege

The King himself Founder and Patron.

Capacity to purchase;

capaces ad habendum perquirendum percipiendum et possidendum terras [et]* tenementa prata pascua pasturas libertates privilegia franchesias jurisdictiones et hereditamenta quaecunque sibi et successoribus suis in feodo et perpetuitate, vel pro termino vitae vitarum vel annorum, seu aliter quocunque modo, ac etiam bona et catalla, ac omnes alias res, cujuscunque fuerint generis naturae speciei sive qualitatis (Statuto de alienatione in manum mortuam non obstante); Necnon ad dandum concedendum [dimittendum]* et assignandum eadem terras tenementa et hereditamenta, bona et catalla, et omnia facta et res necessarias faciendum et exequendum de et concernentia eadem, per nomen praedictum; Et quòd per nomen Praesidis Concilii et Sodalium Regalis Societatis Londini pro Scientia naturali promovenda praedictam placitare et implacitari, respondere et responderi, defendere et defendi de caetero in perpetuum valeant et possint, in quibuscunque Curiis placeis et locis, et coram quibuscunque Judicibus et Justiciariis et aliis personis et officiariis nostris heredum et successorum nostrorum, in omnibus et singulis actionibus, tum realibus, tum personalibus, placitis sectis querelis causis materiis rebus et demandis quibuscunque, cujuscunque sint aut erunt generis naturae vel speciei, eisdem modo et forma, prout aliqui ligei nostri intra hoc Regnum nostrum Angliae, personae habiles et in lege capaces, aut ut aliquod corpus corporatum vel politicum intra hoc Regnum nostrum Angliae, habere perquirere recipere possidere dare et concedere, placitare et implacitari, respondere et responderi, defendere vel defendi valeant et possint, valeat et possit; Et quòd iidem Praeses Concilium et Sodales Regalis Societatis praedictae et successores sui habeant in perpetuum Commune Sigillum, pro causis et negotiis suis et successorum suorum quibuscunque agendis deserviturum; et quòd benè liceat et licebit eisdem Praesidi Concilio et Sodalibus Regalis Societatis praedictae, et successoribus suis pro tempore existentibus, Sigillum illud de tempore in tempus frangere mutare et de novo facere, prout eis meliùs fore videbitur expediri.

 Damus insuper et concedimus per praesentes Praesidi Concilio et Sodalibus Regalis Societatis praedictae, eorumque in perpetuum successoribus, in favoris nostri regii erga ipsos nostraeque de ipsis peculiaris existimationis praesenti et futuris aetatibus testimonium, haec honoris

margin notes: and to grant; to sue and be sued; and to have a Common Seal, alterable at at pleasure); Grant of Arms, viz. Argent, in a Canton Dexter the three Lions of England: and also of a Crest, and Supporters.

 * From the Patent Roll.

insignia sequentia, viz.: In Parmae argenteae angulo dextro tres leones nostros Anglicos; et pro Cristo galeam corona flosculis interstincta adornatam, cui supereminet aquila nativi coloris, altero pede scutum leonibus nostris insignitum tenens; Telamones scutarios, duos canes sagaces albos, colla coronis cinctos (prout in margine luculentiùs videre est*): à praedictis Praeside Concilio et Sodalibus ipsorumque successoribus, prout feret† occasio, in perpetuum gestanda producenda‡ possidenda.

<small>The Council shall consist of Twenty-one (of whom the President or his Deputy shall be always one).</small>

Et, quòd intentio nostra regia meliorem sortiatur effectum, ac pro bono regimine et gubernatione praedictae Regalis Societatis de tempore in tempus, volumus, ac per praesentes pro nobis heredibus et successoribus nostris concedimus eisdem Praesidi Concilio et Sodalibus Societatis Regalis praedictae, et successoribus suis, quòd de caetero in perpetuum Concilium praedictum erit et consistet ex viginti et una personis (quarum Praesidem pro tempore existentem, vel ejus Deputatum, semper unum esse volumus);

<small>All other persons who shall be received and admitted as Members, by the President and Council, or any eleven or more of them (of whom, &c.) or by two thirds or more of those Eleven or more, *within* two months; and at all times *after* those two months, by the President, Council, and *Fellows*, or by any Twenty-one or more of them (of whom the President or his Deputy to be one), or by *two third* parts or more of the said Twenty-one or more; and shall be registered; shall be called *Fellows* of the said Royal Society, for life, unless regularly amoved.</small>

Et quòd omnes et singulae aliae personae, quae intra duos menses proximè sequentes post datum praesentium per Praesidem et Concilium, vel per aliquos undecim vel plures eorum (quorum Praesidem pro tempore existentem, vel ejus Deputatum, semper unum esse volumus), vel per duas tertias partes vel plures praedictorum undecim vel plurium, et in omni tempore sequenti per Praesidem Concilium et Sodales, sive per aliquos viginti et unum vel plures eorum (quorum Praesidem pro tempore existentem, vel ejus Deputatum, semper unum esse volumus), sive per duas tertias partes vel plures praedictorum viginti et unius vel plurium, in eandem Societatem accipientur et admittentur ut Membra Regalis Societatis praedictae, et in Registro per ipsos conservando annotatae fuerint, erunt vocabuntur et nuncupabuntur Sodales Regalis Societatis praedictae, quamdiu vixerint, nisi ob causam aliquam rationabilem, secundùm Statuta Regalis Societatis praedictae condenda, quemvis eorum amoveri contigerit: quos§ quantò eminentiùs omnis generis doctrinae bonarumque literarum studio clarescant, quantò ardentiùs hujusce Societatis honorem studia et emolumentum‖ promoveri cupiant, quantò vitae integritate morumque probitate ac pietate emineant, et fidelitate

---

* A representation of the Arms appears on the first skin of the Charter.

† This word is omitted from the Patent Roll.

‡ *Sic.*   § " Quas " in the Roll.   ‖ Or *emolumenta*.

animique erga nos Coronam et dignitatem nostram sincero affectu polleant, eò magis idoneos et dignos, qui in Sodalium ejusdem Societatis numerum adsciscantur, omnino censeri volumus.

Et, pro meliori executione voluntatis et concessionis nostrae in hac parte, assignavimus nominavimus constituimus et fecimus, ac per praesentes pro nobis heredibus et successoribus nostris assignamus nominamus constituimus et facimus, praedilectum et fidelem nobis Willielmum, Vicecomitem Brouncker, Cancellarium praecharissimae Consortis nostrae Reginae Catharinae, esse primum et modernum Praesidem Regalis Societatis praedictae; volentes quòd praedictus Willielmus, Vicecomes Brouncker, in officio Praesidis Regalis Societatis praedictae, à datu praesentium usque ad festum Sancti Andreae proximùm sequentem post datum praesentium, continuabit, et quousque unus alius de Concilio Regalis Societatis praedictae pro tempore existente ad officium illud debito modo electus praefectus et juratus fuerit, juxta ordinationem et provisionem in his praesentibus inferius expressam et declaratam (si praedictus Willielmus, Vicecomes Brouncker, tam diu vixerit); sacramento corporali in omnibus et per omnia officium illud tangentia benè et fideliter exequendum, secundùm veram intentionem harum praesentium, coram praedilecto et perquam fideli Consanguineo et Consiliario nostro Edwardo, Comite Clarendon, Cancellario nostro Angliae, priùs praestito (cui quidem Edwardo, Comiti Clarendon, Cancellario nostro praedicto, sacramentum praedictum administrare plenam potestatem et authoritatem damus et concedimus), in haec verba sequentia, viz.: *I, William, Viscount Brouncker, doe promise to deale faithfully and honestly in all things belonging to the trust committed to me as President of the Royall Society of London for improving naturall Knowledge, dureing my employment in that capacity. So help me God!*

Assignavimus etiam constituimus et fecimus, ac per praesentes pro nobis heredibus et successoribus nostris facimus, dilectos nobis et fideles Robertum Moray, Militem, unum à Secretioribus nostris Conciliis in Regno nostro Scotiae, Robertum Boyle, Armigerum, Willielmum Brereton, Armigerum, filium primogenitum Baronis de Brereton, Kenelmum Digby, Militem, praecharissimae matri nostrae Mariae Reginae Cancellarium, Gilbertum Talbot,* Militem, Joca-

---

* Sir Gilbert Talbot and Mr. Hill were not in the first Charter: they supply the vacancies of Dr. Wallis and Dr. Wren.

lium nostrorum Thesaurarium, Paulum Neile, Militem, unum Ostiariorum Camerae privatae nostrae, Henricum Slingesby, Armigerum, unum Generosorum praedictae privatae Camerae nostrae, Willielmum Petty, Militem, Timotheum Clarke, in Medicinis Doctorem et unum Medicorum nostrorum, Johannem Wilkins, in Theologia Doctorem, Georgium Ent, in Medicinis Doctorem, Willielmum Aerskine, unum à Poculis nostris, Jonathan. Goddard, in Medicinis Doctorem et Professorem Collegii de Gresham, Willielmum Balle, Armigerum, Matthaeum Wren, Armigerum, Johannem Evelyn, Armigerum, Thomam Henshaw, Armigerum, Dudley Palmer, de Greys Inn in comitatu nostro Middlesexiae, Armigerum, Abrahamum Hill, de London, Armigerum, et Henricum Oldenburg, Armigerum, unà cum Praeside praedicto, fore et esse primos et modernos viginti et unum de Concilio et Sodalibus Regalis Societatis praedictae; continuandos in officiis Concilii praedicti à datu praesentium usque ad praedictum festum Sancti Andreae Apostoli proximùm sequentem, et deinde, quousque aliae idonae personae et habiles et sufficientes in officia praedicta electae praefectae et juratae fuerint (si tam diu vixerint, aut pro aliqua justa et* rationabili causa non amotae fuerint); sacramentis corporalibus coram Praeside pro tempore existente praedictae Regalis Societatis, ad officia sua benè et fideliter in omnibus et per omnia officia illa tangentia exequenda, priùs praestandis, secundùm formam et effectum praedicti sacramenti, mutatis mutandis, Praesidi Regalis Societatis praedictae per Cancellarium nostrum Angliae administrandi (cui quidem Praesidi pro tempore existenti sacramenta praedicta administrare personis praedictis, et aliis quibuscunque in posterum de tempore in tempus in Concilium praedictum eligendis, plenam potestatem et authoritatem pro nobis heredibus et successoribus nostris damus et concedimus per praesentes): Et quòd eaedem personae sic, ut praefertur, ad Concilium praedictae Regalis Societatis electae praefectae et juratae, et in posterum eligendae praeficiendae et jurandae de tempore in tempus, erunt et existent auxiliantes consulentes et assistentes in omnibus materiis rebus et negotiis meliores regulationem gubernationem et directionem praedictae Regalis Societatis, et cujuslibet Membri ejusdem, tangentibus seu concernentibus.

Concedimus etiam Praesidi Concilio et Sodalibus Socie-

* "*Aut*" in the Patent Roll; but see p. 22.

Charta Secunda.

tatis praedictae, et eorum in perpetuum successoribus, quòd ipsi et successores eorum, seu aliqui novem vel plures eorum (quorum Praesidem pro tempore existentem, vel ejus Deputatum, semper unum esse volumus), conventus seu congregationes de seipsis pro experimentorum et rerum naturalium cognitione et indagine, aliisque negotiis ad Societatem praedictam spectantibus, quoties et quando opus fuerit, licitè facere et habere possint in collegio sive aula sive alio loco commodo intra Civitatem nostram Londini, vel [in]* aliquo alio loco commodo intra decem milliaria ab eadem Civitate nostra. or more of them (of whom, &c.), may hold Assemblies at any time or place in London, or within ten miles of it.

Et ulteriùs volumus, ac per praesentes pro nobis heredibus et successoribus nostris concedimus praefatis Praesidi Concilio et Sodalibus Regalis Societatis praedictae, et successoribus suis, quòd Praeses Concilium et Sodales Regalis Societatis praedictae pro tempore existentes, sive aliqui triginta et unus vel plures eorum (quorum Praesidem pro tempore existentem, vel ejus Deputatum, unum esse volumus), seu major pars praedictorum triginta et unius vel plurium, de tempore in tempus perpetuis futuris temporibus potestatem et authoritatem habeant et habebunt nominandi et eligendi, et quòd eligere et nominare possint et valeant, quolibet anno, in praedicto festo Sancti Andreae, unum de Concilio praedictae Regalis Societatis pro tempore existente, qui sit et erit Praeses Regalis Societatis praedictae usque ad festum Sancti Andreae Apostoli exinde proximùm sequentem (si tam diu vixerit, aut interim pro aliqua justa et rationabili causa non amotus fuerit), et exinde quousque unus alius in officium Praesidis Regalis Societatis praedictae electus praefectus et nominatus fuerit; quòdque ille postquam sic ut praefertur electus et nominatus fuerit in officium Praesidis Regalis Societatis praedictae, antequam ad officium illud admittatur, sacramentum corporale coram Concilio ejusdem Regalis Societatis, aut aliquibus septem vel pluribus eorum, ad officium illud rectè benè et fideliter in omnibus officium illud tangentibus exequendum praestabit, secundùm formam et effectum praedicti sacramenti, mutatis mutandis; (cui quidem Concilio, aut aliquibus septem vel pluribus eorum, sacramentum praedictum administrare, pro nobis heredibus et successoribus nostris, plenam potestatem et authoritatem de tempore in tempus, quotiescunque Praesidem eligere opus fuerit, damus et concedimus per praesentes;) et quòd post hujusmodi The President, Council, and Fellows, or any Thirty-one or more of them (of whom the President or his Deputy to be one), or the major part of such Thirty-one or more, may upon every St. Andrew's Day, annually, elect one of the Council to be their President, who shall continue so, (if not dead or amoved,) till the next St. Andrew's Day, and till another shall be elected; having first been sworn in before the Council, or any Seven or more of them.

* From the Patent Roll.

<small>On the Death or Amotion of a President, or if he retire, the Council or any Eleven or more of them may meet to choose a President out of the Council: and the person chosen by them, or the major part of them, being sworn, shall hold during the residue of the year, and until another shall be elected and sworn.</small>

sacramentum sic ut praefertur praestitum, officium Praesidis Regalis Societatis praedictae usque ad festum Sancti Andreae Apostoli exinde proximùm sequentem exequi valeat et possit : Et si contigerit Praesidem Regalis Societatis praedictae pro tempore existentem aliquo tempore, quamdiu fuerit in officio Praesidis ejusdem Regalis Societatis, obire, decedere, vel ab officio suo amoveri, quòd tunc et toties benè liceat et licebit Concilio Regalis Societatis praedictae, eorumque in perpetuum successoribus, sive aliquibus undecim vel pluribus eorum, convenire vel congregari ad eligendum unum de praedicto numero Concilii praedicti in Praesidem Regalis Societatis praedictae ; et quòd ille, qui per Concilium praedictum, vel per praedictos undecim vel plures, vel per majorem partem praedictorum undecim et plurium, electus fuerit et juratus, ut praefertur, officium illud habeat et exerceat durante residuo ejusdem anni, et quousque alius ad officium illud debito modo electus et juratus fuerit, sacramento corporali in forma supra specificata priùs praestando ; et sic toties quoties casus sic acciderit.

<small>On the Death, Amotion, or retirement of any of the Council, (who are hereby made amoveable by the President and Council for sufficient cause.) the President, Council, and Fellows, or any Twenty-one or more of them (of whom, &c.) or the major part of such Twenty-one or more, may supply the vacancy from amongst the Fellows; and the person or persons elected shall hold, (being first sworn,) till the next St. Andrew's Day, and until another or others shall be elected.</small>

Et ulteriùs volumus, quòd quandocunque contigerit aliquem vel aliquos de Concilio Regalis Societatis praedictae pro tempore existente mori, vel ab officio illo amoveri, vel decedere; quos quidem de Concilio Regalis Societatis praedictae et eorum quemlibet pro malè se gerendis aut aliqua alia rationabili causa amobiles esse volumus, ad beneplacitum Praesidis et caeterorum de Concilio praedicto (quorum Praesidem pro tempore existentem, vel ejus Deputatum, unum esse volumus), vel majoris partis eorundem ; quòd tunc et toties benè liceat et licebit praefatis Praesidi Concilio et Sodalibus Regalis Societatis praedictae, eorumque in perpetuum successoribus, vel aliquibus viginti uni vel pluribus eorundem (quorum Praesidem Regalis Societatis praedictae pro tempore existentem, vel ejus Deputatum, unum esse volumus), vel majori parti praedictorum viginti et unius vel plurium, unum alium vel plures alios de Sodalibus Regalis Societatis praedictae, loco sive locis ipsius vel ipsorum sic mortuorum decedentium vel amotorum, ad supplendum praedictum numerum viginti et unius personarum de Concilio Regalis Societatis praedictae, nominare eligere et praeficere ; et quòd ille sive illi sic in officio illo electi et praefecti idem officium habeat et habeant usque ad festum Sancti Andreae Apostoli tunc proximùm sequentem, et exinde quousque unus alius vel plures alii

Charta Secunda.

electus praefectus et nominatus fuerit, electi praefecti et nominati fuerint; sacramento corporali ad officium illud in omnibus et per omnia officium illud tangentia, coram Praeside et Concilio Regali Societatis praedictae, vel aliquibus septem vel pluribus eorum (quorum Praesidem pro tempore existentem, vel ejus Deputatum, semper unum esse volumus), benè et fideliter exequendum, secundùm veram intentionem praesentium, priùs praestando.

Et ulteriùs volumus, ac per praesentes pro nobis heredibus et successoribus nostris concedimus praefatis Praesidi Concilio et Sodalibus praedictae Regalis Societatis, et successoribus suis,* quòd ipsi et successores sui, sive aliqui triginta et unus vel plures eorum (quorum Praesidem pro tempore existentem, vel ejus Deputatum, semper unum esse volumus), sive major pars praedictorum triginta et unius vel plurium, quolibet anno, in praedicto festo Sancti Andreae Apostoli, plenam potestatem et authoritatem habeant et habebunt eligendi nominandi praeficiendi et mutandi decem de Sodalibus Regalis Societatis praedictae, ad supplendum loca et officia decem praedicti numeri viginti et unius de Concilio Regalis Societatis praedictae; quoniam regiam voluntatem nostram esse declaramus, ac per praesentes pro nobis heredibus et successoribus nostris concedimus, quòd decem de Concilio praedicto, et non ampliùs, per Praesidem Concilium et Sodales Regalis Societatis praedictae annuatim mutati et amoti fuerint.

On St. Andrew's Day, Ten of the Council (and no more) are to be changed by the President, Council, and Fellows, or any Thirty-one or more of them (of whom the President or his Deputy always to be one,) or the major part of such Thirty-one or more.

Volumus etiam, et pro nobis heredibus et successoribus nostris concedimus praefatis Praesidi Concilio et Sodalibus praedictae Regalis Societatis, et successoribus suis in perpetuum, quòd si contigerit Praesidem ejusdem Regalis Societatis pro tempore existentem aegritudine vel infirmitate detineri, vel in servitio nostro heredum vel successorum nostrorum versari, vel aliter esse occupatum, ita quòd necessariis negotiis ejusdem Regalis Societatis officium Praesidis tangentibus attendere non poterit, quòd tunc et toties benè liceat et licebit eidem Praesidi sic detento versato vel occupato unum de Concilio praedictae Regalis Societatis pro tempore existente, fore et esse Deputatum ejusdem Praesidis, nominare et appunctuare; qui quidem Deputatus, in officio Deputati Praesidis praedicti sic faciendus et constituendus, sit et erit Deputatus ejusdem Praesidis, de tempore in tempus, toties quoties praedictus Praeses sic abesse contigerit, durante toto tempore, quo praedictus Praeses in officio

The President may appoint One out of the Council to be his Deputy;

who may act as such in his absence, unless the President make some other Deputy out of the Council.

* "*Imperpetuum*," in the Patent Roll.

<small>The Deputy may, in the absence of the President, do all acts that he himself could do if present.</small>

Praesidis continuaverit, nisi interim praedictus Praeses Regalis Societatis praedictae pro tempore existens unum alium de praedicto Concilio ejus Deputatum fecerit et constituerit; Et quòd quilibet hujusmodi Deputatus praedicti Praesidis, sic ut praefertur faciendus et constituendus, omnia et singula, quae ad officium Praesidis praedictae Regalis Societatis pertinent seu pertinere debent, vel per praedictum Praesidem virtute harum Literarum nostrarum Patentium limitata et appunctuata fore* facienda et exequenda, de tempore in tempus, toties quoties praedictus Praeses sic abesse contigerit, durante tali tempore, quo Deputatus praedicti Praesidis continuaverit, facere et exequi valeat et possit, vigore harum Literarum nostrarum Patentium, adeò plenè liberè et integrè, ac in tam amplis modo et forma, prout Praeses praedictus, si praesens esset, illa facere et exequi valeret et posset;

<small>But he must first be sworn before the Council, or Seven or more of them.</small>

sacramento corporali super sancta Dei Evangelia in forma et effectu supra specificatis per hujusmodi Deputatum, ad omnia et singula, quae ad officium Praesidis pertinent benè et fideliter exequenda, coram praefato Concilio praedictae Regalis Societatis, vel aliquibus septem† vel pluribus eorum, priùs praestando; et sic toties quoties casus sic acciderit; cui quidem Concilio vel aliquibus septem vel pluribus eorum pro tempore existente,* sacramentum praedictum administrare potestatem et authoritatem, quoties casus sic acciderit, damus et concedimus per praesentes, absque brevi commissione sive ulteriori warranto in ea parte à nobis heredibus vel successoribus nostris procurando seu obtinendo.

<small>The Society may have a Treasurer, two Secretaries, two or more Curators of Experiments, one Clerk, or more, and two Serjeants at Mace to attend upon the President. All these are to be chosen and named by the President, Council, and Fellows, or any Thirty-one or more of them, (of whom the President or his Deputy to be one,) or by the major part of such Thirty-one or more; and they must be sworn before the President or his Deputy, and the</small>

Et ulteriùs volumus, ac per praesentes pro nobis heredibus et successoribus nostris concedimus praefatis Praesidi Concilio et Sodalibus Regalis Societatis praedictae, et successoribus suis, quòd ipsi et successores sui de caetero in perpetuum habeant et habebunt unum Thesaurarium, duos Secretarios, Curatores experimentorum duos vel plures, Clericum unum vel plures, et praeterea duos Servientes ad Clavas, qui de tempore in tempus super Praesidem attendant: quòdque praedicti Thesaurarius Secretarii Curatores Clericus vel Clerici et Servientes ad Clavas per Praesidem Concilium et Sodales Regalis Societatis praedictae, sive per aliquos triginta et unum vel plures

* *Sic.*

† This number of *seven* is *not* lessened by the third Charter as to the two *new* Oaths there enjoined; but as to this Oath of *Office, five* are made sufficient.

Charta Secunda.

eorum (quorum Praesidem pro tempore existentem, vel ejus Deputatum, unum esse volumus), vel per majorem partem praedictorum triginta et unius vel plurium, eligendi et nominandi, antequam ad officia sua specialia* et respectiva exequenda admittantur, sacramenta sua corporalia in forma et effectu supra specificatis, coram Praeside, vel ejus Deputato, et Concilio ejusdem Regalis Societatis, aut aliquibus septem vel pluribus eorum, officia sua separalia et respectiva in omnibus illa tangentibus rectè benè et fideliter exequenda praestabunt; et quòd post hujusmodi sacramenta† sic ut praefertur praestita, officia sua respectiva exerceant et utantur; quibus quidem Praesidi et Concilio, aut aliquibus septem vel pluribus eorum, sacramenta praedicta de tempore in tempus administrare praedictis separalibus et respectivis officiariis et successoribus suis plenam potestatem et authoritatem damus et concedimus per praesentes: Et assignavimus nominavimus elegimus creavimus constituimus et fecimus, ac per praesentes pro nobis heredibus et successoribus nostris assignamus nominamus eligimus creamus constituimus et facimus, dilectos subditos nostros praedictum Willielmum Balle, Armigerum, fore et esse primum et modernum Thesaurarium, et praedictum‡ Johannem Wilkins et Henricum Oldenburg fore et esse primos et modernos Secretarios praedictae Regalis Societatis, continuandos in eisdem officiis usque ad praedictum festum Sancti Andreae Apostoli proximùm sequentem post datum praesentium: Quòdque de tempore in tempus et ad omnia tempora, in praedicto festo Sancti Andreae Apostoli (si non fuerit dies Dominicus, et si fuerit dies Dominicus, tunc die proximò sequente), Praeses Concilium et Sodales praedictae Regalis Societatis pro tempore existentes, sive aliqui triginta et unus vel plures eorum (quorum Praesidem pro tempore existentem, vel ejus Deputatum, unum esse volumus), sive major pars praedictorum triginta et unius vel plurium, probos et discretos viros de tempore in tempus in Thesaurarium et Secretarios, qui sunt et erunt de numero Concilii Regalis Societatis praedictae, eligere nominare et praeficere valeant et possint; quòdque illi, qui in separalia et respectiva officia praedicta sic ut praefertur electi praefecti et jurati fuerint, officia illa respectiva exercere et gaudere possint et valeant usque ad praedictum festum Sancti

Council, or any seven or more of them.

The first Treasurer named; and also the two first Secretaries.

On every St. Andrew's Day, (unless it be Sunday, and then on the next day,) the President, Council, and Fellows, or any Thirty-one or more of them (of whom, &c.), or the major part of such Thirty-one or more, may elect proper persons out of the Council to be Treasurer and Secretaries; who, after being sworn, are to hold their Offices till the following St. Andrew's Day.

---
* *Sic.*
† "Praedicta" in the Patent Roll, unnecessarily.
‡ *Sic in* Authentic.

<small>If the Elections of President, Council, Treasurer, and Secretaries, or any of them, cannot conveniently be made or finished upon St. Andrew's Day, the President, Council, and Fellows, or any Thirty-one or more of them, (of whom, &c.) or the major part of such Thirty-one, or more, may appoint one or more other day or days, till they shall be finished.</small>

Andreae extunc proximùm sequentem, sacramentis suis praedictis sic ut praefertur priùs praestandis; et sic toties quoties casus sic acciderit. Et si contigerit electiones praedictas Praesidis, Concilii, Thesaurarii, Secretariorum, vel alicujus vel aliquorum eorum, in festo Sancti Andreae praedicto commodè fieri vel perfici non posse, damus et concedimus praedictis Praesidi Concilio et Sodalibus, et successoribus eorum in perpetuum, quòd ipsi, vel aliqui triginta et unus vel plures eorum (quorum Praesidem pro tempore existentem, vel ejus Deputatum, unum esse volumus), vel major pars praedictorum triginta et unius vel plurium, licitè possint nominare et assignare unum alium diem, quàm proximè ad festum Sancti Andreae praedictum commodè fieri poterit, pro electionibus praedictis faciendis vel perficiendis; et sic de die in diem, donec praedictae electiones perficiantur: Et si contigerit aliquem vel aliquos officiariorum praedictorum ejusdem Regalis Societatis obire, decedere, vel ab officiis suis respectivis amoveri, quòd tunc et toties benè liceat et

<small>If any of the said Officers die, retire, or be amoved, the President, Council, and Fellows, or any Twenty-one or more of them (of whom the President or his Deputy to be one), or the major part of such Twenty-one or more, may elect others for the residue of the year, and till new ones shall be elected and sworn.</small>

licebit Praesidi Concilio et Sodalibus praedictae Regalis Societatis, et eorum successoribus in perpetuum, sive aliquibus viginti et uni vel pluribus eorum (quorum Praesidem pro tempore existentem, vel ejus Deputatum, unum esse volumus), seu majori parti praedictorum viginti et unius vel plurium, alium vel alios in officium sive officia illarum personarum sic defunctarum decedentium sive amotarum eligere et praeficere; et quòd ille sive illi sic electus et praefectus electi et praefecti officia praedicta respectiva habeant et exerceant durante residuo ejusdem anni, et quousque alius sive alii ad officia illa respectiva debito modo electus et juratus fuerit, electi et jurati fuerint; et sic toties quoties casus sic acciderit.

<small>The President and Council (every Member of the Council being always duly summoned to extraordinary meetings), or any Nine or more of them (of whom the President or his Deputy to be one), may meet in London or within ten miles of London; and they, or the major part of them, may make Laws, Statutes, and Ordinances, and transact all matters relating</small>

Et insuper volumus, ac de gratia nostra speciali ac ex certa scientia et mero motu nostris concedimus praefatis Praesidi Concilio et Sodalibus Regalis Societatis praedictae, et successoribus suis in perpetuum, quòd Praeses et Concilium praedictae Regalis Societatis pro tempore existentes (praemissa semper in conventibus extraordinariis omnium Membrorum Concilii praedicti debita seu legitima summonitione vel citatione), sive aliqui novem vel plures eorum (quorum Praesidem pro tempore existentem, vel ejus Deputatum, unum esse volumus), pariter congregare et assemblare possint et valeant in collegio sive aula sive alio loco conveniente intra Civitatem nostram Londini, vel in aliquo alio loco convenienti intra

Charta Secunda. 55

decem milliaria ab eadem Civitate nostra; et quòd ipsi sic congregati et assemblati, sive major pars eorum, habebunt et habeant plenam authoritatem potestatem et facultatem de tempore in tempus condendi constituendi ordinandi faciendi et stabiliendi hujusmodi leges statuta jura ordinationes et constitutiones, quae eis, aut eorum majori parti, bona salubria utilia honesta et necessaria juxta eorum sanas discretiones fore videbuntur, pro meliori gubernatione regulatione et directione Regalis Societatis praedictae et cujuslibet Membri ejusdem, omniaque ad gubernationem res bona facultates redditus terras tenementa hereditamenta et negotia Regalis Societatis praedictae spectantia agendi et faciendi; quae omnia et singula leges statuta jura ordinationes et constitutiones sic ut praefertur facienda volumus, et per praesentes pro nobis heredibus et successoribus nostris firmiter injungendo praecipimus et mandamus, quòd de tempore in tempus inviolabiliter observata fuerint, secundùm tenorem et effectum eorundem; ita tamen, quòd praedicta leges statuta jura ordinationes et constitutiones sic ut praefertur facienda, et eorum quaelibet, sint rationabilia, et non sint repugnantia nec contraria legibus consuetudinibus juribus sive statutis hujus Regni nostri Angliae.
to the management of the Society and its affairs; and all their acts shall be valid: But their Statutes must be reasonable, and not contrary to Law.

Et ulteriùs de ampliori gratia nostra speciali ac ex certa scientia et mero motu nostris dedimus et concessimus, ac per praesentes pro nobis heredibus et successoribus nostris damus et concedimus, praefatis Praesidi Concilio et Sodalibus praedictae Regalis Societatis, et successoribus suis in perpetuum, sive aliquibus viginti et uni vel pluribus eorum (quorum Praesidem pro tempore existentem, vel ejus Deputatum, semper unum esse volumus), seu majori parti praedictorum viginti et unius vel plurium, plenam potestatem et authoritatem de tempore in tempus eligendi nominandi et constituendi unum vel plures Typographos sive Impressores, et Chalcographos seu Sculptores; et ipsi vel ipsis per scriptum Communi Sigillo praedictae Regalis Societatis sigillatum, et manu Praesidis pro tempore existentis signatum, facultatem concedendi, ut imprimant tales res materias et negotia praedictam Regalem Societatem tangentes vel concernentes, quales praedicto Typographo vel Impressori, Chalcographo seu Sculptori, vel Typographis vel Impressoribus, Chalcographis vel Sculptoribus, de tempore in tempus per Praesidem et Concilium praedictae Regalis Societatis, vel aliquos septem vel plures eorum (quorum Praesidem pro tempore exis-
The President, Council, and Fellows, or any Twenty-one or more of them, (of whom the President or his Deputy to be always one,) or the major part of such Twenty-one or more, may appoint one Printer or more, and one Engraver or more, and authorise them, by writing under the Common Seal, and signed by the President, to print such things (touching or concerning the Royal Society) as shall be given them in charge by the President and Council, or any Seven or more of them (of whom the President or his Deputy to be one), or the major part of such Seven or more. They must be first sworn before the President

tentem, vel ejus Deputatum, unum esse volumus), vel per majorem partem praedictorum septem vel plurium, commissae fuerint; sacramentis suis corporalibus, antequam ad officia sua exercenda admittantur, coram Praeside et Concilio pro tempore existentibus, vel aliquibus septem vel pluribus eorum, in forma et effectu ultimò specificatis, priùs praestandis; quibus quidem Praesidi et Concilio, vel aliquibus septem vel pluribus eorum, sacramenta praedicta administrare plenam potestatem et authoritatem damus et concedimus per praesentes.

<small>and Council, or Seven or more of them.</small>

Et ulteriùs, quòd praedicti Praeses Concilium et Sodales praedictae Regalis Societatis in philosophicis suis studiis meliorem sortiantur effectum, de ampliori gratia nostra speciali ac ex certa scientia et mero motu nostris dedimus et concessimus, ac per praesentes pro nobis heredibus et successoribus nostris damus et concedimus, praedictis Praesidi Concilio et Sodalibus praedictae Regalis Societatis, et successoribus suis in perpetuum, quòd ipsi et successores sui, sive aliqui novem vel plures eorum (quorum Praesidem pro tempore existentem, vel ejus Deputatum, unum esse volumus), sive major pars praedictorum novem vel plurium, de tempore in tempus habeant et habebunt plenam potestatem et authoritatem de tempore in tempus, et ad talia tempestiva tempora, secundùm eorum discretionem, per assignatum vel assignatos suos, requirere capere et recipere cadavera talium personarum, quae mortem manu carnificis passae fuerunt, et ea anatomizare, in tam amplis modo et forma, et ad omnes intentiones et proposita, prout Praesidens Collegii Medicorum et Societas Chirurgorum Civitatis nostrae London (quibuscunque nominibus duae praedictae corporationes insignitae fuerint) eisdem cadaveribus usi vel gavisi fuerunt, aut uti vel gaudere valeant et possint.

<small>The President, Council, and Fellows, or any Nine or more of them (of whom, &c.) or the major part of such Nine or more, shall have the same Right to demand and receive (by their assign or assigns) the Bodies of executed Criminals, and to anatomize them, as the College of Physicians and the Company of Surgeons of London use or enjoy.</small>

Et ulteriùs, pro melioratione experimentorum artium et scientiarum praedictae Regalis Societatis, de abundantiori gratia nostra speciali ac ex certa scientia et mero motu nostris dedimus et concessimus, ac per praesentes pro nobis heredibus et successoribus nostris damus et concedimus, praefatis Praesidi Concilio et Sodalibus praedictae Regalis Societatis, et successoribus suis in perpetuum, quòd ipsi et successores sui, sive aliqui novem vel plures eorum (quorum Praesidem pro tempore existentem, vel ejus Deputatum, unum esse volumus), sive major pars praedictorum novem vel plurium, de tempore in tempus habeant et habebunt plenam potestatem et authoritatem per

<small>Licence is given to them or any nine (as last above), or the major part of them, to hold a Correspondence, on Philosophical, Mathematical, or Mechanical Subjects, with all sorts of Foreigners by Letters signed by the President or his Deputy, in the presence of the Council, or any Seven or more of them, and in the name of the Society.</small>

Charta Secunda.

literas vel epistolas, sub manu praedicti Praesidis vel ejus Deputati, in praesentia Concilii vel aliquorum septem vel plurium eorum, et in nomine Regalis Societatis, mutuis intelligentiis fruentur* et negotiis† cum omnibus et omnimodis peregrinis et alienis, utrum privatis vel collegiatis, corporatis vel politicis, absque aliqua molestatione interruptione vel inquietate* quacunque: Proviso tamen, quòd haec indulgentia nostra sic, ut praefertur, concessa ad ulteriorem non extendatur usum, quàm particulare beneficium et interesse praedictae Regalis Societatis in materiis seu rebus philosophicis mathematicis aut mechanicis.

Et ulteriùs dedimus et concessimus, ac per praesentes pro nobis heredibus et successoribus nostris damus et concedimus, praefatis Praesidi Concilio et Sodalibus Regalis Societatis praedictae, et successoribus suis in perpetuum, sive Praesidi et Concilio Regalis Societatis praedictae vel majori parti eorum, plenam potestatem et authoritatem erigendi aedificandi et extruendi, aut erigi aedificari et extrui faciendi vel causandi, intra Civitatem nostram Londini, vel decem milliaria ab eadem, unum vel plura Collegium vel Collegia cujuscunque modi et qualitatis, pro habitatione assemblatione et congregatione praedictorum Praesidis Concilii et Sodalium praedictae Regalis Societatis et successorum suorum, ad negotia sua et alias res eandem Regalem Societatem concernentia ordinanda et disponenda.

Licence given to the President, Council, and Fellows, or to the President and Council, or the major part of them, to build a College or Colleges in London, or within ten miles of it.

Et ulteriùs volumus, ac per praesentes pro nobis heredibus et successoribus nostris ordinamus constituimus et appunctuamus, quòd si aliqui abusus vel discrepantiae in posterum orientur et accident de gubernatione aut aliis rebus vel negotiis praedictae Regalis Societatis, unde ejusdem constitutioni stabilimini et studiorum progressui vel rebus et negotiis aliqua inferatur injuria vel impedimentum; quòd tunc et toties per praesentes pro nobis heredibus et successoribus nostris authorizamus nominamus et constituimus praefatum praedilectum et perquam fidelem Consanguineum et Conciliarium nostrum Edwardum, Comitem de Clarendon, Cancellarium nostrum Regni nostri Angliae, per seipsum durante vita sua, et post ejus mortem, tunc Archiepiscopum Cantuariensem, Cancellarium vel Custodem Magni Sigilli Angliae, Thesaurarium Angliae, Custodem Privati Sigilli, Episcopum Londinen-

If any abuses shall happen, or differences arise, they shall be reformed and settled by the Earl of Clarendon (Lord Chancellor) alone, while living; and after his death by the Archbishop of Canterbury, the Chancellor or Keeper of the Great Seal, the Treasurer, Privy Seal, Bishop of London, and two Principal Secretaries, for the time being, or any four or more of them.

---

* *Sic.*
† In the first Charter, "*notitiis*."

General Clauses. sem, et duos Principales Secretarios pro tempore existentes, aut aliquos quatuor vel plures eorum, easdem discrepantias et abusus reconciliare componere et reducere.

Et ulteriùs volumus, ac per praesentes pro nobis heredibus et successoribus nostris firmiter injungendo praecipimus et mandamus omnibus et singulis Justitiariis Majoribus Aldermannis Vicecomitibus Ballivis Constabulariis et aliis officiariis ministris et subditis nostris heredum et successorum nostrorum quibuscunque, quòd de tempore in tempus sint auxiliantes et assistentes praedictis Praesidi Concilio et Sodalibus Regalis Societatis praedictae, corumque in perpetuum successoribus, in omnibus et per omnia, secundùm veram intentionem harum Literarum nostrarum Patentium.

Eò quòd expressa mentio de vero valore annuo vel de certitudine praemissorum sive eorum alicujus, aut de aliis donis sive concessionibus per nos seu per aliquem progenitorum sive praedecessorum nostrorum praefatis Praesidi Concilio et Sodalibus Regalis Societatis praedictae ante haec tempora factis, in praesentibus minimè facta existit; aut aliquo statuto actu ordinatione provisione proclamatione sive restrictione in contrarium inde antehac habito facto edito ordinato sive proviso, aut aliqua alia re causa vel materia quacunque, in aliquo non obstante.

In cujus rei testimonium has Literas nostras fieri fecimus Patentes. TESTE Me ipso, apud Westmonasterium, vicesimo secundo die Aprilis, anno regni nostri decimo quinto.*

Per breve de Privato Sigillo.

HOWARD.

SECOND CHARTER,

Granted by the same to the same, A.D. 1663.

Charles the Second, by the grace of God King of England, Scotland, France, and Ireland, Defender of the Faith, &c., to all to whom these our Letters Patent shall come, greeting.

* This Charter is on four skins of vellum; and, like the first, contains some very fine ornamented capital letters. The Arms of the Society, coloured, appear on the first skin.

We have long and fully resolved with Ourself to extend not only the boundaries of the Empire, but also the very arts and sciences. Therefore we look with favour upon all forms of learning, but with particular grace we encourage philosophical studies, especially those which by actual experiments attempt either to shape out a new philosophy or to perfect the old. In order, therefore, that such studies, which have not hitherto been sufficiently brilliant in any part of the world, may shine conspicuously amongst our people, and that at length the whole world of letters may always recognise us not only as the Defender of the Faith, but also as the universal lover and patron of every kind of truth:

Know ye that we, of our special grace and of our certain knowledge and mere motion, have ordained, established, and granted, and by these presents for us, our heirs, and successors do ordain, establish, and grant, that henceforth for ever there shall be a Society consisting of a President, Council, and Fellows, who shall be called and named The President, Council, and Fellows of the Royal Society of London for promoting Natural Knowledge (of which same Society we by these presents declare Ourself Founder and Patron); And by these presents for us, our heirs, and successors we do make, ordain, create, and constitute the same Society, by the name of The President, Council, and Fellows of the Royal Society of London for promoting Natural Knowledge, one body corporate and politic, in fact, deed, and name, really and fully, and that by the same name they may have perpetual succession; And that they and their successors (whose studies are to be applied to further promoting by the authority of experiments the sciences of natural things and of useful arts, to the glory of God the Creator, and the advantage of the human race), by the same name of The President, Council, and Fellows of the Royal Society of London for promoting Natural Knowledge, may and shall be in all future times persons able and capable in law to have, acquire, receive, and possess lands [and] tenements, meadows, feedings, pastures, liberties, privileges, franchises, jurisdictions, and hereditaments whatsoever to them and their successors in fee and perpetuity, or for term of life, lives, or years, or otherwise in whatsoever manner, and also goods and chattels, and all other things, of whatsoever kind, nature, sort, or quality they may be (the Statute concerning alienation in mortmain notwithstand-

Incorporation and Corporate Name.

The King himself Founder and Patron.

Capacity to purchase;

and to grant;

to sue and be sued;

and to have a Common Seal, alterable at pleasure.

Grant of Arms, viz. Argent, in a Canton Dexter the three Lions of England: and also of a Crest, and Supporters.

ing); and also to give, grant, [demise,] and assign the same lands, tenements, and hereditaments, goods and chattels, and to do and execute all acts and things necessary of and concerning the same, by the name aforesaid; And that by the name of The President, Council, and Fellows of the Royal Society of London for promoting Natural Knowledge aforesaid, they may henceforth for ever be able and have power to plead and be impleaded, to answer and be answered, to defend and be defended, in whatsoever Courts and places, and before whatsoever Judges, Justices, and other persons and officers of us, our heirs, and successors, in all and singular actions, both real and personal, pleas, suits, plaints, causes, matters, things, and demands whatsoever, of whatsoever kind, nature, or sort they may or shall be, in the same manner and form as any of our lieges within this our Realm of England, being persons able and capable in law, or as any body corporate or politic within this our Realm of England, may be able and have power to have, acquire, receive, possess, give, and grant, to plead and be impleaded, to answer and be answered, to defend or be defended; And that the same President, Council, and Fellows of the Royal Society aforesaid and their successors for ever may have a Common Seal, to serve for transacting all causes and affairs whatsoever of them and their successors; and that it may and shall be good and lawful to the same President, Council, and Fellows of the Royal Society aforesaid, and to their successors for the time being, to break, change, and make anew that Seal from time to time, as it shall seem most expedient to them.

We give and grant moreover by these presents to the President, Council, and Fellows of the Royal Society aforesaid, and to their successors for ever, in testimony of our royal favour towards them, and of our peculiar esteem for them, to the present and future ages, these following blazons of honour, that is to say: in the canton dexter of a Shield argent three of our English Lions, and for a Crest a helmet adorned with a crown chequered with florets, which is surmounted by an eagle of natural colour, holding with one foot a shield emblazoned with our lions; Supporters of the shield, two keen-scented white hounds, the necks surrounded by crowns (as is to be seen more clearly in the margin); to be borne, exhibited, and possessed for ever by the aforesaid President,

Second Charter.

Council and Fellows, and their successors, as occasion shall serve.

And that our royal intention may obtain the better effect, and for the good rule and government of the aforesaid Royal Society from time to time, we will, and by these presents for us, our heirs, and successors do grant to the same President, Council, and Fellows of the Royal Society aforesaid, and to their successors, that henceforth for ever the Council aforesaid shall be and consist of twenty-one persons (of whom we will the President for the time being, or his Deputy, to be always one); And that all and singular other persons who within two months next following after the date of these presents shall be received and admitted into the same Society as Members of the Royal Society aforesaid, by the President and Council, or by any eleven or more of them (of whom we will the President for the time being, or his Deputy, to be always one), or by two third parts or more of the aforesaid eleven or more, and in all time following by the President, Council, and Fellows, or by any twenty-one or more of them (of whom we will the President for the time being, or his Deputy, to be always one), or by two third parts or more of the aforesaid twenty-one or more, and shall have been noted in the Register by them to be kept, shall be, be called, and be named Fellows of the Royal Society aforesaid, as long as they shall live, unless it shall happen that any one of them be amoved for any reasonable cause, according to the Statutes of the Royal Society aforesaid, which are to be drawn up; whom, the more eminently they are distinguished for the study of every kind of learning and good letters, the more ardently they desire to promote the honour, studies, and advantage of this Society, the more they are noted for integrity of life, uprightness of character, and piety, and excel in fidelity and affection of mind towards us, our Crown, and dignity, the more we wish them to be especially deemed fitting and worthy of being admitted into the number of the Fellows of the same Society.

And for the better execution of our will and grant in this behalf, we have assigned, nominated, constituted, and made, and by these presents for us, our heirs, and successors do assign, nominate, constitute, and make, our very well-beloved and trusty William, Viscount Brouncker, Chancellor of our very dear consort Queen Catharine, to be the first and present President of the Royal Society

The Council shall consist of Twenty-one (of whom the President or his Deputy shall be always one).

All other persons who shall be received and admitted as Members, by the President and Council, or any eleven or more of them (of whom, &c.) or by two-thirds or more of those Eleven or more, within two months; and at all times after those two months, by the President, Council, and Fellows, or by any Twenty-one or more of them (of whom the President or his Deputy to be one), or by two-third parts or more of the said Twenty-one or more; and shall be registered; shall be called Fellows of the said Royal Society, for life, unless regularly amoved.

William Viscount Brouncker named to be

aforesaid; willing that the aforesaid William, Viscount Brouncker, shall continue in the office of President of the Royal Society aforesaid from the date of these presents until the feast of St. Andrew next following after the date of these presents, and until one other of the Council of the Royal Society aforesaid for the time being shall have been elected, appointed, and sworn to that office in due manner, according to the ordinance and provision below in these presents expressed and declared (if the aforesaid William, Viscount Brouncker, shall live so long); having first taken a corporal oath well and faithfully to execute [his office] in and by all things touching that office, according to the true intention of these presents, before our very well-beloved and very trusty Cousin and Councillor Edward, Earl of Clarendon, our Chancellor of England: to which same Edward, Earl of Clarendon, our Chancellor aforesaid, we give and grant full power and authority to administer the oath aforesaid in these words following, that is to say:—

I, William, Viscount Brouncker, do promise to deal faithfully and honestly in all things belonging to the trust committed to me, as President of the Royal Society of London for improving Natural Knowledge, during my employment in that capacity. So help me God!

We have also assigned, constituted, and made, and by these presents for us, our heirs, and successors do make, our beloved and trusty Robert Moray, Knight, one of our Privy Council in our Realm of Scotland; Robert Boyle, Esquire; William Brereton, Esquire, eldest son of the Baron de Brereton; Kenelm Digby, Knight, Chancellor to our very dear mother, Queen Maria; Gilbert Talbot, Knight, Treasurer of our Jewels; Paul Neile, Knight, one of the Ushers of our Privy Chamber; Henry Slingesby, Esquire, one of the Gentlemen of our aforesaid Privy Chamber; William Petty, Knight; Timothy Clarke, Doctor in Medicine and one of our Physicians; John Wilkins, Doctor in Divinity; George Ent, Doctor in Medicine; William Aerskine, one of our Cup-bearers; Jonathan Goddard, Doctor in Medicine and Professor of Gresham College; William Balle, Esquire; Matthew Wren, Esquire; John Evelyn, Esquire; Thomas Henshaw, Esquire; Dudley Palmer, of Grey's Inn, in our County of Middlesex, Esquire; Abraham Hill, of London, Esquire; and Henry Oldenburg, Esquire, together with the President aforesaid, to be and become the first and present twenty-one of the Council and Fellows of the Royal Society aforesaid; to be continued in their offices of the Council aforesaid from the date of these presents until the aforesaid feast of St. Andrew the Apostle next following, and thenceforth until other fitting and able and sufficient persons shall have been elected, appointed, and sworn into the offices aforesaid (if they shall live so long, or shall not have been amoved for any just and reasonable cause); first taking corporal oaths before the President for the time being of the aforesaid Royal Society, well and faithfully to execute their offices in and by all things touching those offices, according to the form and effect of the aforesaid oath, *mutatis mutandis*, to be administered to the President of the Royal Society aforesaid by our Chancellor of England; (to which same President for the time being, for us, our heirs, and successors, we give and grant by these presents full power and authority to administer the oaths aforesaid to the aforesaid persons, and to any others whomsoever hereafter from time to time to be elected into the Council aforesaid); And that the same persons, so as it is aforesaid elected, appointed, and sworn, and hereafter to be elected, appointed, and sworn from time to time, to the Council of the aforesaid Royal Society, shall be and become aiding, counselling, and assistant in all matters, business, and affairs touching or concerning the better regulation, government, and direction of the aforesaid Royal Society, and of every Member of the same.

To continue till next St. Andrew's Day, and till others shall be elected and sworn, unless amoved for just cause; having first taken, before the President, the like Oath as he took, mutatis mutandis.

We also grant to the President, Council, and Fellows of the aforesaid Society, and to their successors for ever, that they and their successors, or any nine or more of them (of whom we will the President for the time being, or his Deputy, to be always one), may be able lawfully to make and hold assemblies or meetings of themselves for the examination and investigation of experiments and of natural things, and for other affairs belonging to the Society aforesaid, as often as and whenever it shall be needful, in a College or Hall or other convenient place within our City of London, or in any other convenient place within ten miles of our same City.

The President, Council, and Fellows, or any nine or more of them (of whom, &c.), may hold Assemblies at any time or place in London, or within ten miles of it.

And further we will, and by these presents for us, our heirs, and successors, do grant to the aforesaid President, Council, and Fellows of the Royal Society aforesaid, and to their successors, that the President, Council, and Fellows of the Royal Society aforesaid for the time being, or any

The President, Council, and Fellows, or any Thirty-one or more of them (of whom the President or his Deputy to be one), or the major part

of such Thirty-one or more, may upon every St. Andrew's Day, annually, elect one of the Council to be their President, who shall continue so, (if not dead or amoved,) till the next St. Andrew's Day, and till another shall be elected; having first been sworn in before the Council, or any Seven or more of them.

thirty-one or more of them (of whom we will the President for the time being, or his Deputy, to be one), or the major part of the aforesaid thirty-one or more, may and shall have from time to time in all future times for ever power and authority to nominate and elect, and that they may be able and have power to elect and nominate, every year, on the aforesaid feast of St. Andrew, one of the Council of the aforesaid Royal Society for the time being, who may and shall be President of the Royal Society aforesaid until the feast of St. Andrew the Apostle thereafter next following (if he shall live so long, or shall not be amoved meanwhile for any just and reasonable cause), and thenceforth until another shall have been elected, appointed, and nominated to the office of President of the Royal Society aforesaid; and that he, after that he shall so have been elected and nominated, as it is aforesaid, to the office of President of the Royal Society aforesaid, before he be admitted to that office, shall take a corporal oath before the Council of the same Royal Society, or any seven or more of them, rightly, well, and faithfully to execute that office in all things touching that office, according to the form and effect of the aforesaid oath, *mutatis mutandis* (to which same Council, or to any seven or more of them, we give and grant by these presents for us, our heirs, and successors full power and authority to administer the oath aforesaid from time to time, as often as it shall be needful to elect a President); and that after having so taken such oath, as it is aforesaid, he may be able and have power to execute the office of President of the Royal Society aforesaid until the feast of St. Andrew the Apostle thereafter next following;

On the Death or Amotion of a President, or if he retire, the Council or any Eleven or more of them may meet to choose a President out of the Council: and the person chosen by them, or the major part of them, being sworn, shall hold during the residue of the year, and until another shall be elected and sworn.

And if it shall happen that the President of the Royal Society for the time being, at any time, so long as he shall be in the office of President of the same Royal Society, shall die, retire, or be amoved from his office, that then and so often it may and shall be good and lawful to the Council of the Royal Society aforesaid, and to their successors for ever, or to any eleven or more of them, to assemble or meet for the election of one of the aforesaid number of the Council aforesaid as President of the Royal Society aforesaid; and that he who shall have been elected and sworn by the Council aforesaid, or by the aforesaid eleven or more, or by the major part of the aforesaid eleven and more, as it is aforesaid, may have and exercise that office during the residue of the same year, and until another shall have been in due manner elected and sworn to that office, first taking a corporal oath in the form above specified; and so as often as the case shall so happen.

And further we will, that whenever it shall happen that any one or any of the Council of the Royal Society aforesaid for the time being shall die, or be amoved from that office, or retire (which same [members] of the Council of the Royal Society aforesaid, and every one of them, we will to be amovable for misbehaviour or any other reasonable cause, at the good pleasure of the President and of the rest of the Council aforesaid, of whom we will the President for the time being, or his Deputy, to be one, or of the major part of the same), that then and so often it may and shall be good and lawful to the aforesaid President, Council, and Fellows of the Royal Society aforesaid, and to their successors for ever, or to any twenty-one or more of the same (of whom we will the President of the Royal Society aforesaid for the time being, or his Deputy, to be one), or to the major part of the aforesaid twenty-one or more, to nominate, elect, and appoint one other or several others of the Fellows of the Royal Society aforesaid, in the place or places of him or them so dead, retired, or amoved, to fill up the aforesaid number of twenty-one persons of the Council of the Royal Society aforesaid; and that he or they so elected and appointed in that office may have the same office until the feast of St. Andrew the Apostle then next following, and thenceforth until one other or several others shall have been elected, appointed, and nominated; first taking a corporal oath before the President and Council of the Royal Society aforesaid, or any seven or more of them (of whom we will the President for the time being, or his Deputy, to be always one), well and faithfully to execute that office in and by all things touching that office, according to the true intention of these presents.

On the Death, Amotion, or retirement of any of the Council, (who are hereby made amovable by the President and Council for sufficient cause,) the President, Council, and Fellows, or any Twenty-one or more of them (of whom, &c.) or the major part of such Twenty-one or more, may supply the vacancy from amongst the Fellows; and the person or persons elected shall hold, (being first sworn,) till the next St. Andrew's Day, and until another or others shall be elected.

And further we will, and by these presents for us our heirs, and successors do grant to the aforesaid President, Council, and Fellows of the aforesaid Royal Society, and to their successors [for ever], that they and their successors, or any thirty-one or more of them (of whom we will the President for the time being, or his Deputy, to be always one), or the major part of the aforesaid thirty-one or more, every year, on the aforesaid feast of St. Andrew the Apostle,

On St. Andrew's Day, Ten of the Council (and no more) are to be changed by the President, Council, and Fellows, or any Thirty-one or more of them (of whom the President or his Deputy always to be one,) or the major part of such

Thirty-one or more.	may and shall have full power and authority to elect, nominate, appoint, and change ten of the Fellows of the Royal Society aforesaid, to fill up the places and offices of ten of the aforesaid number of twenty-one of the Council of the Royal Society aforesaid; for we do declare it to be our royal pleasure, and by these presents for us, our heirs, and successors we do grant, that ten of the aforesaid Council, and no more, shall be annually changed and amoved by the President, Council, and Fellows of the Royal Society aforesaid.
The President may appoint *one* out of the Council to be his Deputy;	We will also, and for us, our heirs, and successors do grant to the aforesaid President, Council, and Fellows of the aforesaid Royal Society, and to their successors for ever, that if it shall happen that the President of the same Royal Society for the time being is detained by sickness or infirmity, or is employed in the service of us, our heirs, or successors, or is otherwise occupied, so that he shall not be able to attend to the necessary affairs of the same Royal Society touching the office of President, that then and so often it may and shall be good and lawful to the same President so detained, employed or occupied, to nominate and appoint one of the Council of the aforesaid Royal Society for the time being to be and become the Deputy of the same President; which same
who may act as such in his absence, unless the President make some other Deputy out of the Council.	Deputy, so to be made and appointed in the office of Deputy of the President aforesaid, may and shall be the Deputy of the same President from time to time, as often as the aforesaid President shall happen to be so absent, during the whole time in which the aforesaid President shall continue in the office of President; unless in the meanwhile the aforesaid President of the Royal Society aforesaid for the time being shall have made and appointed one other of the aforesaid Council his Deputy; And that every such Deputy of the aforesaid President so to be made and appointed, as it is aforesaid, may be able and have power
The Deputy may, in the absence of the President, do all acts that he himself could do if present.	to do and execute all and singular things which pertain or ought to pertain to the office of President of the aforesaid Royal Society, or which are limited and appointed to be done and executed by the aforesaid President, by virtue of these our Letters Patent, from time to time, as often as the aforesaid President shall happen to be so absent, during such time as he shall continue the Deputy of the aforesaid President, by force of these our Letters Patent, as fully, freely, and wholly, and in as ample manner and form, as the aforesaid President, if he were present, would

be able and have power to do and execute those things; a corporal oath first to be taken by such Deputy upon the holy Gospels of God, in the form and effect above specified, well and faithfully to execute all and singular things which pertain to the office of President, before the aforesaid Council of the aforesaid Royal Society, or any seven or more of them; and so often as the case shall so happen: to which same Council, or to any seven or more of them, for the time being, we do give and grant by these presents, power and authority to administer the oath aforesaid, as often as the case shall so happen, without procuring or obtaining a writ, commission, or further warrant in that behalf from us, our heirs, or successors. *But he must first be sworn before the Council, or Seven or more of them.*

And further we will, and by these presents for us, our heirs, and successors do grant to the aforesaid President, Council, and Fellows of the Royal Society aforesaid, and to their successors, that they and their successors henceforth for ever may and shall have one Treasurer, two Secretaries, two or more Curators of Experiments, one Clerk or more, and moreover two Serjeants-at-Mace, who may from time to time attend upon the President; and that the aforesaid Treasurer, Secretaries, Curators, Clerk or Clerks, and Serjeants-at-Mace, to be elected and nominated by the President, Council, and Fellows of the Royal Society aforesaid, or by any thirty-one or more of them (of whom we will the President for the time being, or his Deputy, to be one), or by the major part of the aforesaid thirty-one or more, before they be admitted to execute their special* and respective offices, shall take their corporal oaths in the form and effect above specified, before the President, or his Deputy, and the Council of the same Royal Society, or any seven or more of them, rightly, well, and faithfully to execute their several and respective offices in all things touching the same; and that after having so taken such oaths, as it is aforesaid, they may exercise and use their respective offices; to which same President and Council, or to any seven or more of them, we do give and grant by these presents full power and authority to administer the oaths aforesaid from time to time to the aforesaid several and respective officers and their successors: And we have assigned, nominated, chosen, created, appointed, and made, and by these presents for us, our heirs, and successors do assign, *The Society may have a Treasurer, two Secretaries, two or more Curators of Experiments, one Clerk or more, and two Serjeants-at-Mace to attend upon the President. All these are to be chosen and named by the President, Council, and Fellows, or any Thirty-one or more of them, (of whom the President or his Deputy to be one,) or by the major part of such Thirty-one or more: and they must be sworn before the President or his Deputy, and the Council, or any seven or more of them.*

The first Treasurer named; and also the two first Secretaries.

* So in the original; *qu.* several.

nominate, choose, create, appoint, and make, our beloved subjects the aforesaid William Balle, Esquire, to be and become the first and present Treasurer, and the aforesaid John Wilkins and Henry Oldenburg to be and become the first and present Secretaries, of the aforesaid Royal Society; to be continued in the same offices until the aforesaid feast of St. Andrew the Apostle next following after the date of these presents: And that from time to time and at all times on the aforesaid feast of St. Andrew the Apostle (unless it shall be Sunday, and if it be Sunday, then on the day next following), the President, Council, and Fellows of the aforesaid Royal Society for the time being, or any thirty-one or more of them (of whom we will the President for the time being, or his Deputy, to be one), or the major part of the aforesaid thirty-one or more, may be able and have power to elect, nominate, and appoint upright and discreet men, who are and shall be of the number of the Council of the Royal Society aforesaid, as Treasurer and Secretaries, from time to time; and that those who shall so have been elected, appointed, and sworn to the aforesaid several and respective offices, as it is aforesaid, may be able and have power to exercise and enjoy those respective offices until the aforesaid feast of St. Andrew then next following, their aforesaid oaths, as it is aforesaid, first to be taken; and so as often as the case shall so happen. And if it shall happen that the aforesaid elections of President, Council, Treasurer, [and] Secretaries, or of any one or any of them, cannot conveniently be made or finished on the aforesaid feast of St. Andrew, we give and grant to the aforesaid President, Council, and Fellows, and to their successors for ever, that they or any thirty-one or more of them (of whom we will the President for the time being, or his Deputy, to be one), or the major part of the said thirty-one or more, may lawfully name and assign one other day, as near to the feast of St. Andrew aforesaid as can conveniently be done, for making or finishing the aforesaid elections; and so from day to day, until the aforesaid elections be finished: And if it shall happen that any one or any of the aforesaid officers of the same Royal Society shall die, retire, or be amoved from their respective offices, that then and so often it may and shall be good and lawful to the President, Council, and Fellows of the aforesaid Royal Society, and to their successors for ever, or to any twenty-one or more of them (of whom we will the President for the time being, or his

Side notes:

On every St. Andrew's Day, (unless it be Sunday, and then on the next day), the President, Council, and Fellows, or any Thirty-one or more of them (of whom, &c.), or the major part of such Thirty-one or more, may elect proper persons out of the Council to be Treasurer and Secretaries; who, after being sworn, are to hold their Offices till the following St. Andrew's Day.

If the Elections of President, Council, Treasurer, and Secretaries, or any of them, cannot conveniently be made or finished upon St. Andrew's Day, the President, Council, and Fellows, or any Thirty-one or more of them, (of whom, &c.) or the major part of such Thirty-one, or more, may appoint one or more other day or days, till they shall be finished.

If any of the said Officers die, retire, or be amoved, the President, Council, and Fellows, or any Twenty-one or more of them (of whom the President or his Deputy to be

Deputy, to be one), or to the major part of the aforesaid twenty-one or more, to elect and appoint another or others to the office or offices of those persons so deceased, retired, or amoved; and that he or they so elected and appointed may have and exercise the respective offices aforesaid during the residue of the same year, and until another or others shall have been in due manner elected and sworn to those respective offices; and so as often as the case shall so happen.

one,) or the major part of such Twenty-one or more, may elect others for the residue of the year, and till new ones shall be elected and sworn.

And moreover we will, and of our special grace and of our certain knowledge and mere motion do grant to the aforesaid President, Council, and Fellows of the Royal Society aforesaid, and to their successors for ever, that the President and Council of the aforesaid Royal Society for the time being (due or lawful summons or citation being always first made of all the Members of the Council aforesaid to extraordinary meetings), or any nine or more of them (of whom we will the President for the time being, or his Deputy, to be one), may be able and have power both to meet together and assemble in a College or Hall or other convenient place within our City of London, or in any other convenient place within ten miles of our same City; and that they so met together and assembled, or the major part of them, shall and may have full authority, power, and faculty from time to time to draw up, constitute, ordain, make, and establish such laws, statutes, acts, ordinances, and constitutions as shall seem to them, or to the major part of them, to be good, wholesome, useful, honourable, and necessary, according to their sound discretions, for the better government, regulation, and direction of the Royal Society aforesaid, and of every Member of the same, and to do and perform all things belonging to the government, matters, goods, faculties, rents, lands, tenements, hereditaments, and affairs of the Royal Society aforesaid; all and singular which laws, statutes, acts, ordinances, and constitutions so to be made as it is aforesaid, we will, and by these presents for us, our heirs, and successors, firmly enjoining, do order and command, that they shall be inviolably observed from time to time, according to the tenor and effect of the same: so nevertheless, that the aforesaid laws, statutes, acts, ordinances, and constitutions so to be made as it is aforesaid, and every one of them, be reasonable, and not repugnant or contrary to the laws, customs, acts, or statutes of this our Realm of England.

The President and Council (every Member of the Council being always duly summoned to extraordinary Meetings,) or any Nine or more of them, (of whom the President or his Deputy to be one), may meet in London or within ten miles of London; and they, or the major part of them, may make Laws, Statutes, and Ordinances, and transact all matters relating to the management of the Society and its affairs; and all their acts shall be valid: But their Statutes must be reasonable, and not contrary to Law.

The President, Council, and Fellows, or any Twenty-one or more of them, (of whom the President or his Deputy to be always one,) or the major part of such Twenty-one or more, may appoint one Printer or more, and one Engraver or more, and authorise them, by writing under the Common Seal, and signed by the President, to print such things (touching or concerning the Royal Society) as shall be given them in charge by the President and Council, or any Seven or more of them (of whom the President or his Deputy to be one,) or the major part of such Seven or more. They must be first sworn before the President and Council, or Seven or more of them.

And further, of our more ample special grace and of our certain knowledge and mere motion, we have given and granted, and by these presents for us, our heirs, and successors do give and grant to the aforesaid President, Council, and Fellows of the aforesaid Royal Society, and to their successors for ever, or to any twenty-one or more of them (of whom we will the President for the time being, or his Deputy, to be always one), or to the major part of the aforesaid twenty-one or more, full power and authority from time to time to elect, nominate, and appoint one or more Typographers or Printers, and Chalcographers or Engravers, and to grant to him or them, by a writing sealed with the Common Seal of the aforesaid Royal Society, and signed by the hand of the President for the time being, faculty to print such things, matters, and affairs touching or concerning the aforesaid Royal Society, as shall have been committed to the aforesaid Typographer or Printer, Chalcographer or Engraver, or Typographers or Printers, Chalcographers or Engravers, from time to time, by the President and Council of the aforesaid Royal Society, or any seven or more of them (of whom we will the President for the time being, or his Deputy, to be one), or by the major part of the aforesaid seven or more; their corporal oaths first to be taken, before they be admitted to exercise their offices, before the President and Council for the time being, or any seven or more of them, in the form and effect last specified; to which same President and Council, or to any seven or more of them, we do give and grant by these presents full power and authority to administer the oaths aforesaid.

The President, Council and Fellows, or any Nine or more of them (of whom, &c.) or the major part of such Nine or more, shall have the same Right to demand and receive (by their assign or assigns) the Bodies of executed Criminals, and to anatomize them, as the College of Physicians and the Company of Surgeons of London use or enjoy.

And further, in order that the aforesaid President, Council, and Fellows of the aforesaid Royal Society may obtain the better success in their philosophical studies, of our more ample special grace and of our certain knowledge and mere motion, we have given and granted, and by these presents for us, our heirs, and successors do give and grant, to the aforesaid President, Council, and Fellows of the aforesaid Royal Society, and to their successors for ever, that they and their successors, or any nine or more of them (of whom we will the President for the time being, or his Deputy, to be one), or the major part of the aforesaid nine or more, may and shall have from time to time full power and authority to require, take, and receive from time to time, and at such seasonable times, according to their discretion, by their assign or assigns the bodies of such persons as have suffered death by the hand of the executioner, and to anatomize them, in as ample manner and form, and to all intents and purposes, as the President of the College of Physicians and the Company of Surgeons of our City of London (by whatsoever names the two aforesaid corporations shall have been distinguished) have used or enjoyed, or may be able and have power to use and enjoy, the same bodies.

And further, for the improvement of the experiments, arts, and sciences of the aforesaid Royal Society, of our more abundant special grace and of our certain knowledge and mere motion, we have given and granted, and by these presents for us, our heirs, and successors do give and grant, to the aforesaid President, Council, and Fellows of the aforesaid Royal Society, and to their successors for ever, that they and their successors, or any nine or more of them (of whom we will the President for the time being, or his Deputy, to be one), or the major part of the aforesaid nine or more, may and shall have from time to time full power and authority, by letters or epistles under the hand of the aforesaid President or his Deputy, in the presence of the Council, or of any seven or more of them, and in the name of the Royal Society, to enjoy mutual intelligence and affairs with all and all manner of strangers and foreigners, whether private or collegiate, corporate or politic, without any molestation, interruption, or disturbance whatsoever: Provided nevertheless, that this our indulgence, so granted as it is aforesaid, be not extended to further use than the particular benefit and interest of the aforesaid Royal Society in matters or things philosophical, mathematical, or mechanical. *Licence is given to them or any nine (as last above), or the major part of them, to hold a Correspondence on Philosophical, Mathematical, or Mechanical Subjects, with all sorts of Foreigners, by Letters signed by the President or his Deputy, in the presence of the Council, or any Seven or more of them, and in the name of the Society.*

And further we have given and granted, and by these presents for us, our heirs, and successors do give and grant to the aforesaid President, Council, and Fellows of the Royal Society aforesaid, and to their successors for ever, or to the President and Council of the Royal Society aforesaid, or the major part of them, full power and authority to erect, build, and construct, or to make or cause to be erected, built, or constructed, within our City of London, or ten miles of the same, one or more College or Colleges, of whatsoever kind or quality, for the habitation, assembly, and meeting of the aforesaid President, Council, and Fellows of the aforesaid Royal Society, and of their successors, for the ordering and *Licence given to the President, Council, and Fellows, or to the President and Council, or the major part of them, to build a College or Colleges in London, or within ten miles of it.*

arranging of their affairs and other matters concerning the same Royal Society.

<small>If any abuses shall happen, or differences arise, they shall be reformed and settled by the Earl of Clarendon (Lord Chancellor) alone, while living; and after his death by the Archbishop of Canterbury, the Chancellor or Keeper of the Great Seal, the Treasurer, Privy Seal, Bishop of London, and two Principal Secretaries, for the time being, or any four or more of them.</small>

And further we will, and by these presents for us, our heirs, and successors do ordain, constitute, and appoint, that if any abuses or differences hereafter shall arise and happen concerning the government or other matters or affairs of the aforesaid Royal Society, whereby any injury or hindrance may be done to the constitution, stability, and progress of the studies, or to the matters and affairs, of the same; that then and so often, by these presents, for us, our heirs, and successors, we do authorise, nominate, assign, and appoint our aforesaid very well-beloved and very trusty Cousin and Councillor Edward, Earl of Clarendon, our Chancellor of our Realm of England, by himself during his life, and after his death, then the Archbishop of Canterbury, the Chancellor or Keeper of the Great Seal of England, the Treasurer of England, the Keeper of the Privy Seal, the Bishop of London, and the two Principal Secretaries for the time being, or any four or more of them, to reconcile, compose, and adjust the same differences and abuses.

<small>General Clauses.</small>

And further we will, and by these presents for us, our heirs, and successors, firmly enjoining, do order and command all and singular the Justices, Mayors, Aldermen, Sheriffs, Bailiffs, Constables, and other officers, ministers, and subjects whomsoever of us, our heirs, and successors, that they be from time to time aiding and assistant to the aforesaid President, Council, and Fellows of the Royal Society aforesaid, and to their successors for ever, in and by all things, according to the true intention of these our Letters Patent.

Although express mention of the true yearly value or of the certainty of the premises, or of any of them, or of other gifts or grants before these times made by us or by any of our progenitors or predecessors to the aforesaid President, Council, and Fellows of the Royal Society aforesaid, is not made in these presents; or any statute, act, ordinance, provision, proclamation, or restriction to the contrary thereof heretofore had, made, enacted, ordained, or provided, or any other thing, cause, or matter whatsoever, in any wise notwithstanding.

In witness whereof we have caused these our Letters to be made Patent. Witness Ourself, at Westminster, the twenty-second day of April, in the fifteenth year of our reign.

By writ of Privy Seal.

HOWARD.

CHARTA TERTIA,*

Iisdem ab eodem concessa, A.D. MDCLXIX.

CAROLUS SECUNDUS, Dei gratia Angliae Scotiae Franciae et Hiberniae Rex, Fidei Defensor, etc., omnibus ad quos hae Literae nostrae Patentes pervenerint, salutem.

Sciatis, quòd nos de gratia nostra speciali ac ex certa scientia et mero motu nostris dedimus et concessimus, ac per praesentes pro nobis heredibus et successoribus nostris damus et concedimus, dilectis et fidelibus nostris Praesidi Concilio et Sodalibus Regalis Societatis Londini pro Scientia naturali promovenda, et successoribus suis in perpetuum, Totam illam peciam terrae arabilis vocatam Teamshott, continentem per aestimationem viginti acras, jacentem inter viam nostram ducentem à Westmonasterio versùs Chelsey ex parte boreali et occidentali, et peciam prati continentem per aestimationem quatuor acras, parcellam octodecim acrarum prati nuper in tenura Comitis Nottingbamiœ vel assignatorum suorum, ex parte australi, ac clausum prati vocatum Stony Bridge Close ex parte orientali, et peciam terrae arabilis nuper in occupatione Thomae Evans vel assignatorum suorum ex parte occidentali, per particulare inde mentionatam esse annualis redditus sive valoris viginti trium solidorum et quatuor denariorum; Necnon totum illud praedictum clausum prati vocatum Stony Bridge Close, continens per aestimationem quatuor acras, nuper in occupatione Johannis Deakes vel assignatorum suorum, jacens inter rivum vocatum le Common Sewer ex parte orientali, et praedictam peciam terrae vocatam Teamshott ex parte occidentali, et pontem vocatum Stony Bridge ex parte boreali, per particulare inde mentionatum esse annualis redditus sive valoris viginti solidorum; Necnon totam illam unam peciam terrae arabilis

Grant of Lands in Chelsey.

* The warrant for this Charter is preserved among the State Papers. It is dated May 24, 1667.

in communi campo vocato East Field, continentem per aestimationem tres acras, nuper in occupatione Thomae Frances vel assignatorum suorum, jacentem inter praedictam peciam terrae vocatam Teamshott ex parte orientali, peciam terrae arabilis nuper in tenura Comitis Lincolniæ vel assignatorum suorum ex parte occidentali, parcellam prati de Earles Court land ex parte australi, et viam nostram ducentem à Westmonasterio versùs Chelsey praedictam ex parte boreali et occidentali, per particulare inde mentionatam esse annualis redditus sive valoris quatuor solidorum; (quae quidem praemissa sunt aut olim fuerunt parcella terrae nostrae in Chelsey, existentis parcellae terrae Dominicalis Manerii de Chelsey praedicta, ac nuper fuerunt parcella possessionum Johannis, nuper Ducis Northumbriae, et quae nuper per praecharissimum avum nostrum beatae memoriae Jacobum Regem per Literas suas Patentes, gerentes datum apud Westmonasterium, octavo die Maii, anno regni sui Angliae octavo et Scotiae quadragesimo tertio, concessa fuerunt aut mentionata esse concessa Praeposito et Sociis Collegii Regis Jacobi in Chelsey propè London, ex fundatione ejusdem Jacobi, Regis Angliae, et successoribus suis in perpetuum, tenenda de praefato Jacobo Rege, ut de Manerio suo de East Greenwich, in comitatu Cantiae, per fidelitatem tantùm, in libero et communi soccagio, et non in capite, nec per servitium militare;) Ac etiam omnia et singula domus aedificia structuras boscos subboscos arbores, ac totam terram fundum et solum eorundem boscorum subboscorum et arborum, ac omnia alia jura jurisdictiones franchesias privilegia libertates proficua commoditates advantagia emolumenta et hereditamenta nostra quaecunque, cum eorum pertinentiis universis, cujuscunque sint generis naturae seu speciei, seu quibuscunque nominibus sciantur censeantur nuncupentur seu cognoscantur, situata jacentia et existentia, provenientia crescentia renovantia sive emergentia, infra comitatum villas campos loca sive hameletta praedicta, vel alibi ubicunque, praedictis terris et caeteris praemissis vel alicui inde parcellae quoquo modo spectantia; Necnon reversionem et reversiones omnium et singulorum praemissorum superiùs per praesentes praeconcessorum, et cujuslibet inde parcellae, dependentes vel expectantes de in vel super aliquam dimissionem vel concessionem pro termino vel terminis vitae vel vitarum vel annorum, aut aliter, de praemissis superiùs per praesentes praeconcessis seu de aliqua inde parcella quoquo modo factam, existentem de recordo vel non de recordo; Necnon omnia et singula redditus et annualia proficua quaecunque reservata super quibuscunque dimissionibus vel concessionibus de et super praemissis per praesentes praeconcessis, vel de et super aliqua inde parcella.

Dedimus etiam et concessimus, ac per praesentes pro nobis heredibus et successoribus notris damus et concedimus, praefatis Praesidi Concilio et Sodalibus Regalis Societatis Londini pro scientia naturali promovenda, et successoribus suis in perpetuum, quòd ipsi et eorum successores de caetero in perpetuum habeant teneant et gaudeant, ac habere tenere et gaudere valeant et possint, infra praemissa superiùs per praesentes praeconcessa, ac infra quamlibet inde parcellam, tot tanta talia eadem hujusmodi et consimilia jura jurisdictiones libertates franchesias consuetudines privilegia proficua commoditates advantagia emolumenta et hereditamenta quaecunque, quot quanta qualia et quae, ac adeò plenè liberè et integrè, ac in tam amplis modo et forma, prout praedictus Johannes, nuper Dux Northumbriae, aut praedictus Praepositus et Socii Collegii Regis Jacobi in Chelsey propè London, ex fundatione ejusdem Jacobi, Regis Angliae, aut aliquis alius sive aliqui alii, praedicta terras tenementa et caetera praemissa cum suis pertinentiis, aut aliquam inde parcellam, unquam antehac habentes possidentes aut seisiti inde existentes, habens possidens aut seisitus inde existens, unquam habuerunt tenuerunt usi vel gavisi fuerunt, habuit tenuit usus vel gavisus fuit, seu habere tenere uti vel gaudere debuerunt aut debuit, in praemissis superiùs per praesentes praeconcessis, aut aliqua inde parcella, ratione vel praetextu alicujus chartae doni concessionis vel confirmationis per nos seu aliquem progenitorum vel antecessorum nostrorum, nuper Regum vel Reginarum Angliae, antehac habitae factae vel concessae seu confirmatae, aut ratione vel praetextu alicujus Actus Parliamenti vel aliquorum Actuum Parliamentorum, aut ratione vel praetextu alicujus legitimae praescriptionis usus seu consuetudinis antehac habitae seu usitatae, aut aliter, quocunque legali modo jure seu titulo; ac adeò plenè liberè et integrè, ac in tam amplis modo et forma, prout nos aut aliquis progenitorum vel antecessorum nostrorum, nuper Regum vel Reginarum Angliae, praedicta terras tenementa et caetera praemissa, aut aliquam inde parcellam, habuimus et gavisi

Adeò plenè Clauses.

fuimus aut habuerunt et gavisi fuerunt, seu habere et gaudere debuimus aut habere et gaudere debuerunt aut debuit.

Damus ulteriùs, ac per praesentes pro nobis heredibus et successoribus nostris concedimus, praefatis Praesidi Concilio et Sodalibus Regalis Societatis Londini pro scientia naturali promovenda, et eorum successoribus, omnia et singula praemissa superiùs per praesentes praeconcessa, cum eorum pertinentiis universis, adeò plenè liberè et integrè, ac in tam amplis modo et forma, prout ea omnia et singula praemissa, aut aliqua inde parcella, ad manus nostras, seu ad manus aliquorum progenitorum vel antecessorum nostrorum, nuper Regum vel Reginarum Angliae, ratione vel praetextu dissolutionis vel sursum redditionis alicujus nuper monasterii prioratus sive hospitalis, aut ratione vel praetextu alicujus Actus Parliamenti vel aliquorum Actuum Parliamentorum, aut ratione alicujus attincturae sive forisfacturae, aut ratione alicujus excambii vel perquisiti, aut alicujus doni vel concessionis, aut ratione eschaetae, aut quocunque alio legali modo jure seu titulo, devenerunt seu devenire debuerunt, ac in manibus nostris jam existunt seu existere debent vel debuerunt.

Tenure.

HABENDUM tenendum et gaudendum praedicta terras tenementa et hereditamenta, ac caetera omnia et singula praemissa superiùs per praesentes praeconcessa, cum eorum pertinentiis universis, praefatis Praesidi Concilio et Sodalibus Regalis Societatis Londini pro scientia naturali promovenda, et successoribus suis in perpetuum; Tenendum de nobis heredibus et successoribus nostris, ut de Manerio nostro de East Greenwich, in comitatu nostro Cantiae, per fidelitatem tantùm, in libero et communi soccagio, et non in capite, nec per servitium militare; Ac reddendo annuatim nobis heredibus et successoribus nostris de et pro praedicta terra arabili vocata Teamshott viginti tres solidos et quatuor denarios, ac de et pro praedicto clauso prati vocato Stony Bridge Close, viginti solidos, ac de et pro praedicta pecia terrae arabilis in communi campo vocato East Field quatuor solidos, legalis monetae Angliae, ad festa Sancti Michaelis Archangeli et Annunciationis beatae Mariae Virginis, ad Receptam Scaccarii nostri Westmonasterii heredum et successorum nostrorum, seu ad manus Ballivorum seu Receptorum praemissorum pro tempore existentium, per aequales portiones annuatim solvendos in perpetuum.

Rent.

Charta Tertia.

Et ulteriùs de uberiori gratia nostra speciali ac ex certa scientia et mero motu nostris volumus, ac per praesentes pro nobis heredibus et successoribus nostris concedimus praefatis Presidi Concilio et Sodalibus Regalis Societatis praedictae, et successoribus suis, quòd nos heredes et successores nostri de caetero in perpetuum annuatim, et de tempore in tempus, exonerabimus acquietabimus et indempnes conservabimus tam praefatos Praesidem Concilium et Sodales Regalis Societatis praedictae, et successores suos, quàm praedicta terras tenementa et caetera omnia et singula praemissa superiùs expressa et specificata ac per praesentes praeconcessa, et quamlibet inde parcellam, cum eorum pertinentiis universis, de et ab omnibus et omnimodis corrodiis redditibus feodis servitiis annuitatibus pensionibus portionibus ac denariorum summis ac oneribus quibuscunque de praemissis seu aliqua inde parcella nobis heredibus vel successoribus nostris exeuntibus vel solvendis, vel superinde versùs nos heredes vel successores nostros oneratis vel onerandis; praeterquam de redditibus servitiis et tenuris superiùs in his praesentibus nobis heredibus et successoribus nostris reservatis, ac praeterquam de dimissionibus et concessionibus de praemissis seu de aliqua inde parcella antehac factis, ac conventionibus et conditionibus in eisdem existentibus, ac conventionibus et oneribus, quae aliquis firmarius seu aliqui firmarii praemissorum ratione indenturarum et dimissionum suarum facere et exonerare tenetur seu tenentur.

Volumus etiam, ac per praesentes pro nobis heredibus et successoribus nostris firmiter injungendo praecipimus tam Commissionariis pro Thesauro nostro, Thesaurario, Camerario, Subthesaurario, et Baronibus Scaccarii nostri heredum et successorum nostrorum pro tempore existentibus, quàm omnibus et singulis Auditoribus et aliis officiariis et ministris nostris heredum et successorum nostrorum quibuscunque pro tempore existentibus, quòd ipsi et eorum quilibet, super solam demonstrationem harum Literarum nostrarum Patentium, vel Irrotulamenti earundem, absque aliquo alio brevi seu warranto à nobis heredibus vel successoribus nostris quoquo modo impetrando seu prosequendo, plenam integram debitamque allocationem et exonerationem manifestam de et ab omnibus et omnimodis hujusmodi corrodiis redditibus feodis pensionibus portionibus et denariorum summis ac oneribus quibuscunque (praeterquam de servitiis redditibus tenuris ac arreragiis redditus

Exonerations, acquittances, &c.

ac caeteris praemissis in his praesentibus, ut praefertur, reservatis, et per praefatos Praesidem Concilium et Sodales Regalis Societatis praedictae et successores suos solubilibus fiendis* seu performandis) de praemissis per praesentes praeconcessis, seu de aliqua inde parte vel parcella, nobis heredibus vel successoribus nostris exeuntibus seu solvendis, vel superinde versùs nos heredes vel successores nostros oneratis seu onerandis, praefatis Praesidi Concilio et Sodalibus Regalis Societatis praedictae et successoribus suis facient, et de tempore in tempus fieri causabunt: Et hae Literae nostrae Patentes, vel Irrotulamentum earundum, erunt de tempore in tempus tam dictis Commissionariis pro Thesauro nostro, Thesaurario, Cancellario,† et Baronibus Scaccarii nostri heredum et successorum nostrorum pro tempore existentibus, quàm omnibus et singulis Auditoribus, et aliis officiariis et ministris nostris heredum et successorum nostrorum quibuscunque pro tempore existentibus, sufficiens warrantum et exoneratio in hac parte.

Recital of some parts of the Second Charter.

Et cùm nos per Literas nostras Patentes, gerentes datum apud Westmonasterium, vicesimo secundo die Aprilis, anno regni nostri decimo quinto, Praesidi Concilio et Sodalibus Regalis Societatis praedictae factas, inter alia concessimus praefatis Praesidi Concilio et Sodalibus praedictae Regalis Societatis, et successoribus suis in perpetuum, quòd si contigerit Praesidem ejusdem Regalis Societatis pro tempore existentem aegritudine vel infirmitate detineri, vel in servitio nostro heredum vel successorum nostrorum versari, vel aliter esse occupatum, ita quòd necessariis negotiis ejusdem Regalis Societatis officium Praesidis tangentibus attendere non poterit; quòd tunc et toties benè liceat et licebit eidem Praesidi sic detento versato vel occupato unum de Concilio praedictae Regalis Societatis pro tempore existente, fore et esse Deputatum ejusdem Praesidis, nominare et appunctuare; qui quidem Deputatus, in officio Deputati Praesidis praedicti sic faciendus et constituendus, sit et esset Deputatus ejusdem Praesidis de tempore in tempus, toties quoties praedictus Praeses sic abesse contigerit, durante toto tempore, quo praedictus Praeses in officio Praesidis continuaverit, nisi interim praedictus Praeses Regalis Societatis praedictae pro tempore existens unum alium de praedicto Concilio ejus Deputatum fecerit et constituerit; Et quòd quilibet

---

* *Sic.*
† *Sic;* see above.

hujusmodi Deputatus praedicti Praesidis, sic ut praefertur faciendus et constituendus, omnia et singula quae ad officium Praesidis praedictae Regalis Societatis pertinent seu pertinere debent, vel per praedictum Praesidem virtute istarum Literarum nostrarum Patentium limitata et appunctuata fore* facienda et exequenda, de tempore in tempus, toties quoties praedictus Praeses sic abesse contigerit, durante tali tempore, quo Deputatus praedicti Praesidis continuaverit, facere et exequi valeat et possit, vigore istarum Literarum nostrarum Patentium, adeò plenè liberè et integrè, ac in tam amplis modo et forma, prout Praeses praedictus, si praesens esset, illa facere et exequi valeat et possit; sacramento corporali super sancti Dei Evangelia, in forma et effectu in eisdem Literis nostris Patentibus specificatis, per hujusmodi Deputatum, ad omnia et singula quae ad officium Praesidis pertinent benè et fideliter exequenda, coram praefato Concilio praedictae Regalis Societatis vel aliquibus septem vel pluribus eorum, priùs praestando; et sic toties quoties casus sic acciderit; cui quidem Concilio, vel aliquibus septem vel pluribus eorum pro tempore existentibus, sacramentum praedictum administrare potestatem et authoritatem, quoties casus sic acciderit, dedimus et concessimus per easdem Literas nostras Patentes, absque brevi commissione sive ulteriori warranto in ea parte à nobis heredibus et successoribus nostris procurando seu obtinendo; Ac quòd ipsi et successores eorum, seu aliqui novem vel plures eorum (quorum Praesidem pro tempore existentem, vel ejus Deputatum, semper unum esse volumus), conventus seu congregationes de seipsis pro experimentorum et rerum naturalium cognitione et indagine, aliisque negotiis ad Societatem praedictam spectantibus, quoties et quando opus fuerit, licitè facere et habere possint in collegio sive aula sive alio loco commodo intra Civitatem nostram London, vel in aliquo alio loco commodo intra decem milliaria ab eadem Civitate nostra.

Et cùm diversa et varia res potestates libertates et privilegia in eisdem Literis nostris Patentibus praefatis Praesidi Concilio ac Sodalibus Regalis Societatis praedictae concessa, virtute istarum Literarum nostrarum Patentium, non sunt exercenda facienda performanda seu exequenda, nisi per praedictos Praesidem et Concilium, aut aliquos septem vel plures eorum; Et cùm ulteriùs per praedictas Literas nostras Patentes pro nobis heredibus

It takes notice that several Powers, granted by that Charter, cannot be executed but by the President and Council, or seven or more of them, by virtue of that Charter.

* *Sic.*

et successoribus nostris dedimus et concessimus praefatis Praesidi Concilio et Sodalibus praedictae Regalis Societatis, et successoribus suis in perpetuum, sive aliquibus viginti et uni vel pluribus eorum (quorum Praesidem pro tempore existentem, vel ejus Deputatum, semper unum esse volumus), seu majori parti praedictorum viginti et unius vel plurium, plenam potestatem et authoritatem de tempore in tempus eligendi nominandi et constituendi unum vel plures Typographos sive Impressores, et Chalcographos seu Sculptores, et ipsi vel ipsis, per scriptum Communi Sigillo praedictae Regalis Societatis sigillatum, et manu Praesidis pro tempore existentis signatum, facultatem concedendi, ut imprimant tales res materias et negotia praedictam Regalem Societatem tangentes vel concernentes, quales praedictis Typographo vel Impressori, Chalcographo vel Sculptori, vel Typographis vel Impressoribus, Chalcographis vel Sculptoribus, de tempore in tempus per Praesidem et Concilium praedictae Regalis Societatis, vel aliquos septem vel plures eorum (quorum Praesidem pro tempore existentem, vel ejus Deputatum, unum esse volumus), vel per majorem partem praedictorum septem vel plurium commissae fuerint; sacramentis suis corporalibus, antequam ad officia sua exercenda admittantur, coram Praeside et Concilio pro tempore existentibus, vel aliquibus septem vel pluribus eorum, priùs praestandis; cui quidem Praesidi et Concilio, vel aliquibus septem vel pluribus eorum pro tempore existentibus, sacramenta praedicta administrare plenam potestatem et authoritatem dedimus et concessimus per praedictas Literas nostras Patentes; prout in eisdem Literis nostris Patentibus, relatione inde habita, pleniùs liquet et apparet:

<small>This Charter directs that the President's Deputy shall continue in office, *although* the President do appoint one or more others:</small>

Nos, de abundantiori gratia nostra speciali ac ex certa scientia et mero motu nostris, dedimus et concessimus, ac per praesentes pro nobis heredibus et successoribus nostris damus et concedimus, praefatis Praesidi Concilio et Sodalibus praedictae Regalis Societatis, et successoribus suis in perpetuum, quòd de caetero in perpetuum, si contigerit Praesidem ejusdem Regalis Societatis pro tempore existentem aegritudine vel infirmitate detineri, vel in servitio nostro heredum vel successorum nostrorum versari, vel aliter esse occupatum, ita quòd necessariis negotiis ejusdem Regalis Societatis officium Praesidis tangentibus attendere non poterit; quòd tunc et toties benè liceat et licebit eidem Praesidi sic detento versato vel occupato unum de Concilio praedictae Regalis Societatis pro tempore existente, fore et esse Deputatum ejusdem Praesidis, nominare et appunctuare; qui quidem Deputatus, in officio Deputati Praesidis praedicti sic faciendus et constituendus, sit et erit Deputatus ejusdem Praesidis de tempore in tempus, toties quoties praedictus Praeses sic abesse contigerit, durante toto tempore, quo praedictus Praeses in officio Praesidis continuaverit, etiamsi interim Praeses Regalis Societatis praedictae pro tempore existens unum alium vel plures alios de praedicto Concilio ejus Deputatum et Deputatos fecerit et constituerit; cui quidem Praesidi pro tempore existenti duos vel plures de praedicto Concilio ejus Deputatos ipso et eodem tempore facere et constituere potestatem et authoritatem, quoties ei placuerit, damus et concedimus per praesentes pro nobis heredibus et successoribus nostris; Et quòd quilibet hujusmodi Deputatus et Deputati praedicti Praesidis, sic ut praefertur faciendi et constituendi, omnia et singula quae ad officium Praesidis praedictae Regalis Societatis pertinent seu pertinere debent, vel per praedictum Praesidem virtute praedictarum Literarum nostrarum Patentium, vel praesentium, limitata et appunctuata fore* facienda et exequenda, de tempore in tempus, toties quoties praedictus Praeses sic abesse contigerit, durante tali tempore, quo Deputatus et Deputati praedicti Praesidis continuaverit et continuaverint, facere et exequi valeat et possit, valeant et possint, vigore harum Literarum nostrarum Patentium, adeò plenè liberè et integrè, ac in tam amplis modo et forma, prout Praeses praedictus, si praesens esset, illa facere et exequi valeret et posset; sacramento corporali super sancta Dei Evangelia, in forma et effectu in eisdem Literis nostris Patentibus specificatis, per hujusmodi Deputatum et Deputatos, ad omnia et singula quae ad officium Praesidis pertinent benè et fideliter exequenda, coram praefato Concilio praedictae Regalis Societatis, vel aliquibus quinque† vel pluribus eorum, priùs praestando; et sic toties quoties casus sic acciderit: cui quidem Concilio, vel aliquibus quinque vel pluribus eorum pro tempore existentibus, sacramentum praedictum administrare potestatem et authoritatem, quoties casus sic acciderit, damus et concedimus per praesentes, absque brevi commissione sive

And it gives him express Power to appoint two *or* more *Deputies, out of the Council, at one and the same time; who may, each of them, do the same Acts in his absence, as he himself could do if present.*

But they must first be sworn before the Council, or five *or more of them.*

---

* *Sic.*

† N.B. The Oaths of Obedience and Supremacy require *seven*; see further on.

ulteriori warranto in ea parte à nobis heredibus et successoribus nostris procurando seu obtinendo;

For the future the President, Council, and Fellows, or any nine of them) of whom the President or his Deputy to be always one), may hold their Assemblies anywhere within the Realm of ENGLAND.

Ac ulteriùs, quòd de caetero in perpetuum ipsi et successores eorum, seu aliqui novem vel plures eorum (quorum Praesidem pro tempore existentem, vel ejus Deputatum, semper unum esse volumus), conventus seu congregationes de seipsis pro experimentorum et rerum naturalium cognitione et indagine, aliisque negotiis ad Societatem praedictam spectantibus, quoties et quando opus fuerit, licitè facere et habere possint in collegio sive aula sive alio loco commodo intra Regnum nostrum Angliae;

All Powers, &c., which could not be exercised heretofore but by the President and Council, or seven *or more of them, may for the future be exercised by the President and Council, or any* five *or more of them.*

Ac ulteriùs, quòd omnia et singula res potestates libertates et privilegia in praedictis Literis nostris Patentibus praefatis Praesidi Concilio et Sodalibus Regalis Societatis praedictae concessa, virtute istarum Literarum nostrarum Patentium, quae non sunt exercenda facienda performanda seu exequenda, nisi per praedictum Praesidem et Concilium, aut aliquos septem vel plures eorum, de caetero in perpetuum exerceri fieri performari seu exequi possint et valeant per praedictos Praesidem et Concilium, aut aliquos quinque vel plures eorum.

For the future, the President *may appoint one Printer or more, and one Engraver or more, and authorise him or them to print such things (touching or concerning the Royal Society) as shall be given to him or them in charge by the President and Council, or any* five *or more of them (of whom the President or his Deputy to be one), or by the major part of such five or more.*

Ac ulteriùs de uberiori gratia nostra dedimus et concessimus, ac per praesentes pro nobis heredibus et successoribus nostris damus et concedimus, praefatis Praesidi Concilio et Sodalibus praedictae Regalis Societatis, et successoribus suis in perpetuum, quòd de caetero in perpetuum benè liceat et licebit Praesidi Regalis Societatis praedictae pro tempore existenti, de tempore in tempus, eligere nominare et constituere aliquem vel aliquos Typographum sive Impressorem, Typographos sive Impressores, et Chalcographum seu Sculptorem, Chalcographos seu Sculptores, et ipsi vel ipsis facultatem concedere, ut imprimant tales res materias et negotia praedictam Regalem Societatem tangentes vel concernentes, quales praedictis Typographo vel Impressori, Chalcographo seu Sculptori, vel Typographis vel Impressoribus, Chalcographis vel Sculptoribus, de tempore in tempus per Praesidem et Concilium praedictae Regalis Societatis, vel aliquos quinque vel plures eorum (quorum Praesidem pro tempore existentem, vel ejus Deputatum, unum esse volumus), vel per majorem partem praedictorum quinque vel plurium, commissae fuerint; sacramentis suis corporalibus, antequam ad officia sua exercenda admittantur, coram Praeside et Concilio pro tempore existente, vel aliquibus quinque vel pluribus eorum, priùs praestandis; et

They must be first sworn before the President and Council, or any five *or more of them.*

sic toties quoties casus sic acciderit: cui quidem Praesidi et Concilio pro tempore existentibus, vel aliquibus quinque vel pluribus eorum, sacramenta praedicta administrare plenam potestatem et authoritatem damus et concedimus per praesentes.

Et ulteriùs volumus, ac per praesentes pro nobis heredibus et successoribus nostris concedimus praefatis Praesidi Concilio et Sodalibus Regalis Societatis praedictae, et successoribus suis, quòd hae Literae nostrae Patentes, vel Irrotulamentum earundem, stabunt et erunt in omnibus et per omnia bonae firmae validae sufficientes et effectuales in lege ad omnes respectus proposita constructiones et intentiones erga et contra nos heredes et successores nostros, tam in omnibus Curiis nostris, quàm alibi intra Regnum nostrum Angliae, absque aliquibus confirmationibus licentiis vel tolerationibus de nobis heredibus vel successoribus nostris quoquo modo in posterum procurandis aut obtinendis: *General confirmatory Clauses.*

Non obstante malè nominando vel malè recitando aut non recitando praedicta terras tenementa et caetera praemissa, vel aliquam inde parcellam; Et non obstante non inveniendo officium aut inquisitionem praemissorum, aut alicujus inde parcellae, per quae titulus noster inveniri debuit, ante confectionem harum Literarum nostrarum Patentium; Et non obstante malè recitando vel non recitando aliquam dimissionem vel concessionem de praemissis vel de aliqua inde parcella factam, existentem de recordo vel non de recordo; Et non obstante malè nominando vel non nominando aliquamvillam hamelettum parochiam locum vel comitatum, in quibus praemissa vel aliqua inde parcella existunt vel existit; Et non obstante, quòd de nobis* tenentium firmariorum sive occupatorum praemissorum, vel alicujus inde parcellae, plena vera et certa non fit· mentio; Et non obstantibus aliquibus defectibus de certitudine vel computatione aut declaratione veri annui valoris praemissorum, aut alicujus inde parcellae, aut annualis redditus reservati de et super praemissis, vel de et super aliqua inde parcella, in his Literis nostris Patentibus expressis et contentis; Et non obstante Statuto in Parliamento Domini Henrici, nuper Regis Angliae Sexti, progenitoris nostri, anno regni sui decimo octavo, facto et edito; Et non obstante aliquibus aliis defectibus, in non certò nominando naturam genus speciei† quantitatem

* Error for *nominibus*; so also in the Patent Roll.
† *Sic*.

aut qualitatem praemissorum, aut alicujus inde parcellae; Et non obstante Statuto de terris et tenementis ad manum mortuam non ponendis, aut aliquo alio statuto actu ordinatione proclamatione provisione sive restrictione in contrarium inde antehac habito facto edito ordinato seu proviso, in aliquo non obstante: SALVO tamen Andreae Cole, Armigero, et omnibus aliis personis quibuscunque, praeterquam nos heredes et successores nostros, tali jure clameo* interesse et demanda quaecunque, quale ipse vel ipsi seu eorum aliquis habet seu habeant,† aut de jure habere debent, de et in praemissis, seu aliqua parte vel parcella inde.

<small>The President and Deputy-Presidents are enjoined to take the Oath of *Obedience* and the Oath of *Supremacy*, before the Council, or *seven* or more of them, previously to their acting.</small>

Et ulteriùs volumus, et per praesentes pro nobis heredibus et successoribus nostris ordinamus et firmiter injungendo praecipimus, quòd Praeses Societatis praedictae pro tempore existens, et Deputati ejus, antequam ipsi aut eorum aliqui ad executionem officii illius admittantur, tam sacramentum corporale communiter vocatum *The Oath of Obedience*, quàm sacramentum corporale communiter vocatum *The Oath of Supremacy*, super sacrosanctis Dei Evangeliis praestabunt, et eorum quilibet praestabit, coram Concilio ejusdem Societatis, aut aliquibus septem‡ vel pluribus eorum: cui quidem Concilio, aut aliquibus septem vel pluribus eorum, sacramenta praedicta administrare pro nobis heredibus et successoribus nostris plenam potestatem et authoritatem de tempore in tempus, quotiescunque opus fuerit, damus et concedimus per praesentes.

Proviso semper, et voluntas et intentio nostra regia est, quòd terrae et praemissa praedicta per praesentes, ut praefertur, concessa, seu eorum aliqua, non alienabuntur vel vendentur alicui personae sive aliquibus personis quibuscunque; aliquo in praesentibus contento in contrarium inde non obstante.

Eò quòd expressa mentio de vero valore annuo vel de certitudine praemissorum sive eorum alicujus, aut de aliis donis sive concessionibus per nos seu per aliquem progenitorum sive praedecessorum nostrorum praefatis Praesidi Concilio et Sodalibus Regalis Societatis de London, et successoribus suis, ante haec tempora factis, in praesentibus minimè facta existit; aut aliquo statuto actu ordinatione

---

* "*Jus clameum*," &c., in the Charter and in the Roll.

† *Sic.*

‡ N.B. The Oath of Office may be taken before *five* only; see before.

provisione proclamatione sive restrictione in contrarium inde antehac habito facto edito ordinato sive proviso, aut aliqua alia re causa vel materia quacunque, in aliquo non obstante.

In cujus rei testimonium has Literas nostras fieri fecimus Patentes. TESTE Me ipso, apud Westmonasterium, octavo die Aprilis, anno regni nostri vicesimo primo.

Per breve de Privato Sigillo.
PIGOTT.*

THIRD CHARTER,

(Granting Chelsea College and further Privileges,) granted to the same by the same, A.D. 1669.

CHARLES THE SECOND, by the grace of God, King of England, Scotland, France, and Ireland, Defender of the Faith, &c., to all to whom these our Letters Patent shall come, greeting.

Know ye that we, of our special grace and of our certain knowledge and mere motion, have given and granted, and by these presents for us, our heirs, and successors do give and grant, to our beloved and trusty the President, Council, and Fellows of the Royal Society of London for promoting Natural Knowledge, and to their successors for ever, All that piece of arable land called Teamshott, containing by estimation twenty acres, *Grant of Lands in Chelsey.* lying between our highway leading from Westminster to Chelsey on the north and west side, and a piece of meadow, containing by estimation four acres, parcel of eighteen acres of meadow, late in the tenure of the Earl of Nottingham or his assigns, on the south side, and a close of meadow called Stony Bridge Close on the east side, and a piece of arable land, late in the occupation of Thomas Evans or his assigns, on the west side, by the particular thereof mentioned to be of the yearly rent or value of twenty-three shillings and four pence; And also

---

* This Charter is on three skins of vellum. The first skin contains an engraved portrait of Charles II., very much inferior in execution to those in the preceding Charters.

all that the aforesaid close of meadow called Stony Bridge
Close, containing by estimation four acres, late in the
occupation of John Deakes or his assigns, lying between
the stream called the Common Sewer on the east side,
and the aforesaid piece of land called Teamshott on the
west side, and the bridge called Stony Bridge on the
north side, by the particular thereof mentioned to be of
the yearly rent or value of twenty shillings; And also all
that one piece of arable land in the common field called
East Field, containing by estimation three acres, late in
the occupation of Thomas Frances or his assigns, lying
between the aforesaid piece of land called Teamshott on
the east side, a piece of arable land, late in the tenure of
the Earl of Lincoln or his assigns, on the west side, a
parcel of meadow of Earles Court land on the south side,
and our highway leading from Westminster to Chelsea
aforesaid on the north and west side, by the particular
thereof mentioned to be of the yearly rent or value of
four shillings; (which same premises are, or formerly
were, parcel of our land in Chelsey, being parcel of the
Demesne land of the Manor of Chelsea aforesaid, and
lately were parcel of the possessions of John, late Duke
of Northumberland; and which lately by our very dear
grandfather, of blessed memory, King James, by his
Letters Patent, bearing date at Westminster, the eighth
day of May, in the year of his reign of England the
eighth, and of Scotland the forty-third, were granted, or
mentioned to be granted, to the Provost and Fellows of
the College of King James in Chelsea, near London, of
the foundation of the same James, King of England, and
to their successors for ever, to hold of the aforesaid King
James, as of his Manor of East Greenwich, in the county
of Kent, by fealty only, in free and common socage, and
not in chief, nor by Knight service;) And also all and
singular houses, buildings, structures, woods, underwoods,
trees, and all the land, ground, and soil of the same
woods, underwoods, and trees, and all other our rights,
jurisdictions, franchises, privileges, liberties, profits, commodities, advantages, emoluments, and hereditaments
whatsoever, with all their appurtenances, of whatsoever
kind, nature, or sort they may be, or by whatsoever
names they may be known, deemed, called, or recognised,
situate, lying, and being, issuing, growing, renewing, or
arising, within the county, towns, fields, places, or hamlets
aforesaid, or elsewhere wheresoever, to the aforesaid lands

and other the premises, or to any parcel thereof, in any manner belonging; And also the reversion and reversions of all and singular the premises above by these presents before granted, and of every parcel thereof, dependent or expectant of, in, or upon any demise or grant for term or terms of life or lives or years, or otherwise, made of the premises above by these presents before granted, or of any parcel thereof, in any manner, being of record or not of record; And also all and singular the rents and yearly profits whatsoever, reserved upon whatsoever demises or grants of and upon the premises by these presents before granted, or of and upon any parcel thereof.

We have also given and granted, and by these presents for us, our heirs, and successors do give and grant to the aforesaid President, Council, and Fellows of the Royal Society of London for promoting Natural Knowledge, and to their successors for ever, that they and their successors henceforth for ever may have, hold, and enjoy, and may be able and have power to have, hold, and enjoy, within the premises above by these presents before granted, and within every parcel thereof, as many, as great, such, the same, like, and similar rights, jurisdictions, liberties, franchises, customs, privileges, profits, commodities, advantages, emoluments, and hereditaments whatsoever, as, such as, and which, and as fully, freely, and wholly, and in as ample manner and form, as the aforesaid John, late Duke of Northumberland, or the aforesaid Provost and Fellows of the College of King James in Chelsey, near London, of the foundation of the same James, King of England, or any other person or persons ever heretofore having or possessing the aforesaid lands, tenements, and other the premises, with their appurtenances, or any parcel thereof, or being seised thereof, ever had, held, used, or enjoyed, or ought to have had, held, used, or enjoyed, in the premises above by these presents before granted or in any parcel thereof, by reason or pretext of any charter of gift, grant, or confirmation by us or by any of our progenitors or ancestors, late Kings or Queens of England, heretofore had, made, or granted, or confirmed, or by reason or pretext of any Act of Parliament or of any Acts of Parliaments, or by reason or pretext of any lawful prescription, use, or custom heretofore had or used, or otherwise, by whatsoever lawful means, right, or title; and as fully, freely, and wholly, and in as ample manner and form, as we or any of our progenitors or

Adeò plenè Clauses.

ancestors, late Kings or Queens of England, had and enjoyed, or ought to have had and enjoyed, the aforesaid lands, tenements, and other the premises or any parcel thereof.

We give further, and by these presents for us, our heirs, and successors do grant to the aforesaid President, Council, and Fellows of the Royal Society of London for promoting Natural Knowledge, and to their successors, all and singular the premises above by these presents before granted, with all their appurtenances, as fully, freely, and wholly, and in as ample manner and form, as all and singular those premises or any parcel thereof came or ought to have come to our hands, or to the hands of any of our progenitors or ancestors, late Kings or Queens of England, by reason or pretext of the dissolution or surrender of any late monastery, priory, or hospital, or by reason or pretext of any Act of Parliament or of any Acts of Parliaments, or by reason of any attainder or forfeiture, or by reason of any exchange or purchase, or of any gift or grant, or by reason of escheat, or by whatsoever other lawful means, right, or title, and now are, or ought to be, in our hands.

Tenure.

To HAVE, hold, and enjoy the aforesaid lands, tenements, and hereditaments, and all and singular other the premises above by these presents before granted, with all their appurtenances, to the aforesaid President, Council, and Fellows of the Royal Society of London for promoting Natural Knowledge, and to their successors for ever; To hold of us, our heirs, and successors, as of our Manor of East Greenwich, in our county of Kent, by fealty only, in free and common socage, and not in chief, nor by Knight service; And rendering yearly to us, our heirs, and successors of and for the aforesaid arable land called Teamshott twenty-three shillings and four pence, and of and for the aforesaid close of meadow called Stony Bridge Close twenty shillings, and of and for the aforesaid piece of arable land in the common field called East Field four shillings, of lawful money of England, at the feasts of Saint Michael the Archangel and the Annunciation of the Blessed Virgin Mary, at the Receipt of the Exchequer at Westminster of us, our heirs, and successors, or to the hands of the Bailiffs or Receivers of the premises for the time being, by equal portions yearly to be paid for ever.

Rent.

Exonerations, acquittances, &c.

And further, of our more abundant special grace and

of our certain knowledge and mere motion, we will, and by these presents for us, our heirs, and successors do grant to the aforesaid President, Council, and Fellows of the Royal Society aforesaid, and to their successors, that we, our heirs, and successors henceforth for ever yearly and from time to time will discharge, acquit, and save harmless as well the aforesaid President, Council, and Fellows of the Royal Society aforesaid and their successors, as the aforesaid lands, tenements, and other all and singular the premises above expressed and specified, and by these presents before granted, and every parcel thereof, with all their appurtenances, of and from all and all manner of corrodies, rents, fees, services, annuities, pensions, portions, and sums of money, and charges whatsoever from the premises or from any parcel thereof to us, our heirs, or successors issuing or to be paid, or thereupon towards us, our heirs, or successors charged or to be charged; except from the rents, services, and tenures above in these presents to us, our heirs, and successors reserved, and except from demises and grants of the premises or of any parcel thereof heretofore made, and the covenants and conditions being in the same, and the covenants and charges which any farmer or farmers of the premises by reason of his or their indentures and demises is or are bound to do and discharge.

We will also, and by these presents for us, our heirs, and successors, firmly enjoining, do command as well the Commissioners for our Treasury, the Treasurer, Chamberlain, Under-Treasurer, and Barons of the Exchequer of us, our heirs, and successors for the time being, as all and singular Auditors and other officers and ministers of us, our heirs, and successors whomsoever for the time being, that they and each of them, upon the mere showing of these our Letters Patent, or of the Enrolment of the same, without any other writ or warrant from us, our heirs, or successors in any manner to be sued out or prosecuted, shall make and from time to time shall cause to be made to the aforesaid President, Council, and Fellows of the Royal Society aforesaid and their successors full, whole, and due allowance and manifest discharge of and from all and all manner of such corrodies, rents, fees, pensions, portions, and sums of money, and charges whatsoever (except from the services, rents, tenures, and arrears of rent and other the premises in these presents reserved, as it is aforesaid, and by the aforesaid President,

Council, and Fellows of the Royal Society aforesaid and their successors payable, to be done, or to be performed) from the premises by these presents before granted, or from any part or parcel thereof, to us, our heirs, or successors issuing or to be paid, or thereupon towards us, our heirs, or successors charged or to be charged; And these our Letters Patent, or the Enrolment of the same, shall be from time to time, as well to the said Commissioners for our Treasury, the Treasurer, Chancellor,* and Barons of the Exchequer of us, our heirs, and successors, for the time being, as to all and singular Auditors and other officers and ministers of us, our heirs, and successors whomsoever for the time being, a sufficient warrant and discharge in this behalf.

<small>Recital of some parts of the Second Charter.</small>

And whereas we, by our Letters Patent bearing date at Westminster, the twenty-second day of April, in the fifteenth year of our reign, made to the President, Council, and Fellows of the Royal Society aforesaid, among other things, granted to the aforesaid President, Council, and Fellows of the aforesaid Royal Society, and to their successors for ever, that if it shall happen that the President of the same Royal Society for the time being is detained by sickness or infirmity, or is employed in the service of us, our heirs, or successors, or is otherwise occupied, so that he cannot attend to the necessary affairs of the same Royal Society touching the office of President, that then and so often it may and shall be good and lawful to the same President, so being detained, employed, or occupied, to nominate and appoint one of the Council of the aforesaid Royal Society for the time being to be and become the Deputy of the same President; which same Deputy, so to be made and appointed in the office of Deputy of the President aforesaid, may and should be the Deputy of the same President from time to time, as often as it shall happen that the aforesaid President is so absent, during the whole time in which the aforesaid President shall continue in the office of President, unless in the meanwhile the aforesaid President of the Royal Society aforesaid for the time being shall have made and appointed one other of the aforesaid Council his Deputy; And that every such Deputy of the aforesaid President so to be made and appointed, as it is aforesaid, may be able and have power to do and execute all and singular things which pertain

* "Chamberlain," &c., above.

or ought to pertain to the office of President of the aforesaid Royal Society, or which are limited and appointed to be done and executed by the aforesaid President by virtue of those our Letters Patent, from time to time, as often as it shall happen that the aforesaid President is so absent, during such time as the Deputy of the aforesaid President shall continue, by force of these our Letters Patent, as fully, freely, and wholly, and in as ample manner and form, as the President aforesaid, if he were present, may be able and have power to do and execute the same; a corporal oath first to be taken upon the holy Gospels of God, in the form and effect in our same Letters Patent specified, by such Deputy, well and faithfully to execute all and singular things which pertain to the office of President, before the aforesaid Council of the aforesaid Royal Society, or any seven or more of them; and so as often as the case shall so happen; to which same Council, or to any seven or more of them, for the time being, we gave and granted, by our same Letters Patent, power and authority to administer the oath aforesaid, as often as the case shall so happen, without procuring or obtaining a writ, commission, or further warrant in that behalf from us, our heirs, and successors; And that they and their successors, or any nine or more of them (of whom we will the President for the time being, or his Deputy, to be always one), may lawfully be able to make and have assemblies and meetings of themselves for the examination and investigation of experiments and of natural things, and for other affairs belonging to the Society aforesaid, as often as and whenever it shall be needful, in a College or Hall or other convenient place within our City of London, or in any other convenient place within ten miles from our same City: And whereas divers and various matters, powers, liberties, and privileges granted in our same Letters Patent to the aforesaid President, Council, and Fellows of the Royal Society aforesaid, by virtue of those our Letters Patent, are not to be exercised, done, performed, or executed, unless by the aforesaid President and Council, or any seven or more of them: And whereas further, by our aforesaid Letters Patent, for us, our heirs, and successors we gave and granted to the aforesaid President and Council of the aforesaid Royal Society, and to their successors for ever, or to any twenty-one or more of them (of whom we will the President for the time being, or his

It takes notice that several Powers, granted by that Charter, cannot be executed but by the President and Council, or seven or more of them, by virtue of that Charter.

Deputy, to be always one), or to the major part of the aforesaid twenty-one or more, full power and authority from time to time to elect, nominate, and appoint one or more Typographers or Printers, and Chalcographers or Engravers, and to grant to him or them, by a writing sealed with the Common Seal of the aforesaid Royal Society, and signed by the hand of the President for the time being, faculty to print such things, matters, and affairs touching or concerning the aforesaid Royal Society as shall be committed to the aforesaid Typographer or Printer, Chalcographer or Engraver, or Typographers or Printers, Chalcographers, or Engravers, from time to time, by the President and Council of the aforesaid Royal Society, or any seven or more of them (of whom we will the President for the time being, or his Deputy, to be one), or by the major part of the aforesaid seven or more; their corporal oaths to be first taken, before they be admitted to exercise their offices, before the President and Council for the time being, or any seven or more of them; to which same President and Council, or to any seven or more of them for the time being, we gave and granted by our aforesaid Letters Patent full power and authority to administer the oaths aforesaid; as in our same Letters Patent, reference being had thereto, it is more fully shown and appears:

This Charter directs that the President's Deputy shall continue in office, although the President do appoint one or more others:

We, of our more abundant special grace and of our certain knowledge and mere motion, have given and granted, and by these presents for us, our heirs, and successors do give and grant, to the aforesaid President, Council, and Fellows of the aforesaid Royal Society, and to their successors for ever, that from henceforth for ever if it shall happen that the President of the same Royal Society for the time being is detained by sickness or infirmity, or is employed in the service of us, our heirs, or successors, or is otherwise occupied, so that he cannot attend to the necessary affairs of the same Royal Society touching the office of President; that then and so often it may and shall be good and lawful to the same President, so being detained, employed, or occupied, to nominate and appoint one of the Council of the aforesaid Royal Society for the time being to be and become the Deputy of the same President; which same Deputy, so to be made and appointed in the office of Deputy of the President aforesaid, may and shall be the Deputy of the same President from time to time, as often as it shall happen that the aforesaid President is so absent, during the whole time in which the aforesaid President shall continue in the office of President, even though in the meanwhile the President of the Royal Society aforesaid for the time being shall have made and appointed one other or several others of the aforesaid Council his Deputy and Deputies; to which same President for the time being we give and grant by these presents for us, our heirs, and successors power and authority to make and appoint two or more of the aforesaid Council his Deputies, at one and the same time, as often as it shall please him: And that every such Deputy and Deputies of the aforesaid President, so as it is aforesaid to be made and appointed, may be able and have power to do and execute all and singular things which pertain or ought to pertain to the office of President of the aforesaid Royal Society, or which are limited and appointed to be done and executed by the aforesaid President by virtue of our aforesaid Letters Patent or of these presents, from time to time, as often as it shall happen that the aforesaid President is so absent, during such time as the Deputy and Deputies of the aforesaid President shall continue, by force of these our Letters Patent, as fully, freely, and wholly, and in as ample manner and form, as the President aforesaid, if he were present, would be able and have power to do and execute the same; a corporal oath to be first taken upon the holy Gospels of God, in the form and effect in our same Letters Patent specified, by such Deputy and Deputies, well and faithfully to execute all and singular things which pertain to the office of President, before the aforesaid Council of the aforesaid Royal Society, or any five or more of them; and so as often as the case shall so happen: to which same Council, or to any five or more of them for the time being, we give and grant by these presents, power, and authority to administer the oath aforesaid, as often as the case shall so happen, without procuring or obtaining a writ, commission, or further warrant in that behalf from us, our heirs, and successors:

And it gives him express Power to appoint two or more Deputies, out of the Council, at one and the same time; who may, each of them, do the same Acts in his absence, as he himself could do if present.

But they must first be sworn before the Council, or five or more of them.

And further, that henceforth for ever they and their successors, or any nine or more of them (of whom we will the President for the time being, or his Deputy, to be always one), may be able lawfully to make and have assemblies or meetings of themselves for the examination and investigation of experiments and of natural things, and other affairs belonging to the Society aforesaid, as

For the future, the President, Council, and Fellows, or any nine of them (of whom the President or his Deputy to be always one), may hold their Assemblies any where within the Realm of ENGLAND.

often as and whenever it shall be needful, in a College or Hall or other convenient place within our Realm of England:

All Powers, &c., which could not be exercised heretofore but by the President and Council, or seven *or more of them, may for the future be exercised by the President and Council, or any* five *or more of them.*

And further, that all and singular things, powers, liberties, and privileges in our aforesaid Letters Patent granted to the aforesaid President, Council, and Fellows of the Royal Society aforesaid, by virtue of those our Letters Patent, which are not to be exercised, done, performed, or executed save by the aforesaid President and Council, or any seven or more of them; henceforth for ever may and shall be able to be exercised, done, performed, or executed by the aforesaid President and Council, or any five or more of them.

For the future, the President *may appoint one Printer or more, and one Engraver or more, and authorise him or them to print such things (touching or concerning the Royal Society) as shall be given to him or them in charge by the President and Council, or any* five *or more of them (of whom the President or his Deputy to be one), or by the major part of such five or more.*

And further, of our more abundant grace, we have given and granted, and by these presents for us, our heirs, and successors do give and grant, to the aforesaid President, Council, and Fellows of the aforesaid Royal Society, and to their successors for ever, that henceforth for ever it may and shall be good and lawful to the President of the Royal Society aforesaid for the time being, from time to time, to elect, nominate, and appoint any Typographer or Printer, Typographers or Printers, and Chalcographer or Engraver, Chalcographers or Engravers, and to grant to him or them faculty to print such things, matters, and affairs touching or concerning the aforesaid Royal Society as shall be committed to the aforesaid Typographer or Printer, Chalcographer or Engraver, or Typographers or Printers, Chalcographers or Engravers, from time to time, by the President and Council of the aforesaid Royal Society, or any five or more of them (of whom we will the President for the time being, or his Deputy, to be one), or by the major part of the aforesaid five or more; their corporal oaths to be first taken, before

They must be first sworn before the President and Council, or any five *or more of them.*

they be admitted to exercise their offices, before the President and Council for the time being, or any five or more of them; and so as often as the case shall so happen: to which same President and Council for the time being, or to any five or more of them, we give and grant by these presents full power and authority to administer the oaths aforesaid.

General confirmatory Clauses.

And further we will, and by these presents for us, our heirs, and successors do grant to the aforesaid President, Council, and Fellows of the Royal Society aforesaid and to their successors, that these our Letters Patent, or the Enrolment of the same, shall stand and be in and by all things good, firm, valid, sufficient, and effectual in law, to all respects, purposes, constructions, and intents, towards and against us, our heirs, and successors, as well in all our Courts as elsewhere within our realm of England, without any confirmations, licences, or tolerations from us, our heirs, or successors in any manner hereafter to be procured or obtained:

Notwithstanding the badly naming or badly reciting, or not reciting, the aforesaid lands, tenements, and other the premises or any parcel thereof; And notwithstanding the not finding an office or inquisition of the premises or of any parcel thereof, whereby our title ought to have been found before the making of these our Letters Patent; And notwithstanding the badly reciting, or not reciting, any demise or grant made of the premises or of any parcel thereof, being of record or not of record; And notwithstanding the badly naming or not naming any town, hamlet, parish, place, or county in which the premises or any parcel thereof are or is; And notwithstanding that full, true, and certain mention is not made of the names of the tenants, farmers, or occupiers of the premises or of any parcel thereof; And notwithstanding any defects of the certainty, or computation, or declaration of the true yearly value of the premises or of any parcel thereof, or of the yearly rent reserved of and upon the premises, or of and upon any parcel thereof, in these our Letters Patent expressed and contained; And notwithstanding the Statute made and enacted in the Parliament of the Lord Henry the Sixth, late King of England, our progenitor, in the eighteenth year of his reign; And notwithstanding any other defects in not certainly naming the nature, kind, sort, quantity, or quality of the premises or of any parcel thereof; And notwithstanding the Statute concerning the not putting of lands and tenements to mortmain, or any statute, act, ordinance, proclamation, provision, or restriction to the contrary thereof heretofore had, made, enacted, ordained, or provided, in anywise notwithstanding: SAVING, nevertheless, to Andrew Cole, Esquire, and to all other persons whomsoever, other than us, our heirs, and successors, such right, claim, interest, and demand whatsoever, as he or they or any one of them has or may have, or of right ought to have, of and in the premises or any part or parcel thereof.

And further we will, and by these presents for us, our *The President*

<small>and Deputy-Presidents are enjoined to take the Oath of *Obedience* and the Oath of *Supremacy*, before the Council, or *seven* or more of them, previously to their acting.</small>

heirs, and successors do ordain, and firmly enjoining do command, that the President of the Society aforesaid for the time being, and his Deputies, before he or any of them be admitted to the execution of that office, shall take, and each of them shall take, as well the corporal oath, commonly called The Oath of Allegiance, as the corporal oath, commonly called The Oath of Supremacy, upon the holy Gospels of God, before the Council of the same Society, or any seven or more of them: to which same Council, or to any seven or more of them, we give and grant by these presents, for us, our heirs, and successors, full power and authority to administer the oaths aforesaid from time to time, whensoever it shall be needful.

Provided always, and our Royal will and intention is, that the lands and premises aforesaid granted by these presents, as it is aforesaid, or any of them, shall not be alienated or sold to any person or persons whomsoever; anything in these presents contained to the contrary thereof notwithstanding.

Although express mention of the true yearly value or of the certainty of the premises or of any of them, or of other gifts or grants before these times made by us or by any of our progenitors or predecessors to the aforesaid President, Council, and Fellows of the Royal Society of London, and to their successors, is not made in these presents; or any statute, act, ordinance, provision, proclamation, or restriction to the contrary thereof heretofore had, made, enacted, ordained, or provided, or any other thing, cause, or matter whatsoever, in anywise notwithstanding.

In witness whereof we have caused these our Letters to be made Patent. Witness Ourself, at Westminster, the eighth day of April, in the twenty-first year of our reign.

By writ of Privy Seal.

PIGOTT.

A LICENSE for purchasing in MORTMAIN to the yearly value of One Thousand Pounds, granted to the President, Council, and Fellows of the ROYAL SOCIETY of London, by King GEORGE the FIRST, in the year MDCCXXV.*

"GEORGE by the Grace of God, of Great Britain, France, and Ireland, King, Defender of the Faith, *etc.*, to all to whom these presents shall come, greeting. WHEREAS our trusty and well-beloved the President, Council, and Fellows, of the Royal Society of our City of London for improving natural knowledge, have by their Petition humbly represented unto us, that our late Royal Predecessor, King Charles the Second, by Letters Patents,† bearing date the Two-and-twentieth day of April, in the Fifteenth year of his reign, did ordain constitute and appoint the said Royal Society of London for improving natural knowledge, and did thereby grant them *Licence to purchase in Mortmain;* that since the grant of the said Letters Patents, several well-disposed Persons have devised and granted to the Petitioners, and their successors, divers lands and hereditaments, and given several sums of money to them, for the use of the said corporation; that the Petitioners being desirous to invest the same money in the most durable manner, for the improvement of the said corporation, have most humbly prayed us to grant to them our Royal Licence to hold and enjoy the lands and hereditaments, which have been devised and granted to them; to purchase hold and enjoy to them, and their successors for ever, for the use and benefit of the said corporation, such manors, lands, tenements, and hereditaments, as they shall think fit to purchase, or shall receive by will, or any deed of conveyance, not exceeding the yearly value of *One thousand pounds*: We are graciously pleased to grant their request. KNOW YE therefore, that we, of our especial grace certain knowledge and meer motion, HAVE given and granted, and by these presents for us our heirs and successors DO give and grant, unto the President, Council, and Fellows of the Royal Society of our city of London for improving natural knowledge aforesaid, and their successors, our especial Licence, full power, and lawful and absolute authority, to hold and enjoy the lands and hereditaments, which have been already devised or granted to the said corporation, as aforesaid; and also to purchase acquire take hold and receive in

---

* Reprinted from Weld's 'History of the Royal Society.'
† *So in the* Original.

Mortmain, in perpetuity or otherwise, to or to the use of or in trust for them or their successors, for the use and benefit of the said corporation, from any person or persons, bodies politic and corporate, their heirs and successors respectively, such manors lands tenements rents or hereditaments, as they shall think fit to purchase, or shall receive by writ, or any deed of conveyance, not exceeding the yearly value of One thousand pounds above all charges and reprizes. AND we do hereby also for us our heirs and successors give and grant our especial Licence, full power, and lawful and absolute authority, to any person or persons, bodies politic or corporate, their heirs and successors respectively, to grant, alien, sell, convey, and dispose of in Mortmain, in perpetuity or otherwise, to or to the use of or in trust for the President Council and Fellows of the Royal Society of our city of London for improving natural knowledge aforesaid, and their successors, any manors lands tenements rents or hereditaments whatsoever, not exceeding the yearly value of One thousand pounds. AND LASTLY, we do hereby, for us our heirs and successors, grant unto the President Council and Fellows of the Royal Society of our City of London for improving natural knowledge aforesaid, and their successors, that these our Letters Patents, or the Inrollment or Exemplification thereof, shall be in and by all things good firm valid sufficient and effectual in the law, according to the true intent and meaning thereof; NOTWITHSTANDING the not rightly naming or describing any of the manor lands tenements rents or hereditaments already devised or granted to the said corporation, or to be granted devised aliened or disposed of in Mortmain to them, and their successors, in fee or otherwise, as aforesaid: or any other omission imperfection defect matter cause or thing whatsoever to the contrary thereof in anywise notwithstanding. IN WITNESS whereof we have caused these our Letters to be made Patents. WITNESS Ourself at Westminster, the Seventeenth day of December, in the Eleventh year of our reign.

"By writ of Privy Seal,

"COCKS."

NOTE.

An enrolment at the Record Office, of which the following is an abstract, reconveys to King Charles II the three Closes granted by the third Charter.

Close Roll, 33 *Chas. II, Part* 3, *No.* 3.

(In English.)

Indenture, 8 Feb., 34 Chas. II, 1681[-2], between the King's most excellent Majesty of the one part, and the President, Council, and Fellows of the Royal

Society (&c.) of the other part; whereby (for 1,300*l*.) the latter bargain and sell to the former "All that piece of arable land called Teamshott," &c., "all that aforesaid Close of meadow called Stonebridge Close," &c., "and also all that one piece of arable land in a common field called Eastfeild," &c., which were granted by the King to the Society by letters patent 8 April, 21 Chas. II.

SEAL OF THE ROYAL SOCIETY.

A NOTE ON THE HISTORY OF THE STATUTES OF THE SOCIETY.*

THE FIRST STATUTES.

Ann. 1663. The second Charter, amending the first granted in 1662, having been granted April 22nd, 1663, the Statutes were drawn up in that year. A copy of them is published in Weld's 'History of the Royal Society.'

THE STATUTES FROM 1663 TO 1752.

During the succeeding ninety years changes were from time to time made in the Statutes; but no new version of the Statutes appears to have been drawn up until the year 1752.†

"The laws of the Royal Society, like those of other communities, were altered from time to time, until they appeared sufficient to embrace every contingency that might occur, while they held their meetings in Gresham College, which they continued to do for near the space of fifty years. But the arrangement of the Society's affairs being somewhat altered upon possessing a house of their own, it became necessary to make different establishments in many particulars and to alter and augment some of their Statutes. However, the greater part of them was still left in the original form, suited to the situation of the Society at Gresham College."—(Preface to Statutes, Edition of 1776.)

Between 1663 and 1752, the following seem to have been the most important changes.

The Election of Fellows.

Ann. 1663. In the original Statutes, Cap. VI, "Of the Election and Admission of Fellows." Sec. 1 provides that candidates be propounded at one meeting, and put to the vote at some other meeting at which twenty-one fellows (as prescribed by Charter) are present; but that every one of his Majesty's subjects having the title and place of Baron, or any higher title and place, and every one of his

---

* Reprinted with additions from 'Proceedings of the Royal Society,' vol. 50, p. 501.

† The British Museum contains a small 8vo edition, dated 1728, but this appears to be a verbatim copy of the Statutes of 1663, except that Cap. VI, Sec. 7, begins with the words "The admission of," instead of "The election and admission of."

Majesty's Privy Council, may be propounded and put to the vote the same day. And Sec. 3 of the same chapter provides that "the name of every person propounded as a Candidate, together with the name of the Fellow proposing, shall be entered in the Journal-book;" by which it appears that "propounding" by *one* Fellow was sufficient.

Ann. 1682. In 1682, however, the following was proposed on August 2, and passed on August 5 :—

"The Statute for Election of Fellows having by long Experience been found insufficient for bringing in persons qualifyed for the ends of the Institution of the Royal Society, few balloting in the negative and presuming the person to be well known to the Member that Proposeth the Candidate, it is thought requisite by the Councell to propose this Statute following,—

"Every person that would propose a Candidate shall first give in his name to some of the Councell, that so in the next Councell it may be discoursed *vivâ voce* whether the person is known to be so qualified as in probability to be usefull to the Society. And if the Councell return no other Answer but that they desire further time to be acquainted with the gentleman proposed, the Proposer is to take that for an Answer. And if they are well assured that the Candidate may be usefull to the Society then the Candidate shall be proposed at the next meeting of the Society and ballotted according to the Statute in that behalf, and shall immediately sign the usual Bond and pay his admission money upon his Admission."

(Neither the Statutes of 1663, nor the Edition of 1752, make any mention of the "Bond for the payment of the contribution;" the words first occur in the Edition of 1776, but the actual Bonds preserved in the Archives of the Society date from January 1, 1674, onwards.)

Ann. 1728. In 1728, January 4th (1727 old style), the following Statute was passed, that of 1682 being apparently repealed :—

"Every Person to be Elected Fellow of the Society shall first at a Meeting of the Society be propounded as a candidate to be approved by the Council, and shall be recommended by three members, one of which at least shall be a member of the Council, and one of them shall at the same Time mention and specify the qualification of the said Candidate. And afterwards such Person shall at another meeting of the Society (whereat there shall be a competent Number for making Elections) be referred back from the Council if approved, and shall then be propounded and put to the Vote for Election Saving and Excepting that it shall be free for every one of his Majesties Subjects who is a Peer or the son of a Peer of Great Britain or Ireland, and for every one of his Majesties Privy Council of either of the said kingdoms to be propounded by any single Person and to be put to the Vote for Election on the same Day, there being present a competent Number for making Elections."

Ann. 1730. This, however, was in turn, very soon, viz., in 1730, changed to the following form, all mention of Council being omitted from the Statute:—

"X. Every person to be elected a Fellow of the Royal Society, shall be propounded and recommended at a meeting of the Society by three or more Members; who shall then deliver to one of the Secretaries a paper, signed by themselves with their own names, specifying the name, addition, profession, occupation, and chief qualifications; the inventions, discoveries, works, writings, or other productions of the candidate for Election; as also notifying the usual place of his habitation.

"A fair copy of which paper, with the date of the day when delivered, shall be fixed up in the common meeting room of the Society at ten several ordinary meetings, before the said candidate shall be put to the ballot: Saving and excepting, that it shall be free for every one of his Majesty's subjects, who is a Peer or the Son of a Peer of Great Britain or Ireland, and for every one of his Majesty's Privy council of either of the said Kingdoms, and for every foreign Prince or Ambassador, to be propounded by any single person, and to be put to the ballot for Election on the same day, there being present a competent number for making Elections."

It appears in this form in the Edition of 1752 as Sec. 10 of Cap. VI.

The Admission of Fellows.

Ann. 1728. In 1728, also on January 4th, the two following Statutes were enacted:—

"II. Every Person who is a Foreigner and every one of his Majesties Subjects whose habitation or usual place of residence is at more than forty miles distance from London, shall be and be deemed as a Fellow of the Society immediately after he shall be Elected, and shall be registered in the Journal Book of the Society as such: Provided always, that no such person shall have liberty to Vote at any Election or meeting of the Society before he shall be qualified pursuant to the Statutes. And if he shall neglect so to qualify himself the first time he comes to London when he may be present at a meeting of the Society and can be admitted; his election shall be declared Void, and his Name shall be cancelled in the Register.

"III. No Person shall be Proposed, Elected, or Admitted a Fellow of the Society upon St. Andrew's Day or the Day of the Anniversary meeting for Electing the Council and Officers."

These appear in the Edition of 1752 as Secs. 8 and 9 respectively of Cap. VI.

As far, then, as the election and admission of Fellows are concerned, no new Statutes were enacted in 1752; the Edition of that year simply adds to the Statutes of 1663 the two enacted in 1727 and the one enacted in 1730.

The Election of Council and Officers.

Ann. 1663. In the original Statutes, Cap. VII, "Of the Election of the Council and Officers" makes arrangements that the eleven members of the existing Council who are to be continued should first be determined, after that the ten new members, and finally the officers. The Statutes of 1752, reproduce the chapter in its original form of 12 sections, with the addition of Sec. 13, enacted in 1735, which provides that in order to lessen the tediousness of the election, Fellows may give in *at the same time* three lists—(1) of eleven old Members of Council to continue, (2) of ten new Members, (3) of Officers.

Ann. 1735.

The Philosophical Transactions.

But the most important changes introduced in 1752, those which probably led to the issue of the new version of the Statutes in that year, relate to the 'Philosophical Transactions.' In the old Statutes, Cap. XIII, "Of the Printer to the Society," provides for the printing and binding of books, catalogues, and such other things by order of the Society or Council; there are no other provisions as to publications. From time to time the Council, acting for the Society, gave the license or imprimatur of the Society to certain books. These were printed by the Society's printer, but not at the cost of the Society; nor were they published at the risk of the Society. The cost and risk was undertaken by the printer or by some other person or persons. The treatment of the 'Philosophical Transactions' was at first somewhat similar. These were begun in 1665, but up to the 46th volume inclusive, published in 1749–50, "the printing of them was always, from time to time, the single act of the respective Secretaries" (Adv. to 'Philosophical Transactions,' vol. 47), though they were licensed by the Council. Thus with regard to the first number the Council (Minutes, March 1, 1664) ordered "that the Philosophical Transactions, to be composed by Mr. Oldenburg, be printed the first Munday of every month, if he have sufficient matter for it, and that that Tract be licensed by the Council of the Society, being first reviewed by some of the Members of the same. And that the President be desired, now to Licence the first papers thereof, being written in four sheets in folio, to be printed by John Martyn and James Allestree." This practice of licensing was, up to 1752, continued with reference to those papers read before the Society which were published in the 'Transactions.'

Ann. 1663.

Ann. 1665.

Ann. 1752. In 1752 it was determined to place the publication of the 'Philosophical Transactions' directly in the hands of the Council, and the Edition of the Statutes of 1752, while leaving Cap. XIII intact, adds the following two new chapters, enacted March 26th of that year :—

Cap. XX, "Of the selecting of Papers laid before the Society, in order for Publication," establishes and lays down regulations for the "Committee of Papers." These regulations are almost verbatim the same as Secs. 1 to 4 of Cap. XIII, "Of the Publication of Papers," of the Statutes in force at the present time, except that the Quorum of the Committee of Papers is five, not seven, and a provision is contained that no entry in the Minute-book of the Committee is to be made of Papers "thought improper to be laid before the public."

In the Statute in its original form the Committee "shall be at liberty to call in to their assistance . . . any other members of the Society who are knowing and well skilled in any particular branch of Science that shall happen to be the subject-matter of any paper which shall be then to come under their deliberation," and almost the same words are retained in the Statutes at present in force. The custom of the Committee is now, and for a long time has been, to "call in to their assistance" two or more Fellows, by asking for written reports, and such Fellows so assisting are generally spoken of as "referees." Though the records of the Society show that even in the earliest days of the Society, communications made to the Society were frequently submitted to Fellows in order that their opinions thereon might be obtained, the earliest mention which has been found in the Society's records of a paper being technically "referred"
Ann. 1780. is on May 25, 1780, when a paper by Mr. Ludlow was "referred" to Mr. Cavendish and Dr. Hutton. There does not
Ann. 1831. appear to be a similar record until March 21, 1831, when a paper by Prof. Davy was referred to Mr. Faraday. By 1832, however, the practice of referring papers seems to have become very common. For some time the name of the person (or persons) to whom the paper was referred is stated in the Minutes of the Committee of Papers, and in all these cases, including those just mentioned, the persons in question were members of the then Council. Very soon, however, the name was omitted, the entry being simply "referred." There seems to be no means of ascertaining when "referees" outside the Council were first had recourse to, or when the practice of written reports first began.

Cap. XXI, "Of the manner of Publication of the Papers laid before the Society, and defraying the Expences thereof," provides for the printing and distribution of the 'Philosophical Transactions,' and is to a large extent, even in its very words, the same as Secs. 5 to 9 of

Cap. XIII of the Statutes at present in force, the word "Clerk" being used where "Assistant Secretary" is now used.

Payments by Fellows.

In order to defray the additional expenses thus incurred by the publication and gratis distribution to the Fellows of the 'Philosophical Transactions,' the "admission-money" is by Sec. 2 of Cap. XXI raised from two guineas to five guineas. In Cap. III of the Statutes of 1663, "Of the Payments by the Fellows to the Society," the admission-money is fixed at forty shillings, and indeed, in the Edition of 1752, the same sum of forty shillings is retained in this Chapter, the error apparently escaping notice. The change from forty shillings to forty-two shillings (two guineas) seems to have taken place at some time in the interval.

THE STATUTES FROM 1752 TO 1776.

In 1774 and 1775, the Council were engaged in considering the Statutes, and in 1776 published a new Edition, containing several important changes. An interesting preface to this Edition (from which a quotation is given above), explains that in spite of large changes in the practices of the Society, the Statutes had been kept as far as possible in their original form; and, indeed, the Statutes of 1752 differ from those of 1663 chiefly in the additions described above. In 1776, however, the Council determined to bring the Statutes into more strict conformity with the practice of the Society, and in consequence the Edition of 1776 differs widely from the two earlier versions.

Five whole chapters are omitted, viz., V,—Of Experiments, and the Reports thereof; XI, Of Curators by Office; XIII, Of the Printer to the Society; XIV, Of Operators to the Society; XVII, Of Benefactors; the twenty-one chapters of 1752 being thus reduced to sixteen. The preface explains how the changes in the Society had long rendered these Statutes unnecessary.

The order of the several chapters is largely altered, the new arrangement adopted being that which has on the whole been followed in subsequent editions, and is still maintained.

The Election of Fellows.

Ann. 1776. The regulations for the election of Fellows remain on the whole the same, save that it is precisely stated that twenty-one is "the competent number" for making an election, a majority of two-thirds being necessary, and in the Statute relating to what we now call the "privileged class," the words "Foreign Prince or Ambassador" are replaced by the words "Foreign Sovereign Prince, or the son of a Sovereign Prince, or an Ambassador to the Court of Great Britain."

Composition Fee.

In the Edition of 1752, as stated above, no mention is made of any "bond" or "composition fee," but in the next year, 1753 (June 7),

Ann. 1753. the Statute, Cap. VI, Sec. 8, concerning Foreigners and persons residing more than 40 miles from London, was repealed, and the following substituted:—

"That no one of his Majesties subjects, or any other person residing in his Majesties Dominions, who shall be elected a Fellow of the Society, shall be deemed an actual Fellow thereof, nor shall the name of any such person be Registered in the Journal Book, or printed in the List of Fellows of the Society, until such Person shall have paid his admission Fee, and given the usual Bond, or paid the Sum of Twenty-one pounds for the use of the Society in lieu of contributions: But that upon such payment or giving Bond as aforesaid, it shall be lawful for the Society to give leave for the name of any such person so elected as aforesaid to be entered in the Journal Book, and printed in the list of Fellows of the Society: Provided always that no such person shall have liberty to Vote at any Election or Meeting of the Society, before he shall be duly admitted a Fellow thereof pursuant to the former Statute."

This is the first time that the Statutes contain any reference to a composition fee.

Ann. 1766. In 1766 (December 11) a Statute was passed increasing the composition fee from twenty to twenty-six guineas; and the Statute of 1753 just quoted re-appears, with some slight changes, in the Edition of 1776 as Sec. 8 of Cap. I, the "sum of twenty-one pounds" being altered into "the sum appointed," and this the Chapter on payments by Fellows states to be twenty-six guineas.

Foreign Members.

The Statutes of 1776 contain, what the Statutes of 1752 and 1663 do not, special regulations for Fellows "residing in foreign parts and not subjects of the British Dominions."

Ann. 1664. So early as 1664 a Statute was passed providing that persons "residing in Forraigne parts," who are elected
Ann. 1716. Fellows, should not pay fees; in 1716 a reference
Ann. 1737. occurs to Foreigners who are Fellows; and in 1737 a resolution of Council (which did not become a Statute) proposed that Foreigners resident in London might be on the Home List if they paid contributions. It would appear, therefore, in spite of no

mention of the matter being made in 1752, that, from an early period, a distinction was made between Fellows who were Foreigners and others, and that the Fellows who were Foreigners did not, of necessity, pay contributions to the Society. In the Register of Fellows, however, at this date no distinction of any kind is made.

It was apparently soon felt that the Foreign Members were too numerous and in some cases not of sufficient distinction; for in 1761 (March 19) the Council, in order to ensure that "no persons residing in Foreign parts, not being subjects of the Crown of Great Britain, be elected Fellows unless their Qualifications be very well known as well abroad as at home," enacted a Statute providing that in the case of such persons the certificate should be signed by at least "three Foreign Fellows," as well as at least "by three Fellows named in the Home List." And in 1765 (December 19) on a proposal "to restrain the number of Foreign Members," it was resolved "that no Foreigner be proposed for election that is not known to the learned world, by some publication or invention which may enable the Society to form a judgment of his merit, and that till the number of Foreign Members be reduced to eighty, not more than two shall be admitted in one year." A special mode of procedure in the election of Foreigners as Fellows was, at the same time, resolved upon, providing for an election of two a year; and a subsequent resolution (December 26) provides that Foreign Members paying contributions shall "have their names printed in an alphabetical List next after that of the Home Members, as Foreign Members* contributing towards the expenses of the Society," and so distinct from "other Foreign Members" "who do not contribute." On January 16 of the next year the limitation to eighty was withdrawn, and the above resolutions were then embodied in the form of Statutes. These at the same time provided that the new regulation should not extend to Foreign Princes or their sons, and gave permission to Foreigners resident in Great Britain to become Fellows in the usual way, which permission was extended on January 26, 1769, to Foreigners who had been resident in Great Britain for the space of six months. Soon after, namely on June 10, 1773, the word "Foreigner" appears in the "Register" for the first time, being placed after the names of Stehelin, Le Roy, and Le Duc; thenceforward it is used frequently.

Ann. 1761.
Ann. 1765.
Ann. 1766.
Ann. 1769.
Ann. 1773.

In the Edition of 1776 these regulations, in a somewhat modified form, are introduced as part of Sec. 8 of Cap. I; the limitation to the election of two a year is omitted, and the certificates, signed by at least three Fellows upon the Foreign List, and at

Ann. 1776.

---

* It may be remarked that in the early records of the Society the words "Member" and "Fellow" appear to be used indiscriminately.

least by three Fellows on the Home List, are directed to be suspended from the 30th November until the weekly Meeting on, or next after, the 30th May. Some years afterwards, however (March 8, 1787), this part of Sec. 8 was repealed, and a new Sec. 9 added which provides a somewhat complex mode of procedure in the election, under the title of "Foreign Members,"* of persons "who are neither natives nor inhabitants of his Majesty's dominions." The number is limited to 100. Certificates signed by six or more Fellows are to be presented at some meeting between Easter and the Anniversary. At a meeting immediately before the following Easter a selection of candidates is to be made, and the candidates so selected are to be balloted for at the next meeting immediately after Easter. These regulations are not, however, to apply to Sovereign Foreign Princes or their Sons, or to such Foreigners resident in great Britain as may desire to become Fellows in the usual way.

Ann. 1787.

The Officers of the Society, the Clerk, Librarian, &c.

No changes are made in the Statutes of 1776 for the election of Council and Officers; but to meet the changes in the contributions there are changes in the regulations for the Treasurer. There are also changes in the duties of the Secretaries, chiefly in reference to the Clerk and to the publication of the 'Philosophical Transactions.'

Cap. X. provides regulations for the qualifications, mode of election, duties and remunerations of the Clerk, the Librarian, the Keeper of the Repository, and the House-Keeper.

Ann. 1663. The Statutes of 1663 contain regulations for the Clerk, and prescribe clerkly duties for him; and the Society had at first neither House-Keeper nor Librarian.

Ann. 1710. When in 1710 the Society moved to Crane Court, the office of House-Keeper was established; but the then Clerk was made House-Keeper. As the Library and Repository were increased the offices of Librarian and Keeper of the Repository were established; but both these offices were held by the Clerk, under supervision, during a certain period at all events, of Fellows chosen for that duty under the title of "Inspectors." But the Statutes of 1752 contain no regulations for these offices other than that of the Clerk, the Statutes concerning whom remain exactly the same as in 1663; and in spite of the special regulations present in the edition of 1776, it appears that the Society had never more than one officer to carry out these several duties, and that he was called "the Clerk," until at a later period (1823) the office of Clerk was abolished, and that of Assistant Secretary instituted.

Ann. 1776.

Ann. 1823.

* Foreign *Member* as distinguished from *Fellow*. In the edition of 1776 and thenceforward the term Member, as applied to an ordinary Fellow, is never used.

The Ordinary Meetings of the Society.

Ann. 1776. In the edition of 1776, Cap. XI, "Of the Ordinary Meetings of the Society," Sec. 1 provides that the ordinary Meetings should be held on "Thursdays, beginning at 6 p.m., and continue about an hour, as usual, at the discretion of the President."

Ann. 1769. This Statute was passed in 1769.

Ann. 1663. The Statutes of 1663 (IV, Sec. 1) provide that the ordinary meetings should be held on "Wednesday, beginning about three of the clock in the afternoon, and continuing until six, unless the major part of the Fellows present shall, for that time, resolve to rise sooner, or sit later." And the Statutes of

Ann. 1752. 1752 reproduce exactly the Statute (IV, Sec. 1) of 1663. Nevertheless, the records of the Society show that the day and hour of the ordinary meeting were more than once changed in the interval, as they have been since. The following shows the changes and their respective dates up to the present time:—

```
1663.           On Wednesdays, at 2 p.m.
July   1, 1663, changed to Wednesday, 3 to 6 p.m.
Feb.   5, 1666      ,,     Thursday   at 3 p.m.
April 10, 1672      ,,     Wednesday.
Oct.  30, 1674      ,,     Thursday   at 3 p.m.
Dec.   8, 1690      ,,     Wednesday  ,, 4 ,,
March  1, 1710      ,,     Thursday   ,, 4 ,,
April 20, 1769      ,,     Thursday   ,, 6 ,,
June  15, 1780      ,,     Thursday   ,, 8 ,,
 (?)     1831       ,,     Thursday   ,, 8.30 p.m.*
Feb.  19, 1880      ,,     Thursday   ,, 4.30 ,,
```

Ann. 1831. The first Statute enacting that no meeting should be held on certain days or in certain weeks was passed in 1831; previously to that the Statutes simply said "upon Wednesday," or "upon Thursday." But the practice of having an Autumn recess was of much older date than this; moreover, the Journal Book shows that from the earliest times it was customary to hold no meetings on Ash Wednesday and certain other holy days, and that in particular no meeting was held on the anniversary of the death of Charles I. In 1661 the Journal Book omits the date, January 30, without remark, although a meeting was due upon that day. On January 30, 1666, the Minute appears, "This day being the Anniversary Fast-Day, there was no Meeting of the Society." In 1667, the entry is, "The Society met not, because of the solemne Fast." Similar entries occur in

---

* Careful search has failed to show when this change was made, but it was probably about this time.

subsequent years, the last being on January 30, 1834. After this date the custom was omitted.

The Admission of Strangers to the Meetings of the Society.

Ann. 1752. In the Statutes of 1752, any of His Majesty's subjects having the title and place of a Baron, or having any higher title or place, are permitted to be present at the Meetings of the Society, "with the allowance of the President;" other persons may attend "upon leave obtained of the President and Fellows present."

Ann. 1776. In 1776 the mention of titled persons is omitted, and the Statute simply provides for "strangers" being present.

Ann. 1784. Some years later, viz., in 1784, a new section was added to Cap. XI as follows:—

"VI. That the meetings of the Society may not be wasted by unprofitable debates, contrary to the intent and meaning of the fifth section of this chapter, it is constituted, established, and ordained, that every motion or question, proposed to be ballotted for by the Society, shall be fairly transcribed on paper, and being signed by six or more Fellows of the Society, it shall be by them delivered to one of the Secretaries at a meeting of the Society; and shall thereupon be read immediately after the declaration of the Presents on the table; and after being marked by the Secretary with the date of the day when delivered, it shall be fixed up in the common Meeting-room of the Society at the next ordinary Meeting; and on the Meeting next following the same, it shall be put to the Ballot, unless those who have signed it agree to withdraw it.

"But nothing contained in this Statute is to be construed to extend to matters relative to elections, or the ordinary business of the Society."

The motions or questions proposed to be "ballotted for" must therefore have had reference to matters of science.

Publications, Records, and Library.

Ann. 1776. In Cap. XII, the quorum of the Committee of Papers is raised from five to seven, and the part of the Statute providing that there should be no entry of rejected papers is omitted.

Ann. 1776. In Cap. XIII, "Of the Manner of Publication of the Papers laid before the Society," the word "Librarian" is substituted for that of "Clerk"; also the period during which surplus copies not required by Fellows must remain before they are disposed of by the Council, is extended from one year (as in 1752) to five years.

Ann. 1776. Cap. XIV, "Of the Books and Papers of the Society," differs somewhat from the corresponding Cap. XVI, "Of the Books of the Society," in the Statutes of 1752. The copy of Statutes, the List of Benefactors, and the Register of Fellows is omitted from the Charter Book.* The Statute concerning the Register Books, containing accounts of observations, experiments, &c., and the Statute concerning the Book of Letters, are omitted.

Ann. 1776. A new Statute (Sec. V) is introduced, to the effect that the original copy of every paper read at the Society shall be considered as the property of the Society; and another (Sec. VI) provides for the care of the papers read. And, lastly, a new Statute (Sec. VII) introduces, for the first time, into the Statutes regulations concerning the use of the Library. The Library is to be open Tuesdays and Thursdays, from 11 a.m. to 2 p.m., and Fellows may, by leave of the Society or of the Council, take out four volumes for six weeks. If these are printed books, the Fellow gives merely his note; if MSS., a bond of £50 for each.

THE STATUTES FROM 1776 TO 1847.

The Statutes of 1819.

The next edition appears to be that of 1819; it is, however, merely a reprint of that of 1776, with the additions of Cap. I, Sec. 9, as to Foreign Members, and Cap. XI, Sec. 6, as to the conduct of ordinary meetings, mentioned above (p. 108 and p. 110).

The Statutes of 1823.

Foreign Members, limited to fifty, selected by Council. In the next edition—that of 1823—several important changes are introduced. The number of Foreign Members is limited to fifty; and "they are to be put in nomination as candidates at a meeting of the Council," instead of the previous complex procedure. The regulations for the election of the Council and officers are much simplified, but not materially altered.

Foreign Secretary. A new Statute, Cap. IX, Sec. 4, institutes a new office, that of the "Secretary for Foreign Correspondence." Since 1719 the proceeds of the bequest of Mr. Robert Keck had been "bestowed on some one of the Fellows" appointed "to carry on a foreign correspondence," but the Fellow performing these duties was

---

* The Charter Book never did contain, as provided by the Statute, the Register of Fellows, but only their signatures. The Society possesses, however, a volume now called "The Register," which contains the names, with dates of election, of all the Fellows from the foundation of the Society up to the year 1875. Since that date the Register is continued in a second volume.

appointed by Council at their pleasure, and was styled Assistant to the Secretaries. The new Secretary for Foreign Correspondence was to rank with the two Principal Secretaries.

Assistant Secretary. The office of Clerk is abolished and that of Assistant Secretary created. The old Statute relating to the Clerk is, in consequence, largely modified. The Assistant Secretary is made Librarian and Housekeeper, but all mention of the Keeper of the Repository disappears from the Statutes. The facilities for using the Library are increased. The annual contribution is raised from "a **Contributions raised.** shilling a week," or thirteen shillings a quarter, to "one pound a quarter," the admission fee from five guineas to ten pounds, and the composition fee from twenty-six guineas to forty pounds.

The Statutes of 1831.

The edition of 1831* contains a few changes which are of no great moment, and chiefly refer to payments (Cap. III), the "bond" being omitted.

In 1831 the Statutes relating to the Assistant Secretary were amended, the separate regulations for Librarian and Housekeeper being omitted.

In 1835, the then existing Statute, Cap. I, Sec. 5 (enacted in 1831), that "no election for Fellows, or for Foreign Members, shall take place excepting on the first ordinary meetings of the Society in December, February, April, and June" was repealed.

The Statutes of 1840.

In the next edition, 1840, the most notable change concerns the election of officers and Council. These are to be put in nomination by the President and Council, according to the plan at present in use. A new Chapter, "Of Special General Meetings of the Society" is added. The composition fee is raised to £60 in the case of Fellows elected after December 11, 1834, except such as have contributed papers to the 'Philosophical Transactions;' the Statutes concerning publications are thrown into one chapter; and some slight changes are made in the Statutes concerning the Treasurer and Secretaries. Cap. XI, "Of the ordinary Meetings of the Society," provides for the recess from the third Thursday in June to the third Thursday in November, and, as mentioned above, for the omission of meetings on certain days.

With the important exception of those relating to the election of

---

* One form of this Edition is simply a reprint of that of 1823, with an Appendix of amended Statutes.

Fellows, the Statutes of this edition are very like those at present in force.

The Statutes of 1847.

Very soon after, however, viz., in 1846, a Committee of Council was appointed to consider the mode of Election of Fellows, with the result that in 1847 new Statutes were enacted, regulating the Election of fifteen Fellows annually, according to the plan at present in use. These Statutes mark an epoch in the history of the Society.

The Changes from 1847 to 1888.

The most notable changes which have since then been enacted or proposed are as follows :—

On November 3rd, 1864, the repeal of the Statute relating to the admission of strangers to the meetings was moved, but negatived; and again, on March 21st, 1867, a proposal that the public be admitted to the Ordinary Meetings of the Society was negatived.

In 1865 the privileged class (Cap. I, Sec. 4) was extended to include *Foreign* Sovereign Princes and their sons.

In 1866 the practice of paying for a proportional part of the year was abolished, and the annual payment was made one in advance.

In 1871 a new Statute was enacted prohibiting the payment of dividends to Fellows.

On October 30th, 1873, upon a motion to assimilate the mode of election of the Privileged Class to that of Ordinary Fellows, to place in the hands of the Council the selection of such candidates, and to require "evidence of ascertained special power and disposition to forward the aims of the Society from exceptional, personal, or official advantages of position, or of great eminence in any branch of learning, instead of any qualification based only on accident of lineage or of political status," the Statute concerned was referred to the consideration of a Committee, and on April 23rd, 1874, the Statute in its existing form was enacted.

On December 17th of same year, 1874, a Committee was appointed to consider the election of candidates for Fellowship, which Committee presented, on November 30th, 1875, a long report giving reasons why no changes should be made.

In 1878-9 changes were made in the payment of fees.

In 1879 the Statutes relating to Foreign Members were altered to their present form.

In 1880 (February 19) the hour of meeting was changed from the evening to the afternoon.

In 1885 the time during which the Library is open to Fellows was extended.

In 1888 the Statute, Cap. XI, Sec. 2, was altered to admit of an

Ordinary Meeting being held on the day of Election of Fellows, and Statute, Cap. XIII, Sec. 7, was altered to allow Fellows to receive their copies of the 'Philosophical Transactions' upon a request in writing.

In 1891 a new edition of the Statutes was published containing, among other smaller changes made in that year, the following more important ones:—

In Chapter XI power was given to the Council to omit weekly meetings with a view to increase, when desirable, the Christmas and Easter recess, and greater freedom was allowed in the conduct of the weekly meetings.

In Chapter XIII certain changes were introduced in the hope of expediting the publication of papers.

A new chapter (XVI) was added in order to insert a Statute passed in 1871 prohibiting dividends to Fellows.

In 1896 changes were again made, some in Chapter XI "Of the Meetings of the Society," but more in Chapter XIII "Of the Publication of Papers." Both these chapters, especially the latter, were simplified, some of the regulations previously existing as statutes being withdrawn from the Statutes and embodied in "Standing Orders." In respect to "publication," the main change effected was the institution of Sectional Committees to assist the Council sitting as a Committeee of Papers or otherwise, with regard to the publication of papers and other matters. In the first days of the Society several Committees were formed to take charge of the several branches of science as well as for special objects; but these, after a while, and apparently after a short while, ceased to exist. On May 31, 1838, "Scientific Committees" to assist the Council were again established, but these were found not to work satisfactorily, and on December 20, 1849, were abolished. The Standing Orders adopted at the time of the change of the Statutes in 1896 will be found in the 'Year-book.'

BENEFACTORS OF THE SOCIETY.

At a Meeting of Council holden December 14, 1663, it was
"Ordered, that the Secretary bring in a list of the Names of all the Benefactors to the Society, together with their Donations, and the time when they presented them.

"Ordered, that the Benefactors be registered in loose vellum sheets."

Similar orders were made on December 3, 1674, on April 27, 1682, and on several subsequent dates. Unfortunately these early lists of Benefactors are not now extant, and no list drawn up at the present day can pretend to be complete. The subjoined list is compiled principally by aid of the Index to the MS. Council Minutes, and is complete only in respect of benefactions of £50 and upwards there recorded. The dates given are, in most cases, those of *the Council Meetings* in the minutes of which the gifts are recorded. Many more names would be added if the lists of subscribers to special funds were consulted, but in these cases only the names of the founders of such funds are here given.

KING CHARLES II.

1662. August 13. Granted to the Society a Charter of Incorporation.

1663. August 3. Presented the Society with a mace of silver, richly gilt, weighing 190 oz. avoirdupois.

1667. September 27. Granted the Society Chelsea College and lands. The College was conveyed to the Society by Royal Patent dated April 8, 1669.

KING GEORGE III.

1768. March 24. Ordered the sum of £4000 clear of fees to be paid to the Society, to enable them to send expeditions to observe the Transit of Venus. The surplus left, after paying all the expenses connected with the expeditions, was ordered by the King to be carried to the credit of the Society.

KING GEORGE IV.

1825. December 15. Founded two Gold Medals of the value of Fifty guineas each (see Royal Medals, p. 132).

KING WILLIAM IV.

1833. March 28. The grant of two Royal Medals restored.

QUEEN VICTORIA.

1838. July 5. The grant of two Royal Medals continued.

1663. December 14. W. Balle. Gift of £100 and "an iron Chest having three Locks and Keyes." This chest is still in use.

1664. June 22. Sir John Cutler. Settled an annual stipend of £50 a year upon Robert Hooke, for a Lectureship, empowering the President, Council, and Fellows of the Society to appoint the subjects and number of lectures.

1665-6. February 21. Daniel Colwall. Gift of £100.—"Voted, that the Fifty pounds in cash; that were formerly presented by Mr. Colwall, be delivered out, to be added to another Fifty pounds presented by the same, to pay for the Collection of Rarities, formerly belonging to Mr. Hubbard."

1666-7. January 2. Henry Howard (afterwards sixth Duke of Norfolk). Gift to the Society of "the Library of Arundel House, to dispose thereof as their property" (see p. 168). The Society "ordered that Mr. Howard should be registered as a benefactor."

1673. November 27. Dr. Wilkins, Bishop of Chester. Bequest of £400, invested January 21, 1674-5, in a Fee Farm Rent at Lewes.

1685. November 11. Samuel Pepys. A gift of £50, "to be laid out as the Council shall judge most convenient." The money was used to pay for 50 Plates to Willughby's 'Historia Piscium.'

1708—1718. Sir Isaac Newton. £190.—At the Meeting of the Council on January 21, 1707, the President, Sir Isaac Newton, "proposed to the Councill of the Society that if they would please to accept of free Gifts, of about or 20 pounds, from 10 any of their members, English or Foreigners, to be paid after the death of the Donors, for promoting Natural Philosophy, he had a prospect of obtaining some such Gifts; and the Councill agreed to accept of them with thanks." At the meeting on January 12, 1708-9, the President gave the Society twenty pounds instead of the like suffie he intended after his death; which was order'd to be put up by itself, and to be subject to such End or Benefaction as the President shall direct. On December 14, 1710, "the President acquainted the Councill that he would give towards the easing of the Debt of ye Society for ye House [in Crane Court], besides the twenty pounds he had reserved, One Hundred Pounds." On November 6, 1718, "the Treasurer acquainted the Council that Sir Isaac Newton had lately paid him as a Gift to the Society seventy pounds."

1709. February 23. Dame Mary Sadleir, Relict of Dr. William Croone. Founded the Croonian Lecture (see p. 126) by bequest of One Fifth of the Clear Rent of a house at the corner of Lambeth Hill, for that purpose.

1710. March 17. Lord Halifax. £100.

1710. December 14. Dr. Hans Sloane, Secretary R.S. £100.

1710. December 14. Alexander Pitfield, Treasurer R.S. £100.

1711. May 30. R. Balle. £50.

1711. June 26. T. Isted. £50.

1711. June 26. Sir David Hamilton. £50.

1712. April 8. Richard Waller. £100. Waller built the "Repository" for the Society at a cost of £400 and accepted £300 as payment in full, on condition that he should be registered as a benefactor.

1716. July 5. Francis Aston. Bequest of an estate at Mabelthorpe, in Lincolnshire, consisting of 55 acres, 2 roods, and 2 perches, and "half the overplus of his estate above Debts and Legacies," realising £445 0s. 7d.

1717. June 20. Sir Godfrey Copley, Bart. £100 in trust for the Royal Society, "to be laid out in experiments, or otherwise, for the benefit thereof, as they shall direct and appoint." The will was dated October 14, 1704, and proved in the Prerogative Court, April 11, 1709; first applied to the purchase of a medal in 1736 (see p. 124).

1717. October 24. S. Hill. £50.

1717. October 24. Thomas Paget, D.D. Bequest of two houses in Coleman Street, worth about £100 per annum.

1719. October 26. Robert Keck. Bequest of £500 to the Society "to support their forreign correspondence."

1741. December 16. Martin Folkes. £100, as a present to the Society "to assist them in the present low state of their Revenue."

1754. November 14. Samuel Hickman. Bequest of £100.

1754. November 21. Martin Folkes. Bequest of £200 in money and a portrait of Lord Bacon.

1769. February 2. Robert Smith, D.D. Bequest of £100.

1775. Henry Baker. Bequest of £100, the interest to be applied for an oration or discourse in Natural History or Experimental Philosophy (see Bakerian Lecture, p. 124).

1786. July 27. Earl Stanhope. Bequest of £500.

1796. May 5. William Benson Earle. Bequest of £210 "for the purchase of Books for the Society's Library."

1796. November 24. Count Rumford. Gift of £1000 stock to found the Rumford Medals (see p. 123).

1828. December 11. William Hyde Wollaston, M.D. Gift of

£2000 3 per cent. Consols, to be called the Donation Fund, the dividends to be applied in promoting experimental researches (see p. 121).

1828. December 11. Davies Gilbert. Gift of £1000 to the Donation Fund.

1829. January 22. J. Guillemand. Gift of £100 to the Donation Fund.

1839. March 7. Sir Clifton Wintringham. Bequest of £1,200 3 per cent. Consolidated Bank Annuities, for the annual award of a Silver Cup to the Author of the most satisfactory Experimental Examination of one of certain subjects (see p. 125.)

1843. November 30. Edwin Hill Handley. Bequest of £6,378 19s. Founder of the Handley Fund (see p. 128).

1843. November 30. Thomas Botfield. Bequeathed " such a sum of money, by way of donation, as would have been payable if he had been made a Life Member" of the Royal Society. (£60.)

1854. June 29. B. Oliveira. Gift of £50 for the Promotion of Science.

1864. October 27. Beriah Botfield. Bequest of £70.

1865. December 21. B. Oliveira. Bequest of £4,000, reduced after a chancery suit to £1,506 17s. 1d. (Minutes, October 28, 1869). This was applied to the construction of the Telescope afterwards lent to Dr. Huggins.

1869. April 22. Dr. John Davy, bequeathed the Service of Plate presented to Sir Humphry Davy for the invention of the Safety Lamp, in fulfilment of Sir H. Davy's intentions, to be melted down and sold, in order from the proceeds to found a medal (see p. 128). It produced £736 8s. 5d.

1871. June 15. John Peter Gassiot. Securities representing £10,000 "given to the Royal Society upon Trust, for the purpose of assisting in carrying on and continuing magnetical and meteorological observations . . . . in the Kew Observatory" (see p. 128).

1873. October 30. E. H. Sterling. " Donation of £100 to the funds of the Society."

1874. June 18. Sir Francis Ronalds. Bequest of £500 "for the Augmentation of the Wollaston [Donation] Fund" (see p. 121).

1874. October 29. Henry Dircks. Bequest of one-fourth of his residue, amounting (see Minutes, May 18, 1876) to £878 12s. 10d.

1875. November 30. Sir Charles Wheatstone. Bequest of £500 for the Donation Fund, and several portraits.

1876. February 17. T. J. Phillips Jodrell. Gift of £6,000 to be applied in any manner "most conducive to the encouragement, among our countrymen, of original research in the Physical Sciences" (see p. 129).

1877. (President's Address, 'Roy. Soc. Proc.,' vol. 26, p. 429). A sum of £500 contributed anonymously by five Fellows to the Society's funds.

1879. January 16. Sir Joseph Whitworth. Gift of £2000 to the Fee Reduction Fund.

Sir William (now Lord) Armstrong. Gift of £1000 to the Fee Reduction Fund.

1878. April 11. James Young. A donation of £1,000, "for the general purposes of the Society." This donation was devoted to the "Publication Fund" (June 27, 1878), afterwards merged in the Fee Reduction Fund (November 7, 1878).

1879. February 27. Sydney Ellis. "An unconditional bequest to the Society of £1,000."

1879. April 24. Sir Walter Calverley Trevelyan, Bart. Bequest of £1,500, to the Society, "the interest to be applied to the promotion of scientific research."

1880. December 16. Miss H. E. Pipe. Gift of £105 in aid of the publication of Mr. W. K. Parker's papers.

1881. March 24. Sir Joseph Copley, Bart. Gift of £1666 13s. 4d. 3 per cent. Consols, "to provide in perpetuity a yearly bonus of £50 to be given to the recipient of the Copley Medal."

1884. January 17. Sir William Siemens. Bequest of £1,000 free of legacy duty, to the Scientific Relief Fund.

1884. October 30. G. Bentham. Bequest of £1000 to the Scientific Relief Fund; afterwards reduced to £567 by an informality in the will.

1885. April 23. James Budgett. Gift of £100 in aid of the publication of Professor W. K. Parker's Researches.

1886. February 18. Dr. Ludwig Mond. Donation of 500 guineas to the Scientific Relief Fund.

1886. November 30. Sir William G. (now Lord) Armstrong. Donation of £7,800 to the Scientific Relief Fund (see p. 120).

1888. March 15. Dr. J. F. Main. A telescope and the piers built for it at St. Moritz.

1891. February 19. Henry Bowman Brady. Bequest of all his books and papers relating to the Protozoa, and £300 free of duty, upon trust for the purchase of works on the same or kindred subjects.

1891. October 29. His Excellency Dr. Robert Halliday Gunning gave the Society his bond for £1000 to found the Gunning Fund (see p. 131).

1893. May 18. Earl of Derby. Bequest of £2,000.

1892. December 8. Dr. Ludwig Mond. Gift of £2,000 "to assist in carrying on the Catalogue of Scientific Papers."

1894. June 21. Dr. Ludwig Mond. Contribution towards the Cost of the Subject Index to the Catalogue of Scientific Papers. "One-half of the total expenditure in excess of the sum of £1,500 available for this purpose out of the £2,000 already placed at the disposal of the Society [see above], provided the Society or others are willing to contribute the remainder of such sum."

THE TRUSTS OF THE ROYAL SOCIETY.*

The following succinct account of the various trusts which the Society administers, their origin and progress, the application of the income of the funds, and their present financial position, follows the order in which the trusts are arranged on the annual balance sheet of the Society. Full particulars of capital, income, and expenditure in each case are clearly given in that sheet (see 'Year-book'). A larger amount of detail as to the foundation of the older funds will be found in Weld's 'History of the Royal Society,' and in an anniversary address delivered by the late Mr. Spottiswoode, as treasurer, in 1874.

No. 1. THE SCIENTIFIC RELIEF FUND.

This most excellent and valuable institution originated in the year 1859, in a proposition of Mr. J. P. Gassiot that a fund of this kind should be founded for the aid of such scientific men, or their families, as may from time to time require assistance. A circular announcing the project was issued by the Society, in May, 1859, and by the following July £2500 had been subscribed. By the end of 1864, the amount of £5000 had been reached, and by 1868 the fund consisted of £6052 17s. 8d., New 3 per cent. Annuities.

Until 1884 the amount remained stationary at a little under £6500, but legacies, from the late Sir W. Siemens, of £1000, and from Mr. Bentham, of about £500, gave it a sensible help.

In November, 1885, however, a noble offer was made by Sir William, now Lord Armstrong, to present a sum of about £6500 to the fund on the understanding that an equal sum should be raised by subscription, and further that the fund might be used in cases of urgent necessity for the remission of the fees of Fellows.

Although by the beginning of 1887 it was not found possible to

* Reprinted in the main from a paper by Sir John Evans, K.C.B., Treasurer R.S., in 'Roy. Soc. Proc.,' vol. 57, p. 202.

raise more than about £4200 by subscription, Lord Armstrong, in February, 1887, munificently increased his contribution to £7800, so that in all £12,000 were added to the fund. Since that date about £800 more have accrued from bequests from Mr. H. B. Brady and others, and from donations. The permanent invested capital of the fund now consists of

> £6000 London and North-Western Railway 4 per cent. Guaranteed Stock;
>
> £7200 Great Northern Railway 3 per cent. Debenture Stock; and
>
> £4340 South Eastern Railway 5 per cent. Debenture Stock;

producing an income of about £670.

The administration of the fund is entrusted to a committee consisting of ten members of whom two retire annually, and applications for grants are made through the Presidents of chartered and incorporated scientific societies, under regulations which will be found in the 'Year-book of the Royal Society.'

No. 2. THE DONATION FUND.

In 1828 the late William Hyde Wollaston, M.D., at one time President of the Society, gave the sum of £2000 3 per cent. Consols, to be called the Donation Fund, the dividends to be applied from time to time in promoting experimental researches, or in rewarding those by whom such researches may have been made, or in such other manner as shall appear to the President and Council for the time being most conducive to the interests of the Society in particular, or of science in general. The application of the funds extends to individuals of all countries, but not to members of the Council of the Society. The dividends are not to be hoarded parsimoniously, but expended liberally. About £1400 more were contributed to the fund by Dr. Davies Gilbert (who gave £1000) and others. In 1874 and 1875 two legacies of £500 each were received from Sir Francis Ronalds, F.R.S., and Sir Charles Wheatstone, F.R.S., and the fund for some years consisted of £6339 Consols, which in 1888 was converted into £5030 Great Northern Railway Perpetual 4 per cent. Guaranteed Stock, producing an income of about £200 per annum. In the year 1879 the late Sir Walter C. Trevelyan bequeathed a sum of £1500, the interest to be applied in the promotion of scientific rasearch. This was invested in the purchase of £1396 Great Northern Railway 4 per cent. Debenture Stock, now converted into £1861 6s. 8d. 3 per cent. Debenture Stock, and forms practically a part of the Donation Fund. The interest of the Jodrell Fund is also transferred to it (see No. 11, p. 129), so that the annual income is about £390.

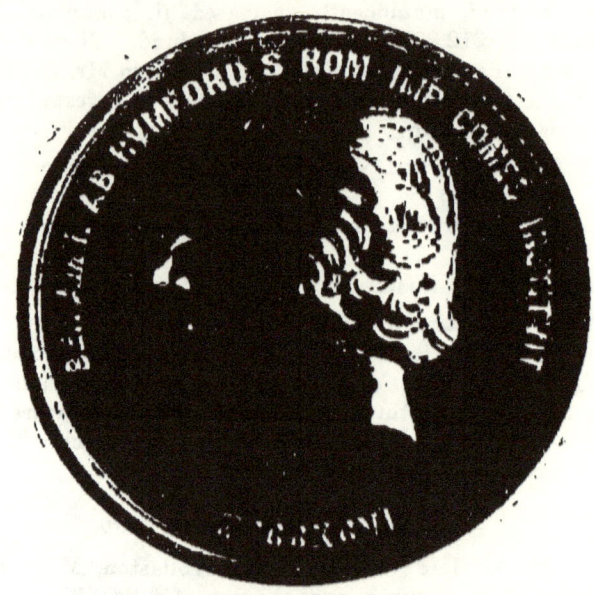

THE RUMFORD MEDAL (p. 123).

No. 3. The Rumford Fund.

Count Rumford, in a letter to Sir Joseph Banks, dated 12th July, 1796, informed him, as president of the Society, that he had purchased and transferred £1000 Stock in the funds of this country, to the end that the interest of the same should be given once every second year as a premium to the author of the most important discovery or useful improvement which shall be made or published by printing, or in any way made known to the public in any part of Europe during the preceding two years on heat or on light, the preference always being given to such discoveries as shall, in the opinion of the President and Council, tend most to promote the good of mankind. The premium is to take the form of two medals, the one of gold and the other of silver, to be together of the value of two years' interest on the £1000, or £60 sterling. In case of there being no new discovery in heat or light during any term of years which, in the opinion of the President and Council, is of sufficient importance to deserve the premium, direction is given to invest its value in the purchase of additional stock in the English Funds, and the interest of this additional capital is to be given in money, with the two medals, at each succeeding adjudication. In a subsequent letter, Count Rumford suggests that the premium should be limited to new discoveries tending to improve the theories of fire, of heat, of light, and of colours, and to new inventions and contrivances by which the generation, and preservation, and management of heat and of light may be facilitated. Chemical discoveries and improvements in optics, so far as they answer any of these conditions, are to be within the limits of the premium, but the Count wishes especially to encourage such practical improvements in the management of heat and light as tend directly and powerfully to increase the enjoyments and comforts of life, especially in the lower and more numerous classes of society. The first recipient of the medals was Count Rumford himself. Previously to 1846 it was not unfrequently the case that no medal was adjudicated for four years. Indeed between 1818 and 1832 the only recipient was M. Fresnel. As a consequence the invested funds have increased to £2,367 2s. 6d., but the interest is now only $2\frac{3}{4}$ per cent., and will in 1903 be only $2\frac{1}{2}$ per cent. A bonus on the conversion of the Stock, including an additional quarter's interest, and some returned income tax have been recently added to capital. The annual income is at present about £65, and the sum of money that accompanies the medals about £70.

No. 4. Bakerian and Copley Medal Fund.

There has for many years been only one amalgamated fund for these two objects. Through successive accumulations, owing in part

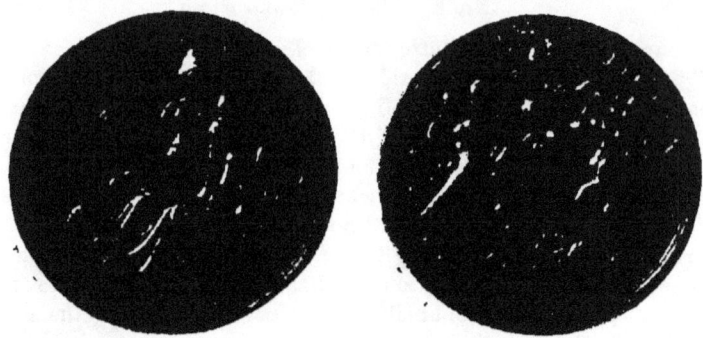

THE COPLEY MEDAL.

to no medal having been awarded in some years, it now consists of £403 9s. 8d. New 2½ per cent. Consols. The Bakerian Lecture originated in 1775, through a bequest of Mr. Henry Baker, F.R.S., of £100, for an oration or discourse, to be spoken or read yearly by some one of the Fellows of the Society, on such part of natural history or experimental philosophy, at such time and in such manner as the President and Council of the Society for the time being shall please to order and appoint. In case no lecture be given, there is a pain of forfeiture attached to the bequest. The payment to the lecturer has for many years been a fixed sum of £4.

The Copley Medal, which has long been regarded as the highest scientific distinction that the Royal Society can bestow, originated in a legacy of £100 from Sir Godfrey Copley, Bart., F.R.S., received in 1709. The testator directed that this sum should be laid out in experiments or otherwise for the benefit of the Society, as they shall direct and appoint. For many years the interest of the fund was paid to Dr. Desaguliers, Curator to the Society,* for various experiments made before them, but in 1736 Martin Folkes, who subsequently became President of the Society, proposed to render Sir Godfrey Copley's donation more beneficial than at that time it was. His suggestion was that instead of the annual experiment, "a medal or other honorary prize should be bestowed on the person whose experiment should be best approved, by which means he apprehended a laudable emulation might be excited among men of genius to try their invention, who, in all probability, may never be moved for the sake of lucre." Eventually, in 1736, it was resolved that a medal of the value of £5, to bear the arms of the Society, should be awarded to the author of the most important scientific discovery or contribution to science by experiment or otherwise. The weight of the medal was fixed at 1 oz. 2 dwts. of fine gold. In 1831 it was resolved

---

* See *ante*, p. 17.

that the Copley Medal shall be awarded to the living author of such philosophical research, either published or communicated to the Society, as may appear to the Council to be deserving of that honour. The particulars of the subject of the research are to be specified in the award, and there is to be no limitation as to the period when the research was made, or the country to which the author may belong.

Owing to the payments for the lecture and the medal being somewhat less than the dividends received, a balance has gradually accumulated in favour of the fund, amounting to over £100. This, however, is now being gradually reduced, for in the year 1881, Sir Joseph Copley, Bart., transferred to the Society a sum of £1666 13s. 4d. 3 per cent. Consols, "to provide in perpetuity a yearly bonus of £50, to be given to the recipient of the Copley Medal." So long as the interest was at 3 per cent., the income of £50 was produced, but now that it is reduced to $2\frac{3}{4}$ per cent., with the near prospect of falling to $2\frac{1}{2}$ per cent., it is insufficient for the gift. So long, however, as there has been a balance in hand in favour of the fund, the Council has thought well to fulfil Sir Joseph Copley's liberal intention.

No. 5. THE KECK BEQUEST.

In the year 1719 a bequest of £500 was received from Mr. Robert Keck, who directed that the profits arising from it were "to be bestowed on some one of the Fellows, whom they shall appoint to carry on a foreign correspondence." For many years this bequest was merged in the general funds of the Society, and the proceeds applied towards the payment of the Foreign Secretary. In 1881 it was again made to appear as a separate trust fund, and £666 13s. 4d. Consols was allotted as the equivalent. This has, at the present time, been converted into £800 Midland Railway 3 per cent. Debenture Stock, and the proceeds are annually paid to the Foreign Secretary, who now receives no other honorarium.

No. 6. THE WINTRINGHAM FUND.

In 1794 a sum of £1200 Consols was bequeathed to the Society by Sir Clifton Wintringham, M.D., a Fellow, payable on the decease of his widow, and subject to certain conditions; the interest or dividends to be for the purchase of a silver cup, of £30 value, to be given to such person as should in ten months after advertisement present the most satisfactory experimental examination of one of three subjects chosen by vote of the Society. It was not, however, until 1842 that, after a tedious law suit, an amount of £1200 Consols was transferred to the Society. It was then found that the conditions of the will were so stringent, and involved so much expense, that it was practically impossible to fulfil them, even when the rate of interest on Consols was 3 per cent. instead of, as at present, $2\frac{3}{4}$, or, as it will be shortly, $2\frac{1}{2}$ per cent., and there being a further provision that in case of failure on the part of the Society to fulfil the intentions of the testator, the income of the fund should be paid over to the Governors of the Foundling Hospital, that institution has in each year received the interest accruing from the fund. The subject has on several occasions been brought before the Council, and also before the legal advisers of the Society, but as yet no way out of the difficulty has been discovered.

No. 7. The Croonian Lecture Fund.

This is one of the earliest institutions connected with the Society, and, in name at least, carries us back to the days of its foundation. At the meeting held on November 28, 1660, when the design for founding the Society was discussed, Mr. Croone, though absent, was nominated as the Register, or as we should now call it Registrar, of the small band of learned men who met weekly at Gresham College. Dr. Croone, as he subsequently became, was from the beginning an active Fellow of the Society, and on his death, in 1684, left a scheme for two lectureships which he intended to found, one of which was for the Royal Society. In his will, however, he made no provision for this purpose, but his widow, who subsequently became Lady Sadleir, remedied the omission, and in her will, dated September 25, 1701, bequeathed to the Society one-fifth of the clear rent of the King's Head Tavern, in or near Old Fish Street, London, at the corner of Lambeth Hill, "for the support of a lecture and illustrative experiment for the advancement of natural knowledge on local motion, or (conditionally) on such other subject as, in the opinion of the President for the time being, should be most useful in promoting the objects for which the Royal Society was instituted," the remainder being paid to the Royal College of Physicians, also for the support of a lecture to be delivered before them; a decree in Chancery, in 1728, empowered the Society to devote the whole nett annual profits of the legacy to the payment for a single lecture and its attendant expenses. The proper subject for the lecture is the nature or laws of muscular motion, to be accompanied by some anatomical demonstration. The first Croonian Lecture was delivered in 1738 by Dr. Stuart, the subject being "The Motion of the Heart." From 1786 to 1885 the property was let for £15 per annum, so that the share of the Society was only about £3, but since 1885 the rent of the estate has been materially increased, and the Society now receives a sum of about £52 yearly as its share, which is paid over by the Royal College of Physicians, which deals with the whole property. The whole of the available balance is in each year paid to the lecturer or for expenses.

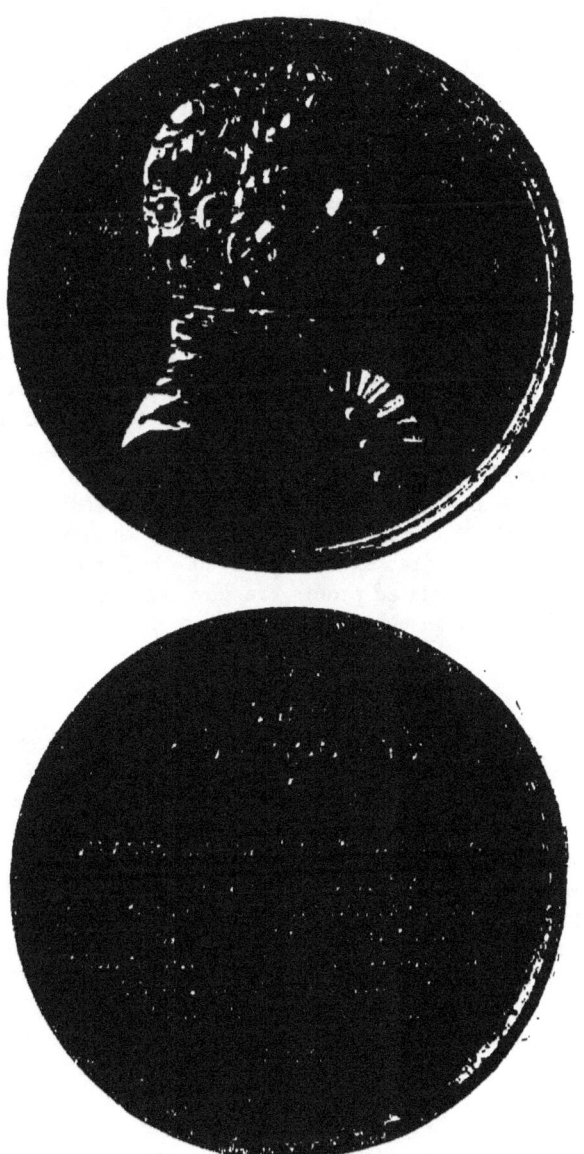

THE DAVY MEDAL (p. 128).

No. 8. The Davy Medal Fund.

By the will of Dr. John Davy, F.R.S., the service of plate presented to Sir Humphry Davy for the invention of the safety lamp, was bequeathed to the Society, to be melted down and sold, in order to found a medal to be given annually for the most important discovery in chemistry. The amount received in 1869 was invested in the purchase of £660 Madras Railway Stock, producing about £33 per annum. Some little time elapsed before the dies could be prepared, and the first medal actually awarded was given, in duplicate, to Bunsen and Kirchhoff in 1877. It was also given in duplicate in 1878, 1882, 1883, and 1893.

No. 9. The Gassiot Trust.

In the year 1871 the late Mr. John Peter Gassiot conveyed to the Society £10,000 Italian Irrigation Bonds, for the purpose of assisting in carrying on and continuing magnetical and meteorological observations with self-recording instruments, and any other physical investigations that may from time to time be practicable and desirable in the Kew Observatory, in the Old Deer Park, Richmond, Surrey. (See "Description of Kew Observatory," p. 138.)

The proceeds are paid over to the Kew Committee appointed in accordance with the trust deed. From time to time some of the Irrigation Bonds are drawn, and a profit has been made on reinvestment. These accumulated profits are now represented by a sum of £500 2¾ per cent. Consols, which forms a kind of reserve or insurance fund.

No. 10. The Handley Fund.

By the will of Mr. E. H. Handley, dated 1840, the reversion of his property was bequeathed to the Society after the death of his sister, the income to be applied as a reward for important inventions in art or discoveries in science, physical and metaphysical, or for assistance in the prosecution of any such invention or discovery, but with power to the President and Council to apply the income as they may deem best for the advancement of science.

Owing to the Statute of Mortmain, a considerable portion of the property did not pass by this will, but eventually, in 1876, the sum of £6378 19s. was received, which, after paying Legacy Duty at the rate of 10 per cent. and legal expenses, left sufficient to purchase £6047 7s. 9d. Reduced 3 per cents. When the rate of interest was threatened a few years ago, this was converted into £4798 Lancashire and Yorkshire Railway 4 per cent. Guaranteed Stock, producing about £192 per annum. Of late years this has been applied towards the cost of preparing the Catalogue of Scientific Papers.

No. 11. The Jodrell Fund.

The late Mr. T. J. Phillips Jodrell, in 1876, placed at the disposal of the Society the sum of £6000, at first with the intention of encouraging in this country original research in the physical sciences, but subsequently, in the same year, with directions to apply the proceeds as part of the ordinary revenue of the Society. In 1879 £1000 was, by Mr. Jodrell's directions, transferred to the Fee Reduction Fund, and the remaining £5000 is represented by the sum of £5182 14s. 10d. 2¾ per cent. Consols, which stand in the name of the fund.

On the death of Mr. Jodrell, in 1889, the proceeds of the fund, in accordance with a letter from him of April 5, 1878, devolved to and were incorporated with the Donation Fund. The income is at present about £140, but this will be reduced when the diminution in the interest of Consols takes place.

No. 12. Fee Reduction Fund.

This fund originated in 1878, the object being to relieve future Fellows of the Society of the £10 paid as an admission fee and of £1 out of the £4 annual subscription. These advantages, however, do not extend to the Privy Councillors and other privileged Fellows who join the Society. Most liberal sums were subscribed: Sir Joseph Whitworth contributing £2000, Sir William (now Lord) Armstrong and Mr. James Young £1000 each. The demand upon the fund keeps on, of course, increasing from year to year, but the excess of income over expenditure has been regularly invested, and the fund now consists of £5000 Metropolitan 3½ per cent. Stock and £9333 London and North Western Railway 3 per cent. Debenture Stock, producing an income of about £450 per annum. The payments on account of Fellows amounted last year to £362, and inasmuch as in each year the payment in respect of the subscriptions of Fellows increases to the extent of £10 or £12, it is evident that, in the course of time, the question will have to be considered whether some modification in the amount of the reduction or some addition to the capital of the fund must not be made. There is, however, at present nearly £90 per annum left for investment; so that there is no immediate danger of the fund failing.

No. 13. The Darwin Memorial Fund.

In 1885 the Committee of the International Darwin Memorial Fund resolved to transfer to the Royal Society the balance that remained in their hands, in trust, to devote the proceeds from time

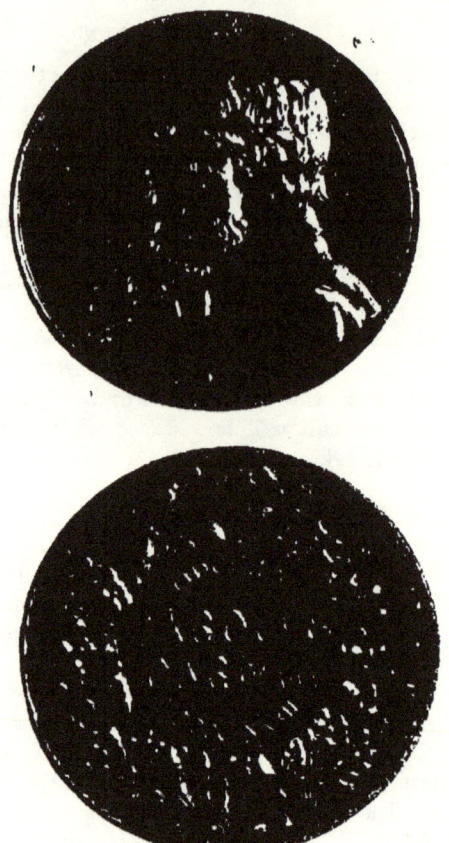

The Darwin Medal.

to time towards the promotion of biological studies and research. The amount has been invested in the purchase of £2500 South Eastern Railway 4 per cent. Debenture Stock, which now forms the capital of the fund. The annual income is nearly £100. In accordance with a resolution of the Council, a medal, either in silver or in bronze, is awarded biennially in reward of work of acknowledged distinction (especially in Biology) in the field in which Mr. Darwin himself laboured. The medal is accompanied by a grant of £100, and the balance of the proceeds is from time to time to be added to the capital fund. The first medal was awarded to Alfred Russel Wallace.

No. 14. The Joule Memorial Fund.

In 1890 the Joule Memorial Committee transferred to the Society the balance in their hands, the proceeds to be applied for the encouragement of research, both in England and abroad, especially amongst younger men, in those branches of physical science more immediately connected with Joule's work. According to the regulations made by the Council (see ' Year-book '), a studentship or grant is to be made every second year to assist research as already specified. These grants are to be made alternately in Great Britain and abroad. The fund consists of £1000 London Brighton and South Coast Railway Guaranteed 5 per cent. Stock and £47 19s. 2d. 2½ per cent. annuities, the annual income being about £50.

No. 15. The Brady Library Fund.

The late Mr. Henry Bowman Brady bequeathed to the Society in 1891 all his books and papers relating to the Protozoa, and also a sum of £300, the interest of which, or the principal, or both, are from time to time to be applied in the purchase of works on the same or kindred subjects to be added to the collection. The fund now consists of £280 2¾ per cent. Consolidated Stock, and £33 14s. 10d. on deposit at the bank.

No. 16. The Gunning Fund.

In 1891 His Excellency Dr. Robert Halliday Gunning gave the Society his bond for £1000 bearing interest at 4 per cent. to form a fund the annual income of which shall be applied triennially towards the promotion of Physical Science and Biology in such manner as to the President and Council may appear most desirable. The three-years' income, amounting to £120, has now been received, and the amount has been voted by the President and Council for the purpose. The Rules for the administration of this Fund will be found in the 'Year-book.'

No. 17. The Buchanan Medal Fund.

This fund dates from February, 1894, when a sum of £276 12s. and the dies for a medal were offered to the Society by the Committee of the Buchanan Fund. The amount has been invested in the purchase of £258 9s. 2d. Metropolitan 3 per cent. Stock, producing rather less than £8 per annum. The medal, which is to be of gold and of the value of about twenty guineas, is to be awarded every three or five years for distinguished service in Hygienic Science or Practice, in the direction either of original research or of professional, administrative, or constructive work. The balance in hand is to accompany the medal, which is to have no limit as to nationality. The first medal was given to Lady Buchanan by the subscribers to the fund.

The Buchanan Medal (p. 131).

In addition to the medals included in the above Trusts, two medals are annually presented by Her Majesty the Queen, the award of which is entrusted to the Society:—

Royal Medals.

The Royal Medals were founded by H.M. King George IV, the proposal to found them being conveyed in a letter from Sir Robert Peel to Sir Humphry Davy, in a letter dated December 3, 1825. They were at first awarded for the most important discoveries completed and made known to the Royal Society in "the year preceding the day of their award," but soon after the foundation this was changed to "within five years preceding the day of such award." H.M. King William IV continued the foundation under the condition that the

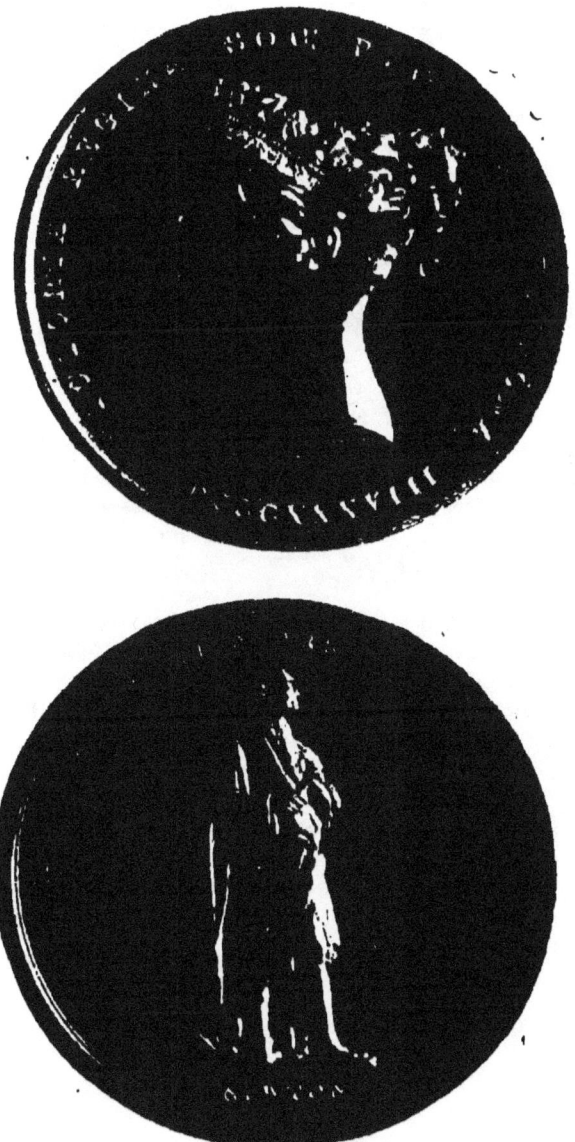

THE ROYAL MEDAL.

subject matter of the inquiry should be previously settled and propounded by the Council three years preceding the day of the award.

Her Majesty Queen Victoria, upon ascending the throne was

graciously pleased to continue the grant of two Royal Medals annually, under the annexed resolutions, proposed by the Council and approved by Her Majesty :—

"That the Royal Medals be given for such Papers only as have been presented to the Royal Society, and inserted in their 'Transactions.'

"That the triennial cycle of subjects be :—

"1. Astronomy; Physiology, including the Natural History of Organised Beings.
"2. Physics; Geology, or Mineralogy.
"3. Mathematics; Chemistry.

"That, in case no Paper coming within these stipulations should be considered deserving of the Royal Medal, in any given year, the Council have the power of awarding such medal to the author of any other Paper on either of the several subjects forming the cycle, that may have been presented to the Society and inserted in their 'Transactions'; preference being given to the subjects of the year immediately preceding; the award being, in such case, subject to the approbation of Her Majesty."

On June 13, 1850, it was resolved that these regulations "should be altered, substituting for them regulations to the following effect:—That the Royal Medals in each year should be awarded for the two most important contributions to the advancement of Natural Knowledge, published originally in Her Majesty's dominions within a period of not more than ten years, and not less than one year of the date of the award, subject, of course, to Her Majesty's approval."

It was at the same meeting resolved—"That it is desirable that, in the award of the Royal Medals, one should be given in each year to each of the two great divisions of Natural Knowledge."

It is upon these lines that the Royal Medals are still awarded.

INSTITUTIONS UPON WHICH THE ROYAL SOCIETY IS REPRESENTED.

UNIVERSITIES.

	Representative.	Appointed.
Oxford University—		
Savilian Professorship of Geometry (Elector).	The President.	*Ex officio.*
Savilian Professorship of Astronomy (Elector).	,,	,,
Sedleian Professorship of Natural Philosophy.	,,	,,
Professorship of Experimental Philosophy.	,,	,,
Wykeham Professorship of Physics.	,,	,,
Waynflete Professorship of Chemistry.	,,	,,
Waynflete Professorship of Mineralogy.	,,	,,
Professorship of Geology.	,,	,,
Cambridge University—		
Lowndean Professorship of Astronomy and Geometry (Elector).	,,	,,

PUBLIC SCHOOLS.

Governing bodies of :—

Charterhouse.	Professor G. H. Darwin.	Mar. 14, 1895.
Christ's Hospital.	Professor Armstrong.	Jan. 16, 1896.
Dulwich College.	Professor G. C. Foster.	Jan. 19, 1893.
Eton College.	Sir H. E. Roscoe.	Dec. 20, 1888.
Harrow School.	Sir A. Geikie.	June 16, 1892.
Rugby School.	Professor Rücker.	Mar. 10, 1892.
Shrewsbury School.	Dr. Pye-Smith.	July 7, 1887.
Westminster School.	Professor Bonney.	Oct. 27, 1881.
Winchester College.	Rev. Professor Price.	Oct. 26, 1881.

OTHER INSTITUTIONS.

Athenæum Club (Committee).	The President.	*Ex officio.*
British Institute of Preventive Medicine.	,,	May 18, 1893.
British Museum (Trustee).	,,	*Ex officio.*
City and Guilds of London Institute (Governor).	,,	,,
Hunterian Museum (Trustee).	,,	,,
Imperial Institute.	Sir J. Evans, K.C.B.	Nov. 30, 1893.
Sir John Soane's Museum.	Professor Church.	Jan. 28, 1897.

The President of the Royal Society is also *ex officio* an honorary Member of the Royal Irish Academy.

OTHER PUBLIC FUNCTIONS PERFORMED BY THE ROYAL SOCIETY.

1. Government Grant for Scientific Investigations.—Administrators. For the History of this Grant see p. 158; for the Regulations see 'Year-book,' p. 74.

2. Kew Observatory.—Lessees under the Crown and Trustees of an endowment by the late J. P. Gassiot for the purposes of the Observatory. (See p. 137.)

3. Lawes Agricultural Trust.—Electors of four members of the Managing Committee. (See p. 155.)

4. Meteorological Council.—Nominators.

    The Council is the official descendant of the Meteorological Department of the Board of Trade, the history of which is given in the Report by the Committee of Inquiry nominated by the Royal Society, the Board of Trade, and the Admiralty respectively, which was printed and presented to Parliament in 1866. This Department was superseded in 1867 by the Meteorological Committee of the Royal Society. In 1877 the Committee transferred their charge to the Meteorological Council as now constituted. The Council is a paid body, and consists of a chairman and four members, nominated by the President and Council of the Royal Society, and approved by the Lords Commissioners of the Treasury, with the Hydrographer of the Admiralty as an official member. The following are the present members:—

    Lieut.-General Strachey, R.E., F.R.S. (Chairman).
    Mr. Alexander Buchan.
    Professor G. H. Darwin, F.R.S.
    Mr. F. Galton, F.R.S.
    Admiral W. J. L. Wharton, F.R.S., Hydrographer of the Admiralty.
    Mr. R. H. Scott, F.R.S. (Secretary).

5. Physick Garden of Chelsea.

    The history of the early connection of the Physick Garden with the Royal Society will be found at p. 153. At present the Society has only a reversionary interest in the garden.

6. Royal Observatory, Greenwich.—Visitors.

    The Royal Society were appointed visitors and directors in 1710, a function which they continued to perform until the accession of King William IV, when, by the new warrant then issued, the President and six of the Fellows of the Royal Astronomical Society were added to the list. The following constitute the existing Board of Visitors:—

The President of the Royal Society—Lord Lister.
The President of the Royal Astronomical Society—Dr. A. A. Common.

Nominated as Fellows of the Royal Society
- Professor W. G. Adams.
- Rev. Professor B. Price.
- Lord Rayleigh.
- Earl of Rosse.
- Professor Rücker.
- Professor Sir G. G. Stokes, Bart.

Nominated as Fellows of the Royal Astronomical Society
- Professor Sir R. S. Ball.
- Professor R. B. Clifton.
- Dr. A. A. Common.
- Dr. J. W. L. Glaisher.
- Dr. W. Huggins.

Savilian Professor of Astronomy at Oxford—Professor H. H. Turner.
Plumian Professor of Astronomy at Cambridge—Professor G. H. Darwin.
Hydrographer of the Admiralty—Admiral W. J. L. Wharton.

7. Standard Weights and Measures.—Custodians.

The Imperial Standard Yard and Pound in actual use for all important comparisons are at the Standards Office. Four copies of each of them are deposited in other places in case of injury or loss of the standards. One of each of these copies is in the custody of the Royal Society.

DESCRIPTION OF THE KEW OBSERVATORY.

The Kew Observatory is situated in the Old Deer Park, about 1,200 yards from the Richmond Railway Station, some 10 miles to the West of the City of London. Its latitude is 51° 28′ 6″ N., and its longitude 0° 18′ 47″ W.

The present building was erected by King George III, in 1769, for observing the transit of Venus, which occurred that year. An earlier observatory, from which it derived its name, was situated in the Kew Palace Grounds, about three-quarters of a mile from the present building. Though the latter lies within the postal district of Richmond, and is approached from the Richmond railway station, its long-established name of "Kew" Observatory has been retained. The site of the present building was originally occupied by an old monastery, which was partly destroyed in the general destruction of religious houses in the sixteenth century, and finally demolished in 1769.

The Government having decided in 1841 to cease to maintain the Observatory, it passed in 1842 into the hands of the British Associa-

Kew Observatory in 1891, from the south-east.

tion for the Advancement of Science, who continued to manage it through a committee until 1871.

Mr. J. P. Gassiot, then Chairman of the British Association Committee for the management of the Observatory, having put in trust with the Royal Society an endowment of £10,000 for the purposes of the Observatory, the management was in that year transferred to the Royal Society, under whose control it has remained, and since that date the Kew Committee has consisted entirely of Fellows of the Society appointed by the Council. The following is a list of members since 1871, the names of the present committee being distinguished by asterisks:—

*Captain W. de W. Abney, C.B.; *Prof. W. G. Adams; *Captain E. W. Creak, R.N.; Captain Sir F. Evans, K.C.B.; *Prof. G. Carey Foster; *Mr. F. Galton, (Chairman since 1888); Mr. J. P. Gassiot; Lieutenant-General Sir J. H. Lefroy, K.C.M.G.; *Prof. J. Perry; Admiral Sir G. H. Richards, K.C.B.; *The Earl of Rosse, K.P. *Prof. A. W. Rücker; Mr. de la Rue (Chairman, 1883–1888) General Sir E. Sabine (Chairman 1871-83); *Mr. R. H. Scott; *Mr. W. N. Shaw; Major-General W. J. Smythe; Mr. Spottiswoode; *Lt.-General R. Strachey, C.S.I.; Mr. E. Walker; General J. T. Walker, C.B.; *Rear-Admiral W. J. L. Wharton, C.B.; Sir Charles

Wheatstone. The staff employed at the Observatory has increased from eight in 1871 to fifteen in 1896.

The chief executive officer under the Committee is styled "Superintendent," the present occupant of the post being Dr. C. Chree. The previous superintendents under the Royal Society's Committee were Mr. S. Jeffery, 1871-76, and Mr. G. M. Whipple, 1876-93. Amongst those who held the post prior to 1871 may be mentioned Sir Francis Ronalds, Mr. John Welsh, and Prof. Balfour Stewart. In addition to the general management of the Observatory, the duties of the Superintendent include the response to inquiries on various scientific matters from Government Departments, especially the Meteorological Office, as well as from individuals engaged in scientific pursuits.

The relations between the Observatory and the Meteorological Office have been very close ever since 1867, as the Observatory has since that date acted as the central observing station for that Office.

DESCRIPTION OF OBSERVATORY.

BASEMENT (see plan No. I).

Magnetograph Room.—This room contains the Magnetographs (1), which were erected in their present form by Mr. Welsh in 1856. The instruments show variations in the Declination, Horizontal Force Component, and Vertical Force Component. Light from fixed gas jets is reflected from mirrors attached to the magnets on to photographic paper. The paper is wound round drums driven by clock-work, and thus a continuous record is obtained of variations either in the direction or intensity of the earth's magnetic force ('B.A. Report,' 1859, pp. 200—228).

The magnetograph curves are standardised by means of direct observations on the strength of the magnets, made from time to time, and the employment of the results of the absolute observations, carried out weekly in a wooden hut (1, Plan II) situated in the garden.

The Barograph (2) is a modified form of that originally designed by Ronalds. A beam of light passes through the chink left between a horizontal stop and the surface of the mercury in the tube of a barometer, and falls upon photographic paper. When the mercury rises in the barometer tube, the beam of light is narrowed, and the trace correspondingly reduced in width, the reverse happening, of course, when the mercury falls ('Report of the Meteorological Committee,' 1867, p. 40).

Photographic Room.—This immediately adjoins the magnetograph room, see Plan I.

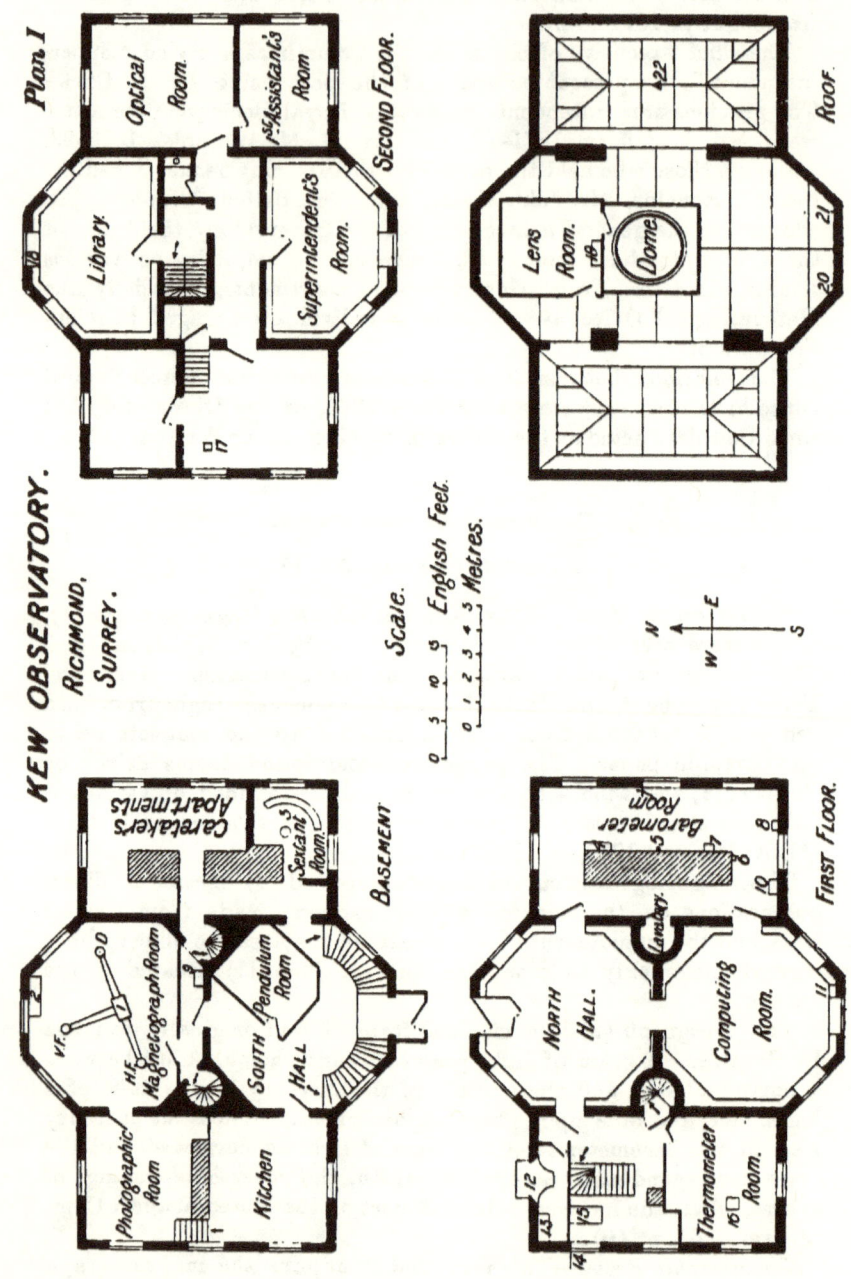

South Hall.—In the passage adjoining the south hall is placed the standard clock, by French (9), the temperature of this part of the Observatory being very constant. The greater part of the south hall is taken up by a double-walled wooden structure in which various observers have at various epochs swung pendulums to determine gravity (see 'Roy. Soc. Proc.', vol. 14, pp. 425—439; vol. 17, pp. 488—499; and 'Phil. Trans.', vol 181, pp. 537—558).

The wooden structure is also used for chronometer trials; its temperature can be raised and kept steady at 100° F. by means of a copper stove.

Sextant Room.—This contains an apparatus (3) for testing the accuracy of graduation in the arc of sextants, which was designed by Mr. T. Cooke ('Roy. Soc. Proc.', vol. 16, pp. 2–6). It consists essentially of five collimating telescopes, with gas jets behind them, which illuminate objects, in the shape of crosses, situated at the principal foci. The collimators are fixed on a slate slab, carried by brickwork. The emergent beams of light converge to a common centre, and are inclined at certain known angles. The readings given by a sextant for the magnitude of these angles supply the data for determining the error at various points in its arc.

First Floor.

North Hall.—This is an octagonal-shaped room, surrounded by glass cupboards, most of which contain instruments no longer in use. Some of these are of considerable historic interest, such as Ronalds' apparatus for examining atmospheric electric potential, Wheatstone's galvanometer, Lord Kelvin's early form of mirror electrometer, and various old patterns of magnetic instruments.

Barometer Room.—The standard barometers (4) were mounted by Welsh, in 1855 ('Phil. Trans.' 1856, p. 507). The barometers are read by means of a cathetometer (5), constructed by Munro. Their cisterns are at a height of 34 ft. above mean sea level. The room also contains the ordinary working standard barometer (6), made by Newman; this is compared from time to time with the Welsh standards, and is used to standardise the barograph, observations being made with it at 10 A.M., noon, 2 P.M., 4 P.M., and 10 P.M. There are also receivers (7) and (7'), in which ordinary mercury barometers and aneroid barometers respectively can be compared at low pressures.

A standard clock (8), by Dent, is used in the tests of watches commenced in 1884; it is electrically connected with a chronograph (10), which daily receives the Greenwich time signal.

The room likewise contains a balance by Oertling, and a dividing engine by Perreaux, similar to that employed by Regnault ('Roy.

Soc. Proc.,' vol. 6, pp. 178—188) ; the dividing engine is used *inter alia* for calibrating and dividing mercury thermometers.

Computing Room.—This is a large octagonal room, similar to the North Hall, in which the greater part of the reduction of meteorological observations is effected; it contains a standard clock by Shelton (11).

West Room.—This contains the Thermograph (12) and Electrograph (13).

The Thermograph was designed and fitted up by Beckley under the direction of Dr. Balfour Stewart, in 1866 (see 'Report of the Meteorological Committee,' 1867). The recording part consists essentially of a drum carrying photographic paper which is driven round by clockwork once in forty-eight hours. There are two thermometers, a dry bulb and a wet bulb, of as nearly as possible the same pattern. Their bulbs are outside the building but inside a screen. The stems first pass horizontally through the wall, and then bend at right angles so as to pass vertically in front of two fixed mirrors. The mirrors reflect beams of light which emanate from gas jets, and are transmitted through condensing lenses. The mercury column of each thermometer has a small air bubble entrapped in it, and only where the bubble is can light pass through to the photographic paper. The bubble rises and falls with the mercury, and thus the photographic trace gives a continuous record of its height, and so indirectly measures the temperature. Alongside the thermograph thermometers in the screen, there are ordinary wet and dry bulb standard thermometers, which are read daily at 10 A.M., noon, 2 P.M., 4 P.M., and 10 P.M. These readings serve to standardise the thermograph curves. There are also in the screen ordinary maximum and minimum thermometers for use in case of failure of the thermograph.

The Electrograph (13), invented by Lord Kelvin, consists of a quadrant electrometer containing a needle to which a small mirror is attached; from this a beam of light is reflected on to photographic paper. The needle is connected electrically with the Water Dropper (14). The curve obtained is intended to show variations in the electric potential at the point outside the building where the jet from the water-dropper breaks into drops. The curve is standardised from time to time by means of a portable electrometer. The position of the base line answering to zero potential is determined by direct experiment daily at 11 A.M. and 4.30 P.M.

Near the electrograph is the chronometer oven (15), employed for testing Navy chronometers at a moderately high temperature; the temperature is regulated by means of a Kullberg's governor.

Thermometer Room.—The Thermometer Comparing Apparatus (16) was designed by Mr. F. Galton. The thermometers to be tested are compared with one or more standards in a vertical position, readings being taken in the majority of instances at intervals of 10°. There are special arrangements for securing and maintaining a uniform temperature.

SECOND FLOOR.

New Addition to West Wing.—These rooms, built in 1892, are not yet much used. They contain a Hypsometer (17), of the form in use at the Bureau International at Sèvres (see Dr. Guillaume's 'Thermométrie de Précision,' p. 113), and an air pump with other apparatus employed in investigating the behaviour of aneroid barometers.

Superintendent's Room.—This contains a considerable part of the Library.

First Assistant's Room.—This room is chiefly devoted to the magnetic computing work; it contains an apparatus for testing the shades of sextants ('Roy. Soc. Proc.,' vol. 35, p. 42).

Optical Room.—This is chiefly used for testing and marking binoculars, Navy telescopes and air meters; it also contains part of the Library.

The Library.—A room similar in size to the Superintendent's room, lined with book-cases. It contains a large glycerine barometer (18) erected by Jordan in 1879, not now in action ('Roy. Soc. Proc.,' vol. 30, p. 105).

THE ROOF.

The Dome contains the photoheliograph erected in 1856 by Dr. Warren De la Rue. For some years the instrument has been used only for eye observations of sun-spots. Work done with it in earlier years is described in the 'Phil. Trans.,' (vol. 159, pp. 1—110, and vol. 160, pp. 389—496).

The Lens Room.—This contains the self-recording apparatus (19), designed by Beckley ('B.A. Report,' 1858, p. 306, and 'Report of Met. Com.,' 1867) for the Robinson anemometer, which is placed above the dome. A long rod is geared to the anemometer spindle by means of an endless screw. At the lower end of this rod is a gearing by which a small horizontal cylinder is made to effect one complete revolution for every 50 miles of wind. The cylinder is encircled by a spiral knife-blade shaped strip of metal, and the edge of this strip touches a chronograph cylinder beneath it, at one point only at a time. During a complete revolution of the small cylinder each point of the spiral strip comes in contact with the chronograph. The chronograph sheet being of metallic register paper, the contacts of the spiral strip are recorded. There is a similar arrangement for recording the wind direction, the small cylinder with its spiral strip making in this case a complete revolution for a complete revolution of the wind vane.

The Lens Room likewise contains an apparatus for examining photographic lenses which was devised by Major L. Darwin ('Roy. Soc. Proc.,' vol. 52, pp. 403—451).

The parapet of the roof supports two sunshine recorders. One (21) the original "Campbell" pattern, consists of a spherical lens fitted in a wooden bowl, the intensity of sun light between two successive solstices being measured by the amount of wood charred ('Roy. Soc. Proc.,' vol. 23, pp. 578—582). The other recorder (20) is of the modern "Campbell-Stokes" pattern, burning a line in a strip of card-board, which is renewed every evening after sunset.

On the roof there is a stand with a camera apparatus (22). By means of this and a similar camera, fixed at a distance of 800 yards from the Observatory, observations were taken some years ago on the height and velocity of clouds ('Roy. Soc. Proc.,' vol. 49, pp. 467—480).

THE GARDEN AND ENCLOSURE. (See Plan II.)

The Magnetic House (1) is a small wooden structure built originally at the cost of General Sabine, once chairman of the Kew Committee. In it absolute observations of the Magnetic Declination, Inclination, and Horizontal Force are taken about once a week. The instruments are of the ordinary "Kew" pattern, the unifilar being by Jones, and the dip circle by Barrow. Observations have been made continuously since 1850.

Experimental House (2) is a wooden building used for testing self-recording instruments.

The Workshop (3), and *Clinical House* (4), are under one roof, the building being substantially built of brick. The Clinical House is devoted to the testing of clinical thermometers, a very large number of which are examined every year.

An addition (5) has recently been made to the north side of the Clinical House. It is fitted up with a fume closet, resistance box, galvanometer, and other appliances for use in connexion with platinum resistance thermometers.

In the centre of the garden are placed the rain gauges. In the Beckley self-recording gauge (6) the funnel empties into a small cistern, floating on mercury, to which a pen is attached. As the cistern fills with water it sinks, carrying with it the pen, which leaves a trace on a sheet of paper wound round a drum driven by clockwork. After a fall of 0·2 inch of rain, the cistern discharges itself by means of a siphon, and rises to its initial position ('Report

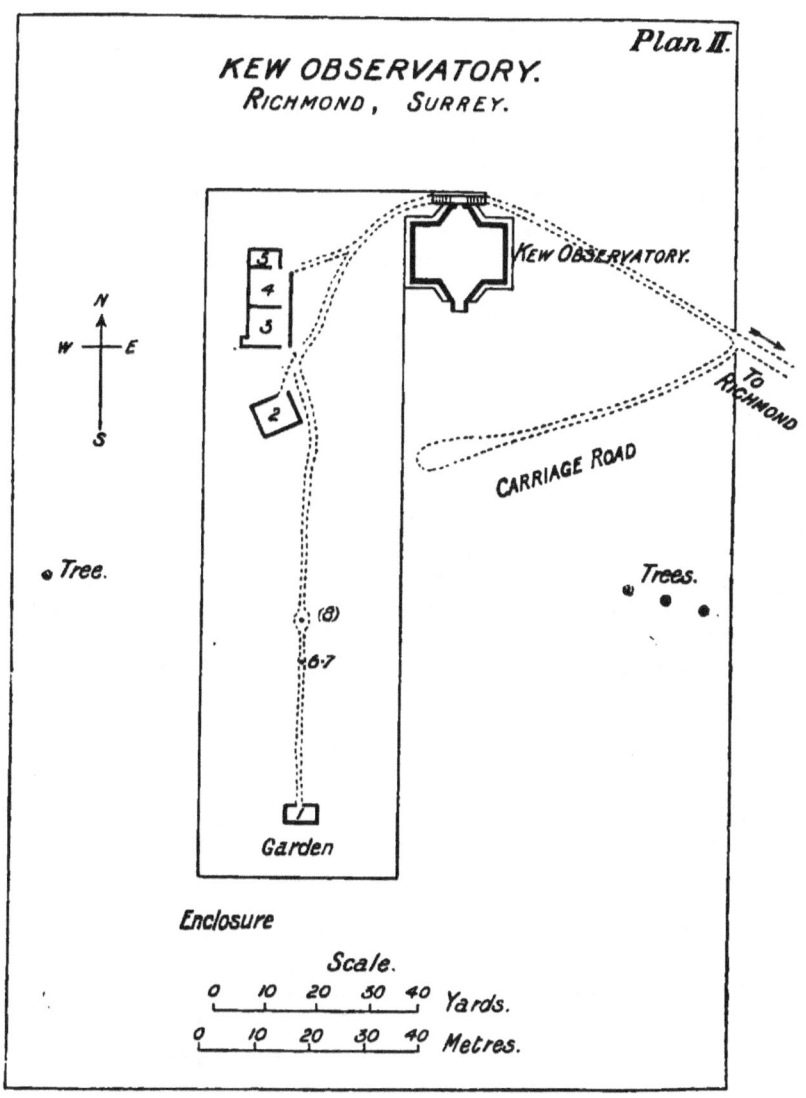

of Met. Committee,' 1869, p. 36, and 'B. A. Report for 1869,' Trans. of Sections, p. 52). The check gauge (7) is of the ordinary Meteorological Office pattern.

The receiving surfaces of the rain gauges are 21 inches above the surface of the ground. The diameter of the Beckley gauge is 11 inches, that of the check gauge 8 inches.

On a stand (8) a little to the north of the rain gauges are some black bulb maximum thermometers *in vacuo*. On the grass near the stand are minimum thermometers of various kinds. These several thermometers are read daily at 10 A.M.

Eye observations of the amount of sky covered by clouds, with the nature of the clouds and apparent directions of motion, are taken daily at 10 A.M., noon, 2 P.M., 4 P.M., and 10 P.M. The scale used is 0 for a perfectly clear sky, 10 for a completely clouded one.

Surrounding the garden is grass land, fully 5 acres in extent, which was added to the Observatory holding leased from the Crown in 1894. It is enclosed within a 6-foot park paling.

Verification Work.

This work took its origin at the middle of the present century in the want then felt in England for magnetic and meteorological instruments of greater accuracy and trustworthiness than those previously in use. It rapidly expanded, and in the natural process of growth has come to include the examination of instruments and appliances whose connexion with magnetism and meteorology is remote.

Magnetic Instruments.—One of the most important branches of the verification work is the determination of the constants of magnetic instruments. A considerable proportion of the magnetometers and inclinometers hitherto used in magnetic surveys have been examined at the Observatory. Since the construction of the magnetographs, in 1856, twenty-one Observatories have been supplied with similar instruments, and the majority of these had been previously tried at Kew.

Thermometers.—In 1850 a standard thermometer, verified, it appears, by Regnault, was obtained from Paris, along with a dividing engine and other necessary apparatus for calibrating and examining thermometers. Within a few years from that date, in addition to verification work, a large number of standard thermometers had been made. The construction of these thermometers still forms a part of the Observatory work, although not to such a large extent as was formerly the case. Since 1850 over 700 standard thermometers have been made up, of which fully 600 have been issued to other Observatories, physical investigators, and instrument makers.

At first the thermometers verified were intended almost exclusively for meteorological work. Towards the middle of the decade 1860–1870, however, clinical thermometers began to be verified, and in the course of a few years the number of thermometers increased beyond the capabilities of the simple testing apparatus originally in use.

To meet the exigencies of the case an apparatus was designed by Mr. F. Galton, which allowed of the nearly simultaneous comparison of a large number of thermometers at any specified temperature between the freezing and boiling points of water. This apparatus is still employed for ordinary meteorological instruments, a second smaller one of similar type being now devoted almost exclusively to clinical thermometers.

For temperatures below the freezing point of water, down to 12° F. or lower, use is made of freezing mixtures; and a considerable number of minimum thermometers are tested annually at the freezing point of mercury, which is reached by the aid of compressed carbonic acid gas.

For temperatures above the boiling point of water corrections are at present obtained by means of calibration; but experiments are in progress which aim at replacing or extending the results so obtained by direct observations in molten metal, or some other suitable medium.

In 1878 a hydraulic press was erected for testing deep-sea thermometers—mainly on behalf of the Admiralty—under pressures similar to those they experience at great depths. In the same year the practice was introduced of etching a distinguishing mark—a monogram of KO—on ordinary thermometers, whose errors do not exceed certain limits.

Barometers.—The testing of mercury barometers dates from 1853, and comprises the ordinary patterns used both on land and sea. There has been no such development of numbers here as has occurred in the case of thermometers; but, on the whole, only a slight increase. The testing of aneroid barometers was instituted considerably more recently, but in this case the number tested annually has shown a considerable rise.

Hydrometers.—The testing of hydrometers also dates from 1853. At first the examination was practically limited to hydrometers intended for ocean meteorology, but of late years there have been a large number intended for commercial and excise purposes.

Anemometers.—These instruments are tried on a staging erected on the observatory roof, at such a height as to place them on a level with the standard Robinson anemometer. The records of each individual anemometer are compared with those of the standard for a sufficient variety of wind velocities.

Rain Gauges.—Ordinary rain gauges have the mean diameters of their receiving surfaces measured, and the necessary corrections determined to the rainfall recorded. More complicated gauges of the self-recording pattern are set up in the neighbourhood of the standard Beckley gauge, and their records over a considerable time compared with those of the standard.

Sunshine Recorders.—Only a small number of these instruments have been examined. The method of testing comprises an examination into the proper working of the instrument, and a comparison of its record with that of the standard "Campbell-Stokes" instrument.

Theodolites.—The number of theodolites tested is also comparatively small, though it apparently tends to increase. These instruments are examined for their optical qualities and accuracy of graduation.

Sextants.—The original testing apparatus was designed by Mr. F. Galton in 1862, and was succeeded in 1866 by a more elaborate apparatus designed by Mr. T. Cooke. In 1888 the Admiralty made a regulation that all sextants used by cadets of H.M. Navy must be certificated at Kew. Sextant shades are separately examined by means of a special apparatus already alluded to.

Compasses.—Prior to 1890 only a small number of compasses were verified, and these consisted mainly of small azimuth compasses for use by travellers. Of late years a very considerable number of ships' compasses have been examined. During the present year the test for ships' compasses has been revised and extended, with the assistance of Captain Creak, F.R.S., of the Hydrographic Department, so as to bring it more into line with the Admiralty test, and with the scientific requirements of the day.

Telescopes and Binoculars.—The testing of navy telescopes and binoculars, on behalf of the Admiralty, was undertaken in 1889, and a good deal of similar work has since then been also performed for instrument makers and private persons.

Lenses.—Since 1891 photographic lenses have been tested, with the aid of the apparatus devised by Major L. Darwin, to which reference has already been made. This departure has, however, met with somewhat limited public recognition, little over 100 lenses having been as yet sent for examination. These are included under the heading "Miscellaneous" in the subsequent table.

Watches and Chronometers.—The rating of watches was commenced in 1884, the system of verification following pretty closely that previously adopted at Geneva. Three classes of certificates, A, B, C, are issued—A denoting the highest grade—according to the severity of the test for which the watch is entered; and an annual list is published of those watches which obtain 80 per cent. and upwards of full marks in the competition for a class A certificate. The number of watches tested annually has fluctuated considerably, a maximum of 1,521 having been reached in 1893. Of late years the tendency has been to a reduction in the numbers entered for the lower classes, B and C, of certificates, and an increase in the number entered for class A.

The rating of marine chronometers commenced in 1886. Two classes of certificates, A and B, of which A is the higher, are granted to instruments sent for the ordinary trials. In answer to special applications, more prolonged trials on the Greenwich system have been carried out for the Italian and Portuguese Governments.

Other Miscellaneous Forms.—In addition to the above classes of instruments, a considerable variety of other forms have been tested, amongst which may be mentioned barographs, thermographs, air meters, artificial horizons, and rain measures.

The following table (p. 150) gives particulars as to the numbers of the several forms of instruments which have been examined at the Observatory since 1853.

Experimental Work.

In addition to experimental work initiated by the Committee or the Meteorological Office, investigations are carried out at the Observatory on behalf of societies or individuals who have obtained the approval by the Committee of the particular research, and who undertake to defray the expense either from their own private resources or from grants voted by public bodies.

A long list of original papers bearing on work done at Kew will be found in an appendix to the 'History of the Observatory,' by Mr. R. H. Scott ['Proc. Roy. Soc.,' 1885, pp. 77—84 (pp. 41—48 of separate off-print)]. Here reference will only be made to a few of the researches and developments which were of special novelty at the time, or have since become intimately associated with the name of the Observatory.

Self-recording Apparatus.—As early as 1843 Sir F. Ronalds, at that time Superintendent, seems to have had a species of self-recording electrometer in regular action. In 1845 he carried out a large number of experiments in photography, and, within a year or two from that date, a barograph and an electrograph, recording photographically, appear to have been in use. In 1851 a six months' trial of a photographic magnetograph was in progress. The present Kew pattern magnetograph is a modification erected in 1856 by Mr. Welsh, Sir F. Ronalds' successor.

Balloon Ascents.—In 1852 Mr. Welsh made several balloon ascents, in which a large number of meteorological observations were taken at different heights up to 22,000 feet ('Phil. Trans.,' 1853, p. 311).

Sun-spot Observations.—In 1856 the photoheliograph was erected, and the observations of sun-spots, &c., made with it, formed the basis of a number of papers by Mr. De la Rue, Professor Balfour Stewart, and others in the 'Phil. Trans.,' 'Proc. Roy. Soc.,' 'Phil. Mag.,' &c., from 1865 onwards.

Atmospheric Electricity.—In 1861, the water-dropper invented by Lord Kelvin—then Professor William Thomson—came into operation, and in 1868 the results on Atmospheric Electricity obtained with it

Number of Instruments tested—1853-1895

Years.	Self-recording magnetic instruments.	Magnetometers.	Inclinometers (dip circles).	Thermometers other than clinical.	Clinical thermometers.	Mercury barometers.	Aneroid barometers.	Hydrometers.	Anemometers.	Rain-gauges.
1853—55	—	—	—	2701	—	280	—	1269	—	—
1856—65	5	14	19	5502	—	1645	—	1123	2	—
1866—75	9	30	35	10403	6008	1325	97	584	25	21
1876—85	5	39	63	17743	46717	1683	458	2787	85	101
1886—95	2	34	38	32378	130332	1740	1017	3667	94	106
Totals, 1853—95	21	117	155	68727	183057	6673	1572	9430	206	228

Table—*continued.*

Years.	Sunshine recorders.	Theodolites.	Sextants.	Compasses.	Telescopes.	Binoculars.	Watches.	Chronometers.	Miscellaneous.	Total.
1853—55	—	—	—	—	—	—	—	—	—	4250
1856—65	—	—	20	1	—	—	—	—	7	8347
1866—75	—	3	13	1	—	—	—	—	33	18587
1876—85	1	18	325	12	—	—	344	—	1375	71756
1886—95	14	57	3480	409	2731	2574	7437	221	1948	188279
Totals, 1853—95	15	78	3847	423	2731	2574	7781	221	3363	291219

were discussed by Professor Everett ('Phil. Trans.' for 1868, p. 347, and elsewhere). A more recent discusssion by the late Superintendent, Mr. Whipple, occurs in the 'B.A. Report' for 1881, p. 443.

Terrestrial Magnetism.—In 1859—71 General Sabine, the then Chairman of the Kew Committee, contributed to the Royal Society a number of papers based on the Kew magnetograph results, dealing *inter alia* with the phenomena of magnetic storms.

Thermometry.—In 1863 Professor Balfour Stewart, then Superintendent, made a large number of experiments with the air thermometer ('Phil. Trans.,' 1863, pp. 425—435). He found for the mean coefficient of expansion of air between 0° and 100° C. the value 0·0036728, while for the freezing point of mercury on the scale of the air thermometer he found —37·93° F. or —38·85° C.

Pendulum Observations.—In 1865 experiments were made by Captain Basevi with pendulums, subsequently used for geodetic work in India. Similar experiments have since been carried out on several occasions (see General J. T. Walker in the 'Phil. Trans.' Series A, for 1890, p. 537).

Variations of Temperature, &c., with Height.—During the years 1873-4-5 an extensive series of experiments were conducted for the Meteorological Office on variations of temperature and humidity with height above the ground. Thermometers were exposed in screens of the same pattern at three different heights, the highest 129 feet from the ground, on the ornamental pagoda in the Royal Gardens, Kew, the requisite permission having been obtained from H.M. Office of Works and the Director of the Gardens. Throughout the greater part of the time readings were taken thrice daily. The results, and their relation to those deduced from a similar research made by Dr. Wild at Pulkowa, were discussed by Mr. R. H. Scott ('Quarterly Weather Reports of the Meteorological Office,' 1876, App., pp. [20]—[37]).

Anemometry.—In 1874, at the suggestion of Mr. R. H. Scott, a series of comparisons were made of anemometers of different patterns. The principal experiments were carried out at the Crystal Palace by Mr. Jeffery and Mr. Whipple, the instruments being mounted on a steam merry-go-round. This was driven at various velocities up to 30 miles an hour. The bearing of the results on the questions of the existence and magnitude of a constant "factor" for the Robinson cup anemometer was discussed by Professor Stokes in 1881 ('Roy. Soc. Proc.,' vol. 32, p. 170).

Cloud Measurements.—In 1885, after numerous preliminary experiments which originated in 1878, two cameras were erected, one on the Observatory roof, the other at a horizontal distance of 800 yds., and a series of observations begun to determine the heights and velocities of clouds. The original observations dealt with clouds at all altitudes, but later observations were confined to the zenith. Some of the results were discussed by General Strachey and Mr. Whipple in 1891 ('Roy. Soc. Proc.,' vol. 49, p. 467).

Recent Experimental Work.

Of the experimental work done in recent years, or now in process of execution, it would be premature to speak at length.

Aneroid Barometers.—Experiments have for some time been directed to an elucidation of the elastic phenomena presented by aneroid barometers under varying pressures, with a view to rendering the results obtained under one definite set of conditions at the Observatory more serviceable under the varied conditions which occur in nature.

Atmospheric Electricity.—At intervals during the last two years, observations have been taken of atmospheric electricity at a variety of points near the Observatory. One of their principal objects is to investigate the extent to which the results may be influenced by peculiarities in the pattern of the recording apparatus or in the circumstances of its immediate environment ('Roy. Soc. Proc.,' vol. 60, 1896, p. 96).

Electrical Resistance Thermometers.—Within the last year a series of experiments have been commenced with electrical resistance thermometers. The object is to test their suitability as instruments of precision in scientific research, and also their convenience for the ordinary observer and manufacturer.

For meteorologists, the suitability of resistance thermometers for the measurement of earth temperatures is a matter of considerable importance. To investigate this, two resistance thermometers of a pattern devised by Professor Callendar and Mr. E. H. Griffiths have been buried near the Observatory, along with a delicate platinum resistance thermometer, and an elaborate comparison is being made.

Instruction to Observers.

There is one other sphere of usefulness for the Observatory to which reference should be made, viz., that of a school of instruction. Not a few members of the staffs of other British and Colonial Observatories have received preliminary instruction at Kew; and the taking of magnetic observations has been studied there by a considerable number of officers of H.M. Navy and others intending to proceed on exploratory voyages.

The plans accompanying this description of the Observatory were drawn by Mr. R. S. Whipple, son of the late Superintendent, who likewise gave valuable assistance in the compilation.

For further particulars, especially of the early history of the Observatory, the reader should refer to 'The History of the Kew Observatory,' by Mr. R. H. Scott, F.R.S., already mentioned.

CHARLES CHREE,
Superintendent.

THE BOTANIC GARDENS, CHELSEA, FORMERLY KNOWN AS "THE PHYSICK GARDEN."

In February, 1721 (1722 new style) Sir Hans Sloane by a deed, one part of which is in the possession of the Society, granted unto and to the use of the Society of Apothecaries for ever, subject to a yearly rent of £5 and to certain conditions, a plot of ground formerly leased to that Society by Lord Cheyne, and known as "The Physick Garden." The most important condition is "That the Garden should at all times hereafter be continued as a Physick Garden" by the Society of Apothecaries, which shall yearly present to the Royal Society "fifty specimens or samples of distinct plants, well dryed and preserved, and which grew in the said Garden the same year, together with their respective names or reputed names, and so as the specimens or samples of such plants be different, or specifically distinct, and no one offered twice, until the compleat number of two thousand plants have been delivered."

The deed further provides that if these conditions be not fulfilled, or if the Society shall at any time convert the Garden into buildings for habitations or for any other uses save as a Physic Garden, Sir Hans Sloane, his heirs and assigns, may enter and hold the premises in trust for the Royal Society, which, however, must pay the said rent, and in like manner deliver fifty plants from the Gardens annually to the College of Physicians, and if the Royal Society fail to comply, the Gardens are to be held in trust for the College of Physicians, subject to the same conditions as those originally imposed on the Society of Apothecaries.

The deed recites that the Society of Apothecaries had "lately resolved upon and sett apart an annuall summe for the maintaining of the 'Garden' forever," a consideration for the Grant which is not mentioned in the abstract of the Deed published in the 'Memoirs of the Botanic Garden at Chelsea,' by Mr. Henry Field and Dr. R. H. Semple, printed in 1878.

The Society of Apothecaries duly presented in each year fifty distinct plants to the Royal Society up to 1762, when the tale of two thousand was completed. After that year plants were still presented up to 1774, when a total of 2,550 plants was attained, and from that date the records of the Royal Society appear to contain no entry concerning the Garden until the year 1861, when the Society of Apothecaries, having expressed to the President of the Royal Society their intention of relieving themselves of the responsibility of maintaining the Botanic Gardens at Chelsea, and the matter having been referred to a Committee, the following Minute of Council appears in reply to an enquiry from the Society of Apothecaries as to the decision of the Council :—

"Oct. 24, 1861. Resolved that thanks be returned to the Master and Wardens of the Society of Apothecaries for their obliging communication, and that they be informed that the President and Council of the Royal Society do not feel in a position to take any steps in the matter referred to, until they receive notice of proceedings on the part of the Heirs of Sir Hans Sloane consequent on the determination of the Society of Apothecaries."

The Garden is said to have contained three acres one rood and thirty-five perches of ground, but this area appears to have been exclusive of the foreshore of the River Thames. In the 'Memoirs' already mentioned (p. 88) it is stated that so long ago as 1707 directions were given for wharfing the Garden towards the river, and that a similar order was made in 1728. In 1771 an embankment was made at an expense of about £400. "This embankment was designed only in order to recover ground which had originally belonged to the Garden, but had in process of time been washed away by the river."

In 1870 the Chelsea Embankment was constructed, and, as the 'Memoirs' state, the Apothecaries' Society, "as tenants of the Chelsea Garden," lost their immediate access to the river and sacrificed their portion of the foreshore, while a road intervened between the garden and the river. As compensation, a handsome wall, railing, and entrance gates facing the Embankment were built by the Board of Works.

It is further stated in the 'Memoirs' that a strip of reclaimed land has "been thrown in with the older portion since the construction of the new river-side embankment."

In 1890 the Society had some correspondence with the Society of Apothecaries on occasion of a proposal that the Gardens should be sold for building purposes; but the proposal was abandoned.

THE LAWES AGRICULTURAL TRUST.*

Mr. (now Sir) John Bennet Lawes was the founder of the Rothamsted Experimental Station. He commenced experiments with different manuring substances, first with plants in pots, and afterwards in the field, soon after entering into possession of his hereditary property at Rothamsted† in 1834. At the outset the researches of De Saussure on vegetation chiefly guided him. Of all the experiments so made, those in which the neutral phosphate of lime, in bones, bone-ash, and apatite, was rendered soluble by means of sulphuric acid, and the mixture applied for root-crops, gave the most striking results. The results obtained on a small scale in 1837, 1838, and 1839, were such as to lead to more extensive trials in the field in 1840 and 1841, and subsequently.

In 1843, more systematic field experiments were commenced; and a barn, which had previously been partially applied to laboratory purposes, became almost exclusively devoted to agricultural investigations. The foundation of the Rothamsted Experimental Station may be said to date from that time (1843).

The Rothamsted station has from the commencement been entirely disconnected from any external organisation, and has been maintained entirely at the cost of Sir John Lawes. Within the last few years he has further set apart a sum of £100,000, the Laboratory, and certain areas of land, for the continuance of the investigations after his death. In February, 1889, Trustees were appointed, and the necessary Trust Deed was executed; and in accordance with the provisions of the Deed, a Committee of Management was soon afterwards appointed, and entered upon its duties.

The Trustees are:—

Sir John Lubbock, Bart., F.R.S.　|　Lord Walsingham, F.R.S.
Sir John Evans, K.C.B., Treasurer of the Royal Society.

The Committee consists of nine Members, who are at present:—

Sir John Evans, Treas. R.S. (Chairman).......⎫
Dr. Hugo Müller, F.R.S. (Treasurer).........⎬ Nominated by:— The Royal Society.
Professor M. Foster, Sec. R.S. ....⎪
W. T. Thiselton Dyer, Esq., C.M.G., F.R.S....⎭

---

* This statement is abridged from the Rothamsted "Memoranda" for 1896.

† Rothamsted is in Hertfordshire, twenty-five miles from London, on the Midland Railway; Station, Harpenden. Postal address—Rothamsted, St. Albans. Telegraphic address—Harpenden.

Professor H. E. Armstrong, LL.D., F.R.S. ….	The Chemical Society.
William Carruthers, Esq., F.R.S. …………	The Linnean Society.
Sir John H. Thorold, Bart., LL.D. …………	The Royal Agricultural
Viscount Emlyn* ……………………………	Society of England.

And Sir J. B. Lawes himself.

The Secretary to the Committee is Mr. Herbert Rix, B.A.

From June 1843, up to the present time, Dr. (now Sir) J. Henry Gilbert has been associated with Sir John Bennet Lawes in the conduct of the experiments, and has had the direction of the laboratory.

In 1854–5 a new laboratory was built, by public subscription of agriculturists, and was presented to Sir John Lawes in July 1855, from which date the old barn-laboratory was abandoned, and the new one has been occupied.

The staff usually consists of one to three chemists, two or three general assistants, two to four computers and record-keepers, a laboratory man and other helps. A botanical assistant has also occasionally been employed, with from three to six boys under him.

The field experiments, and occasionally feeding experiments, also employ a considerable but a very variable number of agricultural labourers.

There is now a collection of more than 40,000 bottles of samples of experimentally grown vegetable produce, of animal products, of ashes, or of soils, besides some thousands of samples not in bottles; and, the Laboratory having become very inconveniently full, a new detached building—a "Sample House"—was erected in the autumn of 1888, comprising two large rooms for the storing of specimens, and for some processes of preparation, and also a drying room.

The investigations may be classed under two heads:—

I.—*Field Experiments, Experiments on Vegetation, &c.*

The general scope and plan of the field experiments has been to grow some of the most important crops of rotation, each separately, year after year, for many years in succession on the same land, without manure, with farmyard manure, and with a great variety of chemical manures; the same description of manure being, as a rule, applied year after year on the same plot. Experiments on an actual course of rotation, without manure, and with different manures, have also been made.

II.—*Experiments on Animals, &c.*

Experiments with the animals of the farm were commenced early in 1847, and have been continued, at intervals, nearly up to the present time.

---

* *Vice* Charles Whitehead, Esq., resigned in 1896.

The following points have been investigated:—

1. The amount of food, and of its several constituents, consumed in relation to a given live-weight of animal within a given time.
2. The amount of food, and of its several constituents, consumed to produce a given amount of increase in live-weight.
3. The proportion, and relative development, of the different organs or parts of different animals.
4. The proximate and ultimate composition of the animals in different conditions as to age and fatness, and the probable composition of their increase in live-weight during the fattening process.
5. The composition of the solid and liquid excreta (the manure) in relation to that of the food consumed.
6. The loss or expenditure of constituents by respiration and the cutaneous exhalations—that is, in the mere sustenance of the living meat-and-manure-making machine.
7. The yield of milk in relation to the food consumed to produce it; and the influence of different descriptions of food, on the quantity, and on the composition, of the milk.

On July 29, 1893, the jubilee of the Rothamsted experiments was celebrated at a meeting held at Harpenden and presided over by the President of the Board of Agriculture. A granite boulder, with a suitable inscription, was erected in front of the laboratory, a portrait of Sir John Lawes, painted by Mr. Hubert Herkomer, was presented to him, and framed and illuminated addresses of congratulation, signed by the Prince of Wales on behalf of the subscribers to the fund, were presented to Sir John Lawes and Dr. Gilbert. A piece of plate was also presented to Dr. Gilbert, upon whom her Majesty the Queen subsequently conferred the honour of knighthood. Addresses from a number of scientific and agricultural societies, both English and foreign, were presented. The subscribers to the Jubilee Fund included societies and individuals in the United Kingdom, Australasia, Canada, India, Mauritius, Austria, China, Denmark, France, Germany, Italy, Russia, Switzerland, and the United States of America.

N.B.—It is requested that those wishing to inspect the experiments will give notice, either by letter or telegram, to Sir John B. Lawes, Bart. (Rothamsted, St. Albans), or to Sir J. Henry Gilbert (Harpenden), as to the time of their intended visit.

Communications for the Committee should be addressed to Herbert Rix, Esq., B.A., Secretary to the Lawes Trust Committee, Royal Society, Burlington House, London, W.

HISTORY OF THE GOVERNMENT GRANT FOR SCIENTIFIC INVESTIGATIONS.

I. "Government Grant" of £1000 per annum.

For the origin of the annual Parliamentary Grant for "scientific investigations," it is necessary to go back to the year 1849. On November 16 of that year, a letter addressed confidentially by Lord John Russell to the late Earl of Rosse was read to the Council, together with the draft of Lord Rosse's reply, and on December 20 a Committee, consisting of the Lord Chief Baron, Professor Owen, Sir Roderick Murchison, Dr. Miller, and the officers, was appointed "to consider and report to the Council respecting the application of the proposed Grant by Her Majesty's Government for the promotion of scientific inquiries." This Committee presented their Report to the Council on March 7, 1850, recommending that—

"First, and chiefly, the Grant be awarded in aid of private individual scientific investigation.

"Secondly, in aid of the calculation and scientific reduction of masses of accumulated observations.

"Thirdly, in aid of astronomical, meteorological, and other observations, which may be assisted by the purchase and employment of new instruments.

"Fourthly, and subordinately to the purposes above named, in aid of such other scientific objects as may, from time to time, appear to be of sufficient interest, although not coming under any of the foregoing heads."

The Report, from which the foregoing is quoted, was adopted and a "Committee of Recommendations" appointed.

The sum granted by the Government and administered by that Committee was £1000. On January 6, 1851, Lord John Russell wrote to the President informing him that he should "set apart one thousand pounds, from the fund for Special Service, to be applied by the Council of the Royal Society in the same manner as the Grant made for scientific purposes last year." The same sum was granted in 1852, 1853, and 1854, but, upon the President applying in 1855, "for the annual Grant of £1000," he was informed by a letter from H.M. Treasury that these Grants were special, and that the limited amount of the fund from which they had been made would not admit of "an annual Grant to the Royal Society," but it was suggested that a Parliamentary vote for the amount of the Grant might be taken.

In their reply the Council, while accepting the latter suggestion emphasised the fact that the Government Grant was not "a grant to the Royal Society," but "a contribution on the part of the nation towards the promotion of science generally in the United Kingdom," and that the Council regarded themselves "as Trustees of the Grant, and accountable to the public for its due administration as long as it should be continued."

From that time to the year 1881 the sum of £1000 was annually voted by Parliament for the promotion of science in the United Kingdom, and was administered by the Council of the Society upon the advice of a Committee consisting of the Members of the Council, twenty-one Fellows, not members of the Council, and the Presidents of the Chemical, Geological, Linnean, and Royal Astronomical Societies (Council Minutes, Jan. 27, 1859). This Committee was at first appointed triennially, but after 1862 annually.

II. "GOVERNMENT FUND" OF £4000 A YEAR AND "GOVERNMENT GRANT" OF £1000 A YEAR.

In July, 1856, the attention of the Council was called to a motion which had been made in the House of Commons for the appointment of a Committee to consider the question, whether any measures could be adopted by the Government or Parliament that would improve the position of science or its cultivators in this country, and it was agreed that as the appointment of the Committee had been deferred until the next Session of Parliament with a view of permitting the question to be meanwhile maturely considered by scientific men, it was expedient that the subject should receive the early attention of the Council.

The Government Grant Committee were, therefore, requested to draw up a Report containing such suggestions as might occur to them, and present it to the Council after the recess.

This Report was presented on January 15, 1857, and contained numerous suggestions, one of which was "That the sum placed at the disposal of the Royal Society for the advancement of science be not necessarily limited to the annual Grant of £1000, when on any occasion special reasons may be signed for an additional sum." No such increase of the Grant was made, however, until nearly 20 years later, when (on April 29, 1876) a letter was received from the Lord President of the Council proposing "that further aid should be given to research by according permission to the Government Grant Committee to recommend in certain cases the payment of personal allowances to gentlemen during the time they are engaged in their investigations; that a sum of £5,000, including the above-mentioned £1000, should be taken annually; that the Royal Society should be invited to aid Her Majesty's Government with their advice and assistance in its appropriation and expenditure, and as to the sums to be granted in each case, reporting annually to the Lords of the Committee of Council on Education on the progress made and the desirability or non-desirability of renewing the Grant; and that this experiment should be tried for five years." The Lord President further proposed that "the administration and expenditure of the Grant, and accountability for it, should be vested in the Science and Art Department, that all instruments purchased for investigations should be left in its charge when no longer required," and that the presidents of certain societies "should be *ex-officio* members of the Government Grant Committee."

After some correspondence, it was finally agreed that the Grant of £1000 should remain as before, and that a vote of £4000 should be taken on the conditions expressed in the Lord President's letter.

For five years these two Grants ran concurrently, the Grant of £1000 being known as "The Government Grant," and the Grant of £4000 as "The Government Fund."

Four Sub-Committees were appointed to consider applications and report upon them to the General Committee, namely :—

    A. Mathematics, Physics, and Astronomy.
    B. Biology.
    C. Chemistry.
    D. General Purposes.

The General Committee, which was now called the Government Fund Committee, was constituted in the same way as before, with the addition of several more *ex-officio* members, the Presidents of the following Societies now forming the *ex-officio* list :—The Royal Society of Edinburgh, Royal Irish Academy, Royal Astronomical Society, Mathematical Society, Chemical Society, Linnean Society, Zoological Society, Geological Society, Physical Society, Institution of Civil Engineers, Institute of Mechanical Engineers, General Council of Medical Education, Royal College of Physicians, Royal College of Surgeons, and British Association. It was further agreed on November 30, 1877, that the Royal Society of Edinburgh and the Royal Irish Academy should each send an additional representative besides the President. The Committee, thus constituted, reported to the Council, with whom lay the final decision upon the recommendations.

On January 11, 1877, the Council received and adopted a code of Regulations which had been drawn up by Sub-Committee D. To these the Council, on their own initiative, added the further Rule: " That no proposition or application involving a Grant to an existing

Member of the Committee be entertained." At the next meeting it was reported that two Members of the Government Fund Committee had resigned their seats, as they intended to make applications; and that as one of them was an *ex-officio* Member, the Education Department had been consulted as to the manner in which the Lords of the Committee of Council on Education would wish the place of a Member *ex officio* who resigned to be supplied.

The Secretary of the Department, in reply, while indicating the way in which this should be done, stated that their Lordships trusted that this self-denying ordinance had not been adopted under any misapprehension of their own views or wishes. "They desire, it may be clearly understood, that they had no wish to impose such a rule as that stated in your letter. On the contrary—while fully appreciating the motives which probably induced the Royal Society to impose it—they cannot but express the regret which they would feel if it should lead to the loss of the services of some of the most active and distinguished men of science in aid of the distribution of a Grant which, being of a new and tentative character, peculiarly requires the support of those in whose judgment and knowledge the country would place the greatest reliance." The rule in question was not, however, at that time reversed.

The assignments recommended were each year submitted to the Science and Art Department for approval, and the question of the nature of the vouchers to be rendered having been raised, it was decided that " the receipt of the gentlemen to whom the payments are made will be accepted as a sufficient voucher, without receipts for all the details of the expenditure."

In the following year (1878) a difficulty began to be experienced by the Department in ascertaining when the investigations were completed, and when the instruments used in the investigations should be called in, and a letter was addressed to the Royal Society upon the subject. A circular was in consequence drawn up by the Society, requesting all who had received Grants to give account of their instruments, and the information thus obtained was communicated to the Department. The process of obtaining full and accurate account of instruments, and the question of when to call them in, have always been matters of some difficulty, which of late have been somewhat more successfully met by an annual return, which every grantee is required to make, and the information thus obtained is embodied in a Schedule of Instruments which was commenced in 1883.

III. Government Grant of £4000 a Year.

The Fund of £4000 a year (which had hitherto run concurrently with the Government Grant of £1000) having been initiated as a five years' experiment, a letter was addressed early in 1881 by the Science and Art Department to the Secretary of the Royal Society reminding him that the five years would soon come to an end, and asking for a Report upon the results of the experiment. A "Report by the President and Council" was accordingly drawn up, in which, after reciting the constitution and Regulations of the Fund, they furnished a table of the five years' Grants, with the following totals for the whole period:—

>Number of Applications, 417.
>Total Amount applied for, £50,401.
>Number of Applications recommended, 190.
>Amount for Personal Allowance, £7,800.
>Amount for Non-Personal Expenses, £11,800.
>Number of Grants above £100, 98.
>„   „   below £100, 92.

The report suggests that if unused balances, instead of reverting to the Treasury, "could be reserved and kept in hand, provision might be made for some larger purposes than those to which the Fund has hitherto been devoted;" and with respect to personal grants, while it does not suggest that these should be entirely discontinued, it does not recommend "the present method of administering them." Some correspondence between the Treasury, the Committee of Council on Education, and the Royal Society ensued, and it was finally agreed (March, 1882), (1) that the Grant of £1000, which had hitherto been provided under the Vote for Learned Societies, should be discontinued; (2) that the £4000 which had for the previous five years been provided under the Vote for the Science and Art Department should be replaced by a like sum "as a Grant in aid of the Royal Society;" (3) that this Grant should be managed by a reconstituted Government Grant Committee, and should be "primarily applicable to non-personal payments," but that the Committee should be "at liberty to recommend occasional personal payments from it, which, however, would only be made with the express sanction of the Treasury, obtained in every case;" (4) that accounts and vouchers of the expenditure should be rendered as in the case of the Grant for Meteorological purposes, the money being issued by the Treasury "only upon satisfactory evidence that previous grants had been spent to a sufficient extent, and that no excessive balance was being accumulated over a series of years."

In the correspondence concerning details which followed this general arrangement the Council again insisted, as they had done in 1855, that the Grant was not a Grant to the Royal Society, but to Science. "With regard to the title under which the Vote is proposed to be made," wrote the President, "inasmuch as the Society derives no pecuniary benefit from the Grant, but in administering it undertakes an onerous and difficult task, the President and Council would be glad if the terms could be so modified as to prevent any misapprehension with regard to this point on the part of the public." The Secretary of the Treasury, in his reply, called attention to the fact that "a Grant in aid means a Grant of which the detailed expenditure is not subject to the same detailed appropriation as the expenditure of an ordinary Grant," and that this was "the reason for using the expression here." Ultimately, in a Treasury Letter dated April 8, 1882, it was agreed that the estimate should be submitted to Parliament in the following terms:—

"A. Royal Society.
Grant for Scientific Investigations undertaken with the sanction of a Committee appointed for the purpose."

The question of detailed vouchers was authoritatively settled by the above-quoted letter, dated March 24, 1882, a decision which was confirmed by a letter dated May 7, 1885.

The constitution of the Government Grant General Committee under the new scheme was identical with that of the Government Fund Committee which it superseded, but the Sub-Committees under this scheme were:—

A. Mathematics, Physics, and Astronomy.
B. Biology and Geology.
C. Chemistry and Mineralogy.
D. For the revision of Personal Grants, recommended by the other Sub-Committees.

The Code of Regulations adopted at this time was amended and consolidated on December 6, 1883; and in January, 1887, Sub-Committees A and C were combined into one Sub-Committee, called "A—C."

In 1888 the Regulations were again under consideration, and on July 5 of that year a code, which is in the main the same as that now in force (see 'Year-book'), was adopted, and communicated to Her Majesty's Treasury, by whom it was approved.

In the letter accompanying this code, the Secretary drew the attention of My Lords to the fact that, whereas in 1882 their Lordships had laid it down that "no excessive balance was to be accumulated over a series of years," the Secretary of the Treasury had in 1885 stated, in answer to an appeal for a Grant in aid of observing the Solar Eclipse of 1886, that "My Lords desire to keep State aid to scientific investigations as much as possible within the limits of the £4000 per annum annually placed by Parliament at the disposal of the Government Grant Committee of the Royal Society."

The Secretary explained that it was in consequence of the desire thus expressed by their Lordships that it was now proposed to establish a Reserve Fund, not at any time to exceed £2000. The Secretary further drew attention to the substitution of several relatively small Boards for the previous large Sub-Committees; to the rule admitting extended Grants; to the special precautions under which personal Grants would be made, and which their Lordships would probably consider obviated the necessity of submitting each Grant for their Lordships' approval; and to the additions to the *ex-officio* list.

In 1894 the Council at the instance of the General Committee asked Her Majesty's Treasury to increase the amount of the Grant, but without success.

Some few amendments have been made in the Regulations since 1888. In March, 1894, Instructions for the Government Grant Boards were drawn up, and in February, 1895, Instructions for a Committee appointed for the purpose of administering a Grant. These will all be found in the 'Year-book.'

THE PUBLICATIONS OF THE ROYAL SOCIETY.

The current publications of the Society are three:—the 'Philosophical Transactions' (4to), the 'Proceedings' (8vo), and the 'Catalogue of Scientific Papers' (4to), to which must be added the 'List of Fellows' (4to), and 'The Year-Book of the Royal Society' (8vo), the first number of which for the session 1896–7 has been recently published. Besides these serials, monographs are occasionally issued by the Society, such as the 'Observations of the International Polar Expeditions, 1882-3--Fort Rae,' published in 1886; 'The Eruption of Krakatoa, and Subsequent Phenomena,' edited by G. J. Symons, F.R.S., &c., published in 1888; and 'A Monograph of the Horny Sponges,' by Dr. R. von Lendenfeld, published in 1889.

THE 'PHILOSOPHICAL TRANSACTIONS.'

Some account of the origin of the 'Philosophical Transactions' has already been given in the introductory sketch of the "Foundation and Early History of the Society" (p. 11). The original form was a small quarto with the title 'Philosophical Transactions: giving some Accompt of the present Undertakings, Studies, and Labours of the Ingenious in many considerable parts of the world.' In 1792 a larger quarto was introduced, and has been continued down to the present time. From 1887 the 'Transactions' have been divided into two series: Series A, containing Papers of a Mathematical or Physical character; and Series B, containing Papers of a Biological character. The papers which they comprise have also since 1875 been published in separate form. The volumes for 1817, 1818, 1820–22, are out of print; with these exceptions all the volumes since 1800 may still be obtained at prices which are advertised each year on the wrapper of the 'List of Fellows.' When the 'Transactions' in stock exceed 100, those preceding the last five years may be purchased by Fellows at one-third of the advertised price.

THE 'PROCEEDINGS OF THE ROYAL SOCIETY.'

At a meeting of Council on May 10, 1832, it was " Resolved—That the printing of the Abstracts of such papers as have been printed in the 'Philosophical Transactions' from the year 1800 inclusive be proceeded in; and that the Treasurer and Secretaries be requested to superintend the printing of the Abstracts." The first volume of these Abstracts, comprising the years 1800 to 1814, was published the same year, and the Abstracts for the years 1815 to 1830 in the year following.

Up to this point the series presents merely a collection of abstracts, arranged in the order of the full papers as they had been issued in the 'Philosophical Transactions;' but with the third volume a new order was adopted, the Abstracts being arranged under meetings and following the order in which the papers were read, and each meeting being headed by a brief account of the business which preceded the reading of the papers. The "short" title, in fact, becomes from this time onwards 'Proceedings of the Royal Society,' but the title page still stands, 'Abstracts of the Papers printed in the Philosophical Transactions,' a description which is not strictly accurate since, even so early in the series as the third volume, many Abstracts were published of papers which never appeared in the 'Philosophical Transactions.'

With the seventh volume (1854–55), a still further change began. Many papers were published in full in this and the subsequent volumes which were not published in the 'Philosopical Transactions' at all. These papers were for many years only the briefer or less important communications, the more bulky or more valuable papers being reserved for the quarto form. In time even this distinction became less marked, some papers of great importance appearing only in the 'Proceedings.' In this connection, it may be noted that the Statute (Chap. III, § 5), which stands in the edition of 1871 and previous editions, privileging "All who have become Fellows of the Society after

December the 11th, 1834, and who have contributed a paper, which has been printed *in the 'Philosophical Transactions'*" to compound for their annual contributions for the sum of Forty Pounds, instead of Sixty Pounds, disappears in the next edition; and in the year 1887 a further remnant of the distinction disappears by the removal from the List of Fellows of the marginal letter P, which had hitherto been placed against the names of those Fellows who had contributed a paper to the 'Philosophical Transactions.'

At the present time the 'Proceedings of the Royal Society' has reached the sixtieth volume. All the volumes are still in print except vols. 7, 9, 10, 14, and 15, and are sold at a uniform price of 21*s*. per volume, no reduction being made to the Fellows of the Society.

Catalogue of Scientific Papers.*

The Royal Society's 'Catalogue of Scientific Papers,' is the outcome of a movement which dates back nearly forty years. At the Glasgow meeting of the British Association which was held in 1855, a communication from Professor Henry, of Washington, was read, "containing a proposal for the publication of [a catalogue of] philosophical memoirs scattered throughout the Transactions of Societies in Europe and America, with the offer of co-operation on the part of the Smithsonian Institute." This proposal was referred to a Committee consisting of Mr. Cayley, Mr. Grant, and Professor (now Sir George Gabriel) Stokes; and their report was presented next year at the Cheltenham meeting of the Association. The scheme set forth in this report was that of a catalogue embracing only the mathematical and physical sciences, but comprising a subject catalogue as well as a catalogue according to the names of authors. There were to be paid editors, "familiar with the several great branches respectively of the sciences to which the catalogue relates," and the work was to include, besides Transactions and Proceedings of Societies, journals, ephemerides, volumes of observations, and "other collections not coming under any of the preceding heads."

In this form the scheme came came before the Royal Society in March, 1857, General Sabine having requested, on the part of the British Association, the co-operation of the Society in the undertaking. The scheme, after discussion, was narrowed to a *manuscript* catalogue, the question of printing being deferred; it was to be a catalogue of periodical works in the Royal Society's library only; the suggested American co-operation, moreover, was dispensed with, and the work undertaken at the Society's own charge. In one important respect, however, the scheme was greatly widened, for the idea of confining the catalogue to the mathematical and physical

---

* Reprinted in part from 'Nature,' vol. 45, p. 338.

sciences, which had been put forward in the report to the British Association, was abandoned, and it was decided "that all the sciences should be comprehended." The tentative restrictions were, of course, finally relaxed. It was resolved to extend the indexing to works in other libraries not contained in the library of the Royal Society; and in 1864, when the question of printing had to be determined, it was decided to offer the Catalogue to Government for publication.

The cost to the Society of compiling the material for the first series of the Catalogue was considerable, and many of the Fellows had spent no small amount of time, not only in superintending the progress of the work at home, but in corresponding with Academies abroad, with the view of making the list of serials to be catalogued as complete as might be. It was therefore with some reason that the Lords of the Treasury, in resolving to print the Catalogue at the public expense, stated that they had regard "to the importance of the work, with reference to the promotion of scientific knowledge generally, to the high authority of the source from which it comes, and to the labour gratuitously given by members of the Royal Society for its production." The printing of this first series of the Catalogue covering the scientific serials from the year 1800 to 1863, was commenced by the Stationery Office in 1866, seven Fellows of the Royal Society undertaking to read the proof-sheets gratuitously. The sixth and last volume of the series, completing the alphabet, was issued in 1872.

An additional decade of serials, embracing the years 1864–73, containing about 99,000 titles, and filling two additional quarto volumes (vols. 7 and 8), was completed in January 1876, and published by Her Majesty's Stationery Office in 1879. But when the next decade neared completion it was found, that, even keeping the Catalogue on the old lines, and making no considerable addition to the number of serials catalogued, ten years of memoirs, which formerly filled two volumes, would now fill three; and an additional difficulty arose from the fact that the Treasury now informed the Society that the "'Catalogue of Scientific Papers' would not be continued as a publication of the Stationery Office." Parliament voted, however, a gift towards the charges of publication, and a portion of this gift, supplemented by the Royal Society's own funds, was devoted to the issue of vol. 9, which the Cambridge University Press, aided by a subsidy from the Society, published in 1891. The question how to meet the expense of future volumes was, however, still an unsolved problem until in December, 1892, Dr. Ludwig Mond made the Society the handsome donation of £2000 to assist in carrying on the Catalogue and Index. Partly by aid of this gift, vol. 10 was published in 1894, and vol. 11, completing the decade 1874—83, last year.

In addition to the foregoing, the President and Council have determined to issue a supplementary volume, in which will be catalogued all the most important papers that have appeared from 1800 to 1883 in periodicals not hitherto indexed, and the copy for this volume is now in an advanced stage of preparation. The work for the decade 1883-94 has also made some progress.

The question of a Subject Catalogue has been often considered, and the Society have actually on foot a Subject Index to the existing Catalogue. The preliminary preparation of the copy, involving the reduction of all the titles to one language, is now far advanced, and the scheme of classification is under consideration. A portion of Dr. Ludwig Mond's gift, which has been mentioned above, is devoted to this branch of the work, and in June, 1894, he supplemented this important aid by the still more munificent promise to contribute one-half of the total expenditure upon the Index in excess of that portion of his former gift already devoted to this purpose, provided the Society or others are willing to contribute the remainder of such sum (see p. 120). By this means the Index to the Catalogue will doubtless in due time become an accomplished fact, and thus the whole series from 1800 to 1883, under Authors and Subjects, be completed. And the Society looks forward to being able to continue the whole work up to the year 1900, at which date it is to be hoped that an international organization, the consideration of which was the subject of an international conference held at the instance of the Royal Society in July of last year, may take it up.

THE LIBRARY.

On the 2nd January, 1666-7, Mr. Henry Howard (afterwards sixth Duke of Norfolk) presented the Royal Society with "the Library of Arundel House, to dispose thereof as their property, desiring only that in case the Society should come to faile, it might return to Arundel House; and that this inscription, *Ex dono Henrici Howard Norfolciensis*, might be put upon every book given them." "The Society," it is added, "received this noble donation with all thankfullnesse, and ordered that Mr. Howard should be registered as a benefactor." This gift may be regarded as the nucleus of the Society's Library.

A considerable part of the Arundel Library came originally from the collection of Matthias Corvinus, King of Hungary, a portion of which, after his death, passed into the possession of the celebrated Bilibald Pirckheimer, of Nuremberg, who died in 1530. This portion was purchased by Howard's grandfather, Thomas, Earl of Arundel, during his embassy at Vienna; and it consisted of a great number of printed books and many rare and valuable manuscripts.* It may be mentioned that several of the books, which are still in the Society's possession, contain Bilibald Pirckheimer's book-plate, designed by Albrecht Dürer.

An entry in the Council Minutes of May 18, 1681, shows that the Arundel Library was at that time kept separate from the other books, and it probably remained so for many years. The volumes were afterwards, however, distributed according to subjects, and in process of time many were disposed of. Sales of books were made in 1713. 1745, and at subsequent dates. On June 20, 1872, the Council, on the recommendation of the Library Committee, resolved " to dispose of superfluous books from the collection of works on 'Miscellaneous Literature,'" and these probably included many 'Arundel books.' The most valuable of the printed books of purely literary interest retained by the Society were in 1883 collected together, under the superintendence of the Treasurer, Sir John Evans, in a case made for the purpose. They include a copy of Caxton's Chaucer, and two volumes, printed on vellum, by Fust and Schœffer, named the 'Liber Sextus Decretalium cum glossis' (A.D. 1465), and Cicero's 'Officia et Paradoxa' (A.D. 1466); a very perfect example of Albrecht Dürer's 'Historia Mariæ, Passio Domini, et Apocalipsis,' in one volume (A.D. 1511); a copy of the 'Nuremburg Chronicle'; a very fine copy of 'Euclidis Elementa,' Editio Princeps (Venetiis. Ratdolt, 1482) with illuminated initials; a number of Editiones Principes of the Latin Classics, including many Aldines, a large collection of Luther's and of scarce Reformation tracts, and many other works of literary or typographical interest.

The bulk of the Arundel Manuscripts was sold to the Trustees of the British Museum in 1830 for the sum of £3559, the proceeds being devoted to the purchase of scientific books; these Manuscripts are still kept in the British Museum as a separate collection. A catalogue of all the manuscripts and printed books originally given to the Society by Henry Howard of Norfolk was printed in 1681, and a copy of the same is in the Society's Library.

The scientific books in the Library probably number about 60,000 volumes. In the purchase of books, special attention has for many years past been paid to scientific serials; and the collection of Journals and of the Transactions of Scientific Societies is now a very large one. The Council annually votes a sum of £400 for the purchase and binding of books.

* Weld's 'History,' vol. 1, p. 196.

A Catalogue of the Scientific Books in two octavo volumes is on sale. Part I (1881) containing Transactions, Journals, &c., 5s.; Part II (1883), General Science, 15s. A reduction on these prices is made to Fellows. A List of Additions to the Library made during the year will be found in the 'Year-book.'

The Regulations for the use of the Library are contained in Statutes, Chap. XIV, §§ 7—11 (see 'Year-book'); but the Council have under consideration the issue of more detailed Standing Orders. The books lent out are called in by order of Council usually once a year, at the beginning of the Long Vacation; and, during the month of August, no book is allowed to leave the house, though the Library is kept open for purposes of reference.

Besides the printed books, the Library contains a rich collection of scientific correspondence, official records, and other manuscripts, including the original MS., with Newton's autograph corrections, from which the first edition of the 'Principia' was printed; the celebrated MS. volume of the 'Commercium Epistolicum,' relating to the Leibnitz-Newton controversy on the priority of the invention of fluxions; the MS. of John Aubrey's 'Memoires of Naturall Remarques in the County of Wilts,' written in 1685; a collection of over 300 letters by Leeuwenhoek; a collection of letters and manuscripts by Malpighi; a collection of letters by Henry Oldenburgh and Dr. J. Beale written to Robert Boyle; Henry Oldenburgh's commonplace book containing drafts of his letters to Milton and to Robert Boyle; the autograph MS. of Wallis's 'Treatise on Logic,' published in the folio edition of his works; a large album containing original letters, portraits, and other memorials of Joseph Priestley, collected by James Yates, &c. Many of the manuscripts and most of the MS. letters are given in the 'Catalogue of Miscellaneous Manuscripts,' compiled by the late J. O. Halliwell-Phillipps, F.R.S., in 1840, which is on sale (price 2s.). Among the series not there catalogued are 'The Boyle Papers,' bound in fifty-three volumes, the 'Letter Books,' containing copies of the early scientific correspondence from the foundation of the Society to the end of the 17th century, the 'Register Book' of the Royal Society, containing copies of scientific memoirs communicated to the Society from 1661 to 1738, in twenty-one volumes; the 'Journal Book,' containing minutes of the Society's meetings from 1660 to the present time; the 'Council Minutes' from the foundation of the Society; and a series of guard-books, containing the original MSS. of early memoirs communicated to the Society, arranged under subjects. The MSS. of the 'Philosophical Transactions' and 'Proceedings,' and the papers read before the Society but not published, are bound into volumes and preserved for reference, as, also, are the "Certificates of Candidature," in which the qualifications of candidates are stated, and to which the signatures of supporters are attached.

All the above-mentioned MSS., and others not here specified, are open to the inspection of Fellows, but the loan of them is exclusively vested in the Council.

INSTRUMENTS AND HISTORICAL RELICS IN THE POSSESSION OF THE ROYAL SOCIETY.

Relics of Sir Isaac Newton.

1. Solar Dial cut in stone, made by the hand of Sir Isaac Newton when a boy, taken out in 1844 from the wall of the Manor House at Woolsthorpe, in which he was born, and presented the same year to the Royal Society by the Rev. Chas. Turnor, F.R.S., to whose family the house belonged.
2. Two rules made of the wood of Sir Isaac Newton's apple tree at Woolsthorpe. *Presented by Rev. Chas. Turnor, F.R.S.*
3. Original Reflecting Telescope of Sir Isaac Newton, made with his own hands, in 1671. ('Phil. Trans.,' vol. 7. p. 4004.) *Presented to the Royal Society by Messrs. Heath and Wing, Math. Inst. Makers, Strand, London; Feb. 6, 1766.* 4 parts.
4. The MS. of the 'Principia,' from which the First Edition was printed, with autograph corrections by Sir Isaac Newton.
5. An autograph order, dated July 27, 1720, addressed by Sir Isaac Newton to Dr. John Francis Ffouquier, directing him to apply certain sums belonging to Newton in purchasing, on Newton's account, South Sea Stock. *Presented by Dr. Wollaston, P.R.S.*
6. The original mask of Newton's face, which belonged to Roubiliac, from the cast taken after death. *Presented in 1839 by Prof. Hunter Christie, Sec. R.S.*
7. Sir Isaac Newton's Watch.
8. A lock of Sir I. Newton's Hair. *Presented by Henry Garling, Oct. 25, 1847.*
9. Armchair, formerly belonging to Sir Isaac Newton. Bequeathed in 1812 to Richard Saumarez. *Bequeathed to the Royal Society in 1891 by the late Mr. Thomas Kerslake, of Clevedon.*

Other Relics and Instruments.

1. Air-pump, with double barrel. *Presented to the Royal Society by the Hon. Robert Boyle, in 1662.*

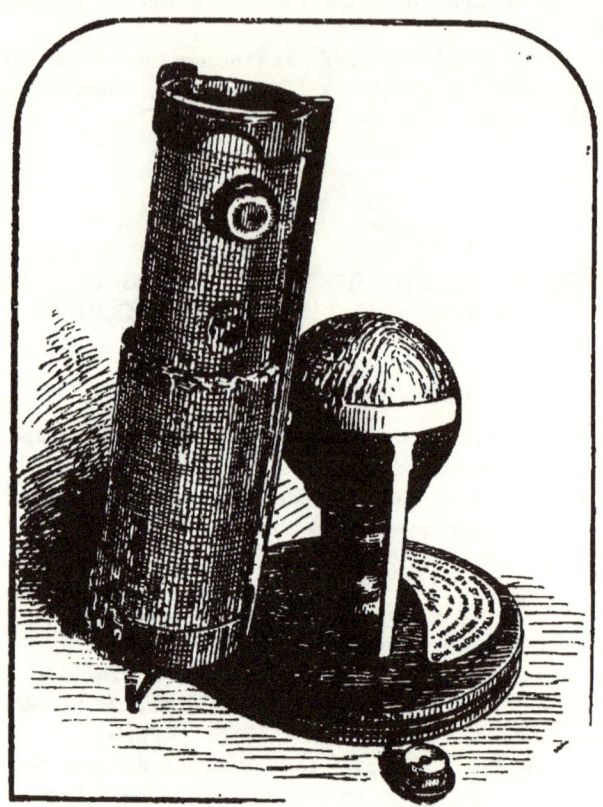

SIR ISAAC NEWTON'S REFLECTING TELESCOPE.

2. Sir William Petty's Double-bottomed boat.

"Upon the reading of a letter, sent out of Ireland to the Secretary, concerning the expectation, which the Committee, that heretofore had given the Society an Account of Sr William Petty's new ship, did entertain for hearing the sense of the Society thereupon, it was

"Ordered, That the Committtee should be put in minde by the Secretary that the Matter of Navigation, being a State-concerne, was not proper to be managed by the Society; And that Sr William Petty, for his private satisfaction, may, when he pleases, have the sense (if he hath it not already) of particular Members of the Society, concerning his new Invention."—*Council Minutes*, May 27, 1663.

"The Papers of the next Philosophical Transactions, having been considered of, and the account therein given concerning the Structure and Advantages of Sr William Petty's Double-bottom'd ship; it was resolved, that the publication of them should be differed, till his Ma^{ty} had been made acquainted with the particulars therein, relating to the said ship."—*Council Minutes*, April 26, 1665.

3. Open Cistern Mercurial Barometer, by Ramsden.
'Phil. Trans.,' 1776, p. 383.
4. Open Cistern Mercurial Barometer, by Newman, under the direction of Mr. Daniell. 'Meteorological Essays.'
5. Open Cistern Mercurial Barometer, by Newman, under the direction of Sir H. Davy, with an Iron Plunging Cylinder, compensating for difference of capacities.
6. Mercurial Standard Thermometer, by Dollond. Brass divided scale, $23\frac{1}{2}$ inches long, with divisions extending from 20° below, to 535° above zero, Fahrenheit.
7. Mercurial Standard Thermometer, by Troughton and Simms. Brass divided scale, 15 inches long; divisions from zero to 215° F.
8. Wedgwood's Pyrometer; or Thermometer for measuring high degrees of heat. 66 parts.
'Phil. Trans.,' 1782, p. 305; 1784, p. 358; 1786, p. 390.
9. Captain Kater's Hygrometer, by Robinson.
10. Jones's Hygrometer, with the stem bent at an acute angle.
'Phil. Trans.,' 1826, p. 53.
11. Hydrometer, by Fordyce.
12. Huygens's Aërial Telescope.

(1) An object-glass of 122 feet focal length, with an eye-glass of 6 inches, and original apparatus for adjustment, made by Huygens, and presented by him to the Royal Society in 1691.
(2) The apparatus for using Huygens's object-glass, constructed by Hooke.
(3) Additional apparatus, by Dr. Pound. *Presented by Dr. Bradley.*
(4) Ditto, by Mr. Cavendish.

} 12 parts.

13. An Object-glass by Huygens, of 170 feet focal length. *Presented to the Royal Society by Sir Isaac Newton, P.R.S.*
14. An Object-glass by Huygens, with two eye-glasses by Scarlet, for a Telescope of 210 feet. *Presented by the Rev. Gilbert Burnet, M.A., F.R.S., in 1724.*
15. An Object-glass (Venetian), of 90 feet focal length: which belonged to Flamsteed. *Presented to the Royal Society by James Hodgson, F.R.S., in 1737.*
16. A 10-inch Protractor, by Ramsden; with vernier to 1'.
17. Convertible Pendulum of Captain Kater; with the Agate Planes.
The basis of the present system of British Weights and Measures.
'Phil. Trans.,' 1818, p. 37.
18. Copy of the Imperial Standard Yard, by Dollond.
'Phil. Trans.,' 1831, p. 345.

19. A brass standard of Length, marked
    Exch\vphantom{}^{r}. Standard, Hen. VII. 1490.
    Exch\vphantom{}^{r}. Standard, Eliz. 1588.
20. Trigonometer, by Bowles. 4 parts.
21. Repeating Circle, of one foot diameter, by Troughton.
    Employed by Captain Kater at the principal Stations of the Trigonometrical Survey. 'Phil. Trans.,' 1819, p. 339.
22. Chronometer, by Arnold.
23. Chronometer, by Arnold.
    Both these Chronometers accompanied Captain Cook on his second and third Voyages.
24. A 12-inch Dipping Needle, by Nairne and Blunt. 2 parts.
    'Phil. Trans.,' 1776, p. 395.
25. A 12-inch Variation Needle. *Ibid.*, p. 385.
26. A Magnetic Variation Needle, with Vernier Microscopes, by Jones; for making observations on the influence of the Aurora Borealis upon the Magnetic Needle.
27. Dr. Gowin Knight's Battery of Magnets. *Presented to the Royal Society by Dr. John Fothergill in 1776.*
    Re-arranged in 1828 by Captain Beaufort and Mr. Barlow.
28. Armed Loadstone.
    Grew's "Catalogue of Rarities" (p. 364) mentions an *Orbicular Loadstone, or Ter[r]ella*, given by Sir Christopher Wren, the size of which, so far as the stone is concerned, agrees with the above; it is conjectured that it may be the same.
29. A Galvanic Battery, made by Dr. Wollaston, in a tailor's thimble. *Presented to the Royal Society by Sir A. W. Franks, June 28, 1879.*
    In a letter to the late William Spottiswoode, P.R.S., which accompanied this present, Sir (then Mr.) Augustus Wollaston Franks says that this little battery was given by his godfather, Dr. Wollaston, to his mother then Miss Sebright. See also an anecdote about this battery in Weld's 'History of the Royal Society,' vol. 2, p. 309.
30. Dr. Priestley's Electrical Machine.
31. Curious Steel Callipers for very accurate measurement, by Paull of Geneva: 1777.
32. Rowning's Universal Constructor of Equations.
    'Phil. Trans.,' 1770, p. 240.
33. The original model for Davy's Safety Lamp.

And other Instruments of less interest.

LIST OF PORTRAITS AND BUSTS IN THE APARTMENTS OF THE SOCIETY*.

⁎ Where the entries after a name are incomplete, particulars are wanting.

Subject.	Description.	Painter, Engraver, or Sculptor.	Donor.	Date of gift.
1. Amici, Giovanni Battista	Photograph	..	Sir C. Wheatstone, F.R.S.	1876
2. Arnott, Neil, F.R.S.	Crayon drawing	Mrs. Carpenter	Mrs. Arnott	1874
3. Arundel, Thomas Howard, Earl of	Oil painting	T. Murray	Sir Isaac Newton, P.R.S.	
4. Aston, Francis, Sec. R.S.	Ditto	F. Kerseboom		
5. Bacon, Sir Francis, Lord Chancellor	Ditto	P. van Somer, on panel	Martin Folkes, Esq., P.R.S.	1754
6. Baily, Francis, F.R.S.	Mezzotinto engraving	T. Lupton, after T. Phillips, R.A.	Rev. R. Sheepshanks	1846
7. Banks, Sir Joseph, Bart., P.R.S.	Oil painting	T. Phillips, R.A.	Don Jose de Mendoza y Rios	1818
8. Ditto	Marble bust	Sir F. Chantrey, R.A.	Sir F. Chantrey, R.A.	1819
9. Barrow, Sir John, Bart., F.R.S.	Oil painting	S. Pearce	J. Barrow, Esq., F.R.S.	1866
10. Bavaria, Charles Theodore, Duke of	Ditto	..	Duke of Bavaria	1785
11. Birch, Thomas, D.D., F.R.S.	Ditto	J. Wills		
12. Boyle, Hon. Robert, F.R.S.	Ditto	F. Kerseboom	Executors of Mr. Boyle	1692
13. Ditto	Ditto	Sir G. Kneller	Sir C. Wheatstone, F.R.S.	1876
14. Ditto	Ditto			
15. Bradley, James, D.D., F.R.S.	Ditto	J. Richardson	Rev. — Peach	1790
16. Brahe, Tycho	Ditto	M. J. Mierevelt		
17. Brodie, Sir Benjamin C., Bart., P.R.S.	Ditto	A. Thompson, after G. F. Watts, R.A.	Sir B. C. Brodie, Bart.	1873
18. Ditto.	Plaster bust	Original model of the bust by W. Behnes	Sir B. C. Brodie, Bart.	1867
19. Brouncker, Viscount, P.R.S.	Oil painting	Sir P. Lely	Viscount Brouncker	
20. Buchanan, George	Ditto	F. Pourbus, Sen.	T. Povey, Esq.	
21. Buckland, Rev. William, F.R.S.	Mezzotinto engraving	S. Cousins, R.A., after T. Phillips, R.A.	Sir C. Wheatstone, F.R.S.	1876
22. Buissière, Paul, For. Mem. R.S.	Oil painting	T. Gainsborough (?)	Peter Buissière, Esq., F.R.S.	

* Reprinted from the 'Proceedings of the Royal Society,' vol. 50, with additions.

Subject.	Description.	Painter, Engraver, or Sculptor.	Donor.
23. Burney, Dr., F.R.S.	Plaster bust		
24. Burrow, Sir James, P.R.S.	Oil painting	J. B. Van Loo	Sir J. Burrow
25. Chandler, Samuel, D.D., F.R.S.	Oil painting.	M. Chamberlain	Executors of Mr. John Chandler, F.R.S.
26. Chardin, Sir John, F.R.S.	Ditto		G. Handford, Esq.
27. Charles II., King, Founder and Patron	Ditto	Sir P. Lely	
28. Ditto	Marble bust	J. Nollekens	Ordered by the Council R.S.
29. Children, John George, Sec. R S.	Oil painting	S. Pearce (?) *	Dr. J. E. Gray, F.R.S.
30. Clift, William, F.R.S.	Ditto	H. Schmidt	Mrs. Owen
31. Colwall, Daniel, F.R.S.	Ditto		D. Colwall, Esq.
32. Combe, Taylor, Sec. R.S.	Ditto	Joseph (?) ‡	Dr. J. E. Gray, F.R.S.
33. Copernicus, Nicholas	Ditto (on panel)	Lorman of Berlin, from an original portrait (see 'Phil. Trans.,' vol. lxvii, p. 33)	Dr. Wolf
34. Cuvier, Georges	Bronze bust		P. J. David, Esq.
35. Dalton, John, F.R.S.	Oil painting	B. R. Faulkner	A Memorial Committee
36. Darwin, Charles, F.R.S.	Etching	P. Rajon, after W. W. Ouless, R.A.	
37. Ditto	Photograph (small oval)		Major Darwin
38. Ditto	Bronze medallion	Allan Wyon	
39. Darwin, Erasmus, F.R.S.	Medallion, in Wedgwood		J. Evans, Esq., Treas. R.S.
40. Davy, Sir Humphry, Bart., P.R.S.	Oil painting	Sir T. Lawrence, P.R.A.	Lady Davy
41. Ditto	Photograph of the statue at Penzance		W. J. Henwood, Esq., F.R.S.
42. Ditto	Wax medallion	J. Tayler	
43. De la Beche, Sir Henry Thomas, F.R.S.	Mezzotinto engraving	W. Walker, after H. P. Bone	Sir C. Wheatstone, F.R.S.

* The portrait of Mr. Children was long in his possession, and given to me by him v left the British Museum. I have failed as yet in getting any clue as to the painter of the I have an idea that it was Mr. Pearce, who afterwards painted the Arctic people. (Lett the donor, Aug. 4, 1873.)

† Included in a list printed in 1834.

‡ The portrait of Mr. Combe was given to me by Mr. Charles Tooke, his nephew, the his sister and T. Tooke, Esq., the author of 'Prices.' Mr. Combe married the daug Dr. E. W. Gray, Sec. R.S., my uncle. I believe the portrait is by Joseph, who painted family. (Letter from donor, Aug., 1873.)

List of Portraits and Busts. 177

Subject.	Description.	Painter, Engraver, or Sculptor.	Donor.	Date of gift.
44. Derham, Rev. William, D.D., F.R.S.	Oil painting	G. White	G. Scott, Esq.	*
45. Descartes, René	Ditto	F. Hals	Dr. Maty	1776
45a. Dollond, George, F.R.S.	Marble bust	— Garland	A. W. Dollond, Esq.	1894
46. Dollond, John, F.R.S.	Oil painting	W. F. Witherington, R.A.	G. Dollond, Esq., F.R.S.	1842
47. Ditto	Marble bust	— Garland	G. Dollond, Esq., F.R.S.	1843
48. Euler, Leonard	Plaster medallion			
49. Evans, John, Treas. R.S.	Bronze medallion	..	John Evans, Esq.	1889
50. Evelyn, John, Sec. R.S.	Oil painting	F. Kerseboom (?)	Mrs. Evelyn	*
51. Fairbairn, Sir William, F.R.S.	Ditto	B. R. Faulkner	Sir W. Fairbairn	1874
52. Ditto	Marble bust	P. Park	T. Fairbairn, Esq.	1862
53. Falconer, Hugh, F.R.S.	Ditto	T. Butler	A Memorial Committee	1866
54. Faraday, Michael, F.R.S.	Oil painting	A. Blaikley (painted between 1851 and 1855)	J. P. Gassiot, Esq., F.R.S.	1873
55. Ditto	Mezzotinto engraving	S. Cousins, R.A., after H. W. Pickersgill, R.A.	J. P. Gassiot, Esq., F.R.S.	1876
56. Ditto	Lithograph	..	Sir C. Wheatstone, F.R.S.	1876
57. Ditto	Marble bust	M. Noble	H. Bence Jones, Esq., F.R.S.	1873
58. Ditto	Plaster bust	J. H. Foley, R.A.	Purchased by the Council, R.S.	1885
59. Flamsteed, Rev. John, F.R.S.	Oil painting	T. Gibson	John Belchier, Esq.	[1785†]
60. Ditto	Ditto	T. Gibson (?)		*
61. Folkes, Martin, P.R.S.	Ditto	W. Hogarth	Martin Folkes, Esq.	
62. Ditto	Plaster bust	..	Earl Stanhope	1871
63. Fontenelle, Bernard le Bovier de, For. Mem. R.S.	Oil painting	H. Rigaud	Dr. Maty, F.R.S.	1776
64. Forbes, Edward, F.R.S.	Plaster bust	J. G. Lough	Miss Lough-Bishop	1889
65. Franklin, Benjamin, F.R.S.	Oil painting	..	Caleb Whitefoord, Esq.	1790
66. Ditto	Plaster bust	..	Earl Stanhope	1871
67. Franklin, Sir John, F.R.S.	Lithograph	J. H. Maguire, after Negelin	Sir C. Wheatstone, F.R.S.	1876

* Included in a list printed in 1834.
† The date of a reference to the gift (Council Minutes, vol. 7, p. 231).

Subject.	Description.	Painter, Engraver, or Sculptor.	Donor.	Date of gift.
68. Gale, Thomas, D.D., Sec. R.S.	Oil painting	J. Riley (?)		*
69. Galileo Galilei	Ditto	After J. Sustermans	Purchased	
70. Gassendi, Pierre	Ditto		Dr. Paget, F.R.S.	*
71. George III., King, Patron	Marble bust	J. Nollekens	Ordered by the Council R.S.	1773
72. Gilbert, Davies, P.R.S.	Oil painting	T. Phillips, R.A.	Davies Gilbert, Esq.	1834
73. Ditto	Marble bust	R. Westmacott, R.A.	The Baroness Basset	1844
74. Graham, Thomas, F.R.S.	Mezzotinto engraving	J. Faed, after J. G. Gilbert	Sir C. Wheatstone, F.R.S.	1876
75. Gray, Edward Whittaker, Sec. R.S.	Oil painting	Sir A. Calcott, R.A.	Sir A. Calcott	1830
76. Gray, John Edward, F.R.S.	Ditto	Mrs. Carpenter	The Botanical Society	1859
77. Haak, Theodore, F.R.S.	Ditto	J. Richardson		
78. Haller. Albert von, For. Mem. R.S.	Ditto	C. von Stoppelaer	Dr. Sharpey, F.R.S.	1877
78a. Ditto	Ditto		Sir J. Paget, F.R.S.	1892
79. Halley, Edmund, Sec. R.S.	Ditto	M. Dahl (?)		*
80. Ditto	Ditto	T. Murray (?)		*
81. Harvey, William, M.D.	Ditto	De Reyn	Dr. Mappletorf	*
82. Herschel, Sir John F. W., Bart., F.R.S.	Oil painting	C. A. Jensen	John Evans, Esq., Treas. R.S.	1877
83. Hey, William, F.R.S.	Plaster bust	(Chantrey executed a marble bust from this plaster)	Rev. J. B. Reade, F.R.S.	1864
84. Hobbes, Thomas	Oil painting	W. Dobson†	Dr. Paget, F.R.S. (?)	*
85. Ditto	Ditto	After W. Dobson	∴	*
86. Holland, Sir Henry, F.R.S.	Lithograph		Sir C. Wheatstone, F.R.S.	1876
87. Holman, Lieut. James, F.R.S.	Oil painting	G. Chinnery	Bequeathed by Lieut. Holman	1858
88. Home, Sir Everard, Bart., P.R.S.	Ditto	T. Phillips, R.A.	Sir E. Home, Bart.	
89. Hood, Thomas	Plaster bust	E. Davis	E. Davis, Esq.	1867
90. Hooker, Sir Joseph Dalton, P.R.S.	Oil painting	Hon. J. Collier	From sixty-eight Fellows, R.S.	1881
91. Humboldt. F. H. Alexander von, For. Mem. R.S.	Bronze statuette			
92. Hunter, John, F.R.S.	Oil painting	R. Home‡	Sir E. Home, Bart.	1850

* Included is a list printed in 1834.
† See Aubrey's 'Letters written by Eminent Persons,' vol. 2, Part II, p. 682, where he mentions a portrait of Hobbes by J. B. Gaspars as presented to the Society.
‡ The dog in this picture is mentioned in 'Phil. Trans.,' vol. 77, p. 257.

List of Portraits and Busts.

Subject.	Description.	Painter, Engraver, or Sculptor.	Donor.	Date of gift.
93. Huxham, John, M.D., F.R.S.	Oil painting	T. Rennel	J. C. Huxham, Esq., F.R.S.	
94. Huxley, Thomas Henry, P.R.S.	Etching (remarque proof)	L. Flemeng, after Hon. J. Collier	Fine Art Society	1885
95. Joule, James Prescott, F.R.S.	Oil painting	Hon. J. Collier	From a number of Fellows, R.S.	1883
95a. Ditto	Plaster bust		B. A. Joule, Esq.	1893
96. Jurin, James, M.D., Sec. R.S.	Oil painting		Rev. W. A. Totton	1868
97. Laplace, Pierre Simon de, For. Mem. R.S.	Plaster bust			
98. Leibnitz, Gottfried Wilhelm, For. Mem. R.S.	Oil painting		Dr. Wilson	1883
99. Liebig, Justus von For. Mem. R.S.	Photograph		Sir C. Wheatstone, F.R.S.	1876
100. Locke, John, F.R.S.	Oil painting	After Sir G. Kneller	J. Belchier, Esq.	1785
101. Lyell, Sir Charles, F.R.S.	Marble bust	W. Theed, after J. Gibson, R.A.	Leonard Lyell, Esq.	1878
102. Macclesfield, Earl of, P.R.S.	Oil painting	T. Hudson (?)	Earl of Macclesfield	1754
103. M'Culloch, John, M.D., F.R.S.	Ditto	B. R. Faulkner	Bequeathed by Mrs. M'Culloch	
104. Malpighi, Marcello, For. Mem. R.S.	Ditto	A. M. Tobar	Signor Malpighi	
105. Mantell, Gideon Algernon, F.R.S.	Ditto	J. J. Masquerier	W. Mantell, Esq.	1859
106. Maskelyne, Nevil, D.D., F.R.S.	Ditto	A. Vanderburgh	Mrs. Mervin Storey	
107. Moivre, Abraham de, F.R.S.	Ditto	J. Highmore	E. Wortley Montague, Esq.	
108. Moll, ——	Lithograph	H. W. Couwenberg	Sir C. Wheatstone, F.R.S.	1876
109. More, Henry, D.D., F.R.S.	Oil painting	Sir P. Lely	Dr. Paget, F.R.S.	
110. Murchison, Sir Roderick Impey, F.R.S.	Mezzotinto engraving	W. Walker, after W. H. Pickersgill, R.A.	Sir C. Wheatstone, F.R.S.	1876
111. Newton, Sir Isaac, P.R.S.	Oil painting	C. Jervas	Sir I. Newton	
112. Ditto	Ditto	J. Vanderbank*	C. B. Vignoles, Esq., F.R.S.	1841
113. Ditto	Ditto	J. Vanderbank	Martin Folkes, Esq., P.R.S.	
114. Ditto	Mezzotinto engraving	J. Faber, after Vanderbank	R. Mallet, Esq.	1882
115. Ditto	Ditto	After Vanderbank	Rev. J. A. Edleston	1851
116. Ditto	Steel engraving	T. O. Barlow, R.A., after Sir G. Kneller	Dr. S. Crompton	1866
117. Ditto	Pencil drawing (signed D. L. Marchant)			

* Painted the year before Newton died.

Subject.	Description.	Painter, Engraver, or Sculptor.	Dono
118. Newton, Sir Isaac, P.R.S.	Lithograph ..	— Baldrey, after L. F. Roubiliac's statue at Trinity College, Cambridge	Rev. C. F.R.S.
119. Ditto	Marble bust ..	L. F. Roubiliac	..
120. Ditto	Plaster statuette	W. Theed.. ..	J. Winter,
121. Ditto	Ditto	H. J. Jones, after L. F. Roubiliac's statue at Trinity College, Cambridge	
122. Northampton, Spencer J. A. Compton, Marquess of, P.R.S.	Oil painting ..	T. Phillips, R.A...	Marquess o ampton
123. Oersted, Jens Christian, For. Mem. R.S.	Plaster bust ..	Bissen, of Copenhagen	Miss Harn
124. Oldenburg, Henry, Sec. R.S.	Oil painting ..	J. van Cleef ..	Purchased
125. Paget, Sir James, Bart., F.R.S.	Steel engraving	T. O. Barlow, R.A., after J. E. Millais, R.A.	T. O. Barl
126. Paget, Thomas, D.D.	Ditto	Mary Beale (?)	
127. Peacock, George, Dean of Ely, F.R.S.	Oil painting ..	D. Y. Blakiston ..	A Comm Subscrit
128. Pepys, Samuel, P.R.S.	Ditto	Sir G. Kneller ..	S. Pepys,
129. Pirogoff, ——.. ..	Photograph		
130. Price, Richard, D.D. F.R.S.	Oil painting ..	B. West, P.R.A. ..	Bequeathe Morgan F.R.S.
131. Priestley, Joseph, F.R.S.	Photograph (from a portrait)	..	Sir C. Wh F.R.S.
132. Pringle, Sir John, F.R.S.	Oil painting ..	Sir J. Reynolds, P.R.A.	Sir J. Pri
133. Ramsden, Jesse, F.R.S.	Ditto	R. Home	Sir E. Ho
134. Rennell, James Major, F.R.S.	Wax relief ..	— Hagbolt ..	Sir J. D. F.R.S.
135. Ditto	Porcelain medallion		
136. Ronalds, Sir Francis, F.R.S.	Plaster bust ..	E. Davis	S. Carter,
137. Ross, Sir James Clark, R.N., F.R.S.	Lithograph ..	After Negelen ..	Lieut.-Co
138. Rosse, William Parsons, Earl of, F.R.S.	Oil painting ..	J. Catterson Smith	Earl of R
139. Sabine, General Sir Edward, P.R.S.	Ditto	S. Pearce	Mrs. Sabi

* The date of a reference to the gift (Council Minutes, vol. 7, p. 231).
† Included in a list printed in 1834.

Subject.	Description.	Painter, Engraver, or Sculptor.	Donor.	Date of gift.
140. Sabine, General Sir Edward, P.R.S.	Marble bust ..	J. Durham	J. P. Gassiot, Esq., F.R.S.	1860
141. Schelling, Friedrich W. J. von	Lithograph ..	..	T. Handley, Esq...	1846
142. Schumacher, Heinrich Christian, For. Mem. R.S.	Oil painting ..	H. Wolf ..	H. Wolf, Esq.	
143. Sedgwick, Rev. Adam, F.R.S.	Mezzotinto engraving	S. Cousins, after T. Phillips, R.A.	Sir C. Wheatstone, F.R.S.	1876
144. Sloane, Sir Hans, Bart., P.R.S.	Oil painting ..	Sir G. Kneller ..	Sir Hans Sloane	
145. Smeaton, John, F.R.S.	Ditto	Mather Brown ..	A. Aubert, Esq., F.R.S.	*
146. Ditto	Ditto	J. Richardson ..	Ditto	*
147. Smith, Henry John Stephen, F.R.S.	Marble bust ..	J. E. Boehm, R.A. (a Replica)	A Committee of Subscribers	1885
148. Somers, John, Lord Chancellor, P.R.S.	Oil painting ..	Sir G. Kneller ..	Sir J. Jekyll	
149. Somerville, Mrs. ..	Marble bust ..	Sir F. Chantrey, R.A.	H.R.H. the Duke of Sussex and other subscribers	1842
150. Southwell, Sir Robert, P.R.S.	Oil painting ..	Sir G. Kneller ..	Sir R. Southwell	
151. Spelman, Sir Henry..	Ditto	D. Mytens		
152. Spottiswoode, William, P.R.S.	Oil painting ..	Hon. J. Collier ..	A Committee of Subscribers	
153. Spratt, Thomas, Bishop of Rochester, F.R.S.	Wood engraving	M. V. Gucht, after Sir P. Lely	Dr. Eldridge Spratt	1880
154. Stephenson, Robert, F.R.S.	Steel engraving	F. Holl, after G. Richmond	Institution of Civil Engineers	1861
155. Stokes, Sir George Gabriel, Bart., P.R.S.	Oil painting ..	H. Herkomer, R.A.	Several Fellows of the Royal Society	1891
156. Sturm, John Christopher	Ditto	Heyman Dullaert..	T. Haak, Esq., F.R.S.	
157. Sussex, H.R.H. the Duke of, P.R.S.	Ditto	T. Phillips, R.A...	The Duke of Sussex	
158. Taylor, Brook, Sec. R.S.	Ditto	A. Ramsay ..	Sir W. Young, Bart., F.R.S.	
159. Ditto	Autotype, after an original picture in the possession of Lady Young	...	Prof. A. G. Greenhill, F.R.S.	1889
160. Viviani, Vincentio, For. Mem. R.S.	Oil painting ..	..	Dr. Wilson ..	1883
161. Waller, Richard, Sec. R.S.	Ditto	T. Murray ..	R. Waller, Esq. ..	1711
162. Wallis, John, D.D., F.R.S.	Ditto	G. Soest	Mrs. Wallis	
163. Watson, Sir William, M.D., F.R.S.	Ditto	L. F. Abbot ..	Sir W. Watson	
164. Watt, James, F.R.S..	Marble bust ..	J. Hoffernan, after Sir F. Chantrey, R.A.	— Watt, Esq. ..	1843

* Included in list printed in 1834.

Subject.	Description.	Painter, Engraver, or Sculptor.	Donor.	Date of gift
165. Wheatstone, Sir Charles, F.R.S.	Oil painting	C. Martin	Sir C. Wheatstone	1876
166. Wilkins, John, Bishop of Chester, Sec. R.S.	Ditto	Mary Beale		*
167. Williamson, Sir Joseph, P.R.S.	Ditto	Sir G. Kneller	Sir J. Williamson	
168. Wollaston, William Hyde, M.D., P.R.S.	Oil painting	J. Jackson, R.A.	Family of Dr. Wollaston	
169. Worcester, Edward Somerset, 2nd Marquess of	Steel engraving	W. Faithorne	H. Dircks, Esq.	1864
170. Wren, Sir Christopher, P.R.S.	Oil painting	Sir P. Lely (? Sir G. Kneller)	S. Wren, Esq.	*
171. Young, Thomas, M.D., F.R.S.	Ditto	H. P. Briggs, R.A., after Sir T. Lawrence, P.R.A.	Hudson Gurney, Esq.	1842

* Included in list printed in 1834.

MISCELLANEOUS.

Subject.	Description.	Painter, Engraver, or Sculptor.	Donor.	Date of gift
1. Representing a Deputation from the Council of the Royal Society consisting of the President (Lord Wrottesley), Mr. Grove, and Mr. Gassiot to Mr. Faraday to urge him to accept the Presidentship, May, 1857	Oil painting	E. Armitage, R.A.	J. P. Gassiot, Esq., F.R.S.	1878
2. Manor House, Woolsthorpe, the birthplace of Sir Isaac Newton	Ditto		Rev. C. Turnor, F.R.S.	
3. Ditto, from another point of view	Ditto		Rev. C. Turnor, F.R.S.	
4. Village Church, Woolsthorpe	Ditto		Rev. C. Turnor, F.R.S.	

NOTE.—In addition to the framed engraved portraits, all of which are included in the above list, the Royal Society possesses a large collection arranged in portfolios; and a number photographs of Fellows.

CATALOGUE OF THE MEDALS IN THE POSSESSION OF THE SOCIETY.

※※※ The sizes of the Medals described in the Catalogue are given in inches and decimals.

1. **Amsterdam. Koninklijke Akademie van Wetenschappen.** Medal founded by M. Hoeufft, 1837, a gold example of which is awarded annually for a Latin poem. Poetry, holding in one hand a lyre, with the other places a laurel wreath upon the head of a poet who holds a scroll on which is inscribed CERTAMINA POETICA. Both are standing. *Legend.* CERTAMINA POESEOS LATINAE. *Exergue.* J. P. MENGER. F.
Reverse. Within a laurel wreath, ACADEMIA REGIA DISCIPLINARVM NEDERLANDICA. *Exergue.* LEGATO IACOBI HENRICI HOEVFFT. 2·96. Æ.

2. **Baglivi, Giorgio, F.R.S.** Bust of Baglivi, r., hair curly, in plain falling collar, doublet buttoned, and cloak. *Leg.* G. BAGLIVUS . MED . IN . ROM . ARCHIL . P . ET . SOC . REG . LOND . COLL . Behind s . v.
Rev. A tripod encircled by a snake, between a mortar, retort and other implements of medicine, &c. *Leg.* VNAM . FACIEMVS . VTRAMQVE. *Ex.* MDCCIIII. 1·55. Æ.

3. **Baly, William.** Bust of Baly, l., almost facing, open shirt. *Leg.* IN HONOREM GULIELMI BALY M.D. OB[T]. 1861. Below, J. S. WYON SC.
Rev. Representation of the façade of the Royal College of Physicians. Inscribed around, OB PHYSIOLOGIAM FELICITER EXCULTAM. Below, SIR R. SMIRKE R.A. ARCH[T]; J. S. & A. B. WYON SC. *Ex.* COLL . REG . MED . LOND. 2·28. Æ.

4. **Batavia. Bataviaasch Genootschap van Kunsten en Wetenschappen.** Medal struck in celebration of the centenary of the Society, 1778–1878. Within a wreath of tropical flowers, SOCIETAS . ART . SCIENT . BAT . IN . MEMORIAM . I . SAEC . FEL . CLAVSI . Below wreath, CH . WIENER . BRUXELLES. Inscribed within a border, A . D . VIII . K . MAI; MDCCLXXVIII–MDCCCLXXVIII.
Rev. A cocoa-nut tree (*Cocos nucifera*, Linn.) with outlines of Java mountains behind, and inscribed within a border, the motto, TEN NUTTE VAN 'T GEMEEN.BATAVIA'S GENOOTSCHAP. 2·89. Æ.

5. **Becquerel, Antoine César, For. Mem. R.S.** Head of Becquerel, *l.*, bare, hair short. *Leg.* ANTOINE CÉSAR BECQUEREL MEMBRE L'ACADÉMIE DES SCIENCES. ˙Below, ALPHÉE DUBOIS.

   Rev. Spaced on the field, OFFERT LE 13 AVRIL 1874 À L'ILLUSTRE DOYEN DES PHYSICIENS PAR SES CONFRÈRES PAR SES AMIS ET PAR SES ADMIRATEURS. 2·0. Æ.

6. **Beneden, Pierre J. van, For. Mem. R. S.** Arms of the University of Louvain with crest and supporters, and the motto, IN FIDE CONSTANS. Below, J. WIENER.

   Rev. Inscription spaced on the field, CIVI SVO PRÆCLARO P. J. VAN BENEDEN PER ANNOS XL . IN UNIV . LOVAN . DOCENTI SCIENTIIS NATURALIBUS DOCTISSIMO CIVITAS MECHLINIENSIS DEDICAVIT A$^{D.}$ MDCCCLXXVII. 1·98. Æ.

7. ——— ——— ——— —— —— ——— —— Head of Van Beneden, *l.*, hair long, bearded. Below, ED . GEERTS . F.

   Rev. Above, branches of laurel and palm intertwined with scroll inscribed PALÆONTOLOGIA . ANATOMIA . ZOOLOGIA. Inscription below, VIRO DOCTISSIMO ET CELEBERRIMO P. J. VAN BENEDEN PER DECEM JAM LUSTRA IN UNIVERSITATE CATHOLICA LOVANIENSI PROFESSORI . MDCCCXXXVI–MDCCCLXXXVI 2·18. Æ.

8. **Berzelius, Jöns Jakob, For. Mem. R.S.** Bust of Berzelius, *r.*, hair short, bare. *Leg.* JACOBUS BERZELIUS . NAT . MDCCLXXIX . DEN . MDCCCXLVIII.

   Rev. Fame flying towards Night, who is seated, her left arm rests on a sphinx, and near are emblems of the sciences. Inscribed around, APERIT AENIGMATA CONDITA LUSTRAT; right and left, C . G . OVARNSTRÖM . INV. P . H . LUNDGREN FEC. *Ex.* SOCIO LONGE NOBILISSIMO PER ANNOS XXX SECRETARIO ACAD . REG . SCIENT . SVEC. 2·22. Æ.

Bigsby, John Jeremiah, F.R.S. *See* London, Geological Society.

Black, Joseph. *See* Glasgow, University.

9. **Brahe, Tycho.** Bust of Brahe, *r.*, hair short, in richly embroidered doublet and mantle; round the neck a chain, to which a medallion portrait is attached. *Leg.* TYCHO BRAHÉ. Below, ROGAT . E.

   Rev. Inscription, spaced on the field, NATUS ELSINBURGHI IN SCANIA AN . M.D.XLV . OBIIT AN . M.DC.I. SERIES NUMISMATICA UNIVERSALIS VIRORUM ILLUSTRIUM. M.D.CCC.XXV. DURAND EDIDIT. 1·64. Æ.

10. **Brussels. Académie Royale des Sciences et Belles-Lettres.** Medal celebrating the 100th anniversary of the foundation of the Academy by the Empress Maria Theresia. Bust of Maria Theresia, *l.*, hair in short curls, wearing bandeau decorated with pearls, drapery falling from the head fastened at the

breast with brooch; in low richly embroidered gown, and mantle fastened with jewel on the shoulder. *Leg.* IMP. MARIA THERESIA . ACAD . CONDIT. Below, B D U V.

Rev. Inscription, spaced on the field, ACADEMIA SCIENT . LIT . ET . ART . BELGICA AB . AVG . IMP . MARIA . THERESIA ANNO . MDCCLXXII . INSTITVTA A . GVILIELMO . I . REGE . AVGVSTO ANNO . MDCCCXVI . RESTITVTA A . LEOPOLDO . I . REGE . AVG . ANNO . MDCCCXLV . AVCTA FESTA . SAECVLARIA . AGIT ANNO . MDCCCLXXII. 2·0. Æ.

Buchanan, Sir George, F.R.S. *See* London, Royal Society.

11. **Canning, George, F.R.S.** Head of Canning, *l.*, top of head bare. Behind, CANNING. On truncation, A. J. STOTHARD D.; below, F. L. CHANTREY . R A. D.

    Rev. Clio, looking to *r.*, leans in almost upright position against low pillar, on which rests her left hand with scroll bearing legend, TO GREAT MEN; in right hand a pen. Below, PUB^D BY S PARKER LONDON. MDCCCXXVII. Right and left, A. J. STOTHARD F. T. STOTHARD R.A. D. 2·46. Æ.

12. **Challenger Medal.** Bust of Athena, *l.*, near her an owl, and behind, forming a background, the terrestrial globe. In the field right and left appears a dolphin, and Neptune, who holds a trident and dredge. Below, two mermaids support a scroll on which is inscribed VOYAGE OF H·M·S· CHALLENGER 1872-76.

    Rev. The genius of the "Challenger" Expedition represented by a Knight in armour, who throws down his gauntlet to the sea. Inscribed around on a scroll, one end of which passes round a trident behind the figure, REPORT ON THE SCIENTIFIC RESULTS OF THE CHALLENGER EXPEDITION 1886-95. Cast. 2·87. Æ.

    This medal was founded to commemorate the work connected with the "Challenger" Expedition. It was presented by Dr. John Murray, F.R.S., to the naval officers and members of the civilian staff of the Expedition, to contributors of memoirs, and to other persons who took part in the promotion of the Expedition, or the publication of the scientific results.

13. **Chesterfield, Philip Dormer Stanhope, Earl of, F.R.S.** Bust of the Earl, *l.*, hair long, in coat, riband, and star of the Garter. *Leg.* PHILIPPUS STANHOPE. Below, I. A. DASSIER . F.

    Rev. Within an ornamental border, COMES DE CHESTERFIELD . MDCCXLIII. 2·15. Æ.

14. **Christiania. K. Norske Frederiks Universitet.** Within a laurel wreath the inscription ACADEMIAE REGIAE NORV . FRIDERICIANAE SACRA SEMISECULARIA D . II SEPTBR . MDCCCLXI.

Rev. Mercury seated, wearing Phrygian cap, offers drink to a lion out of a patera. Inscribed around, EX HAUSTU OLYMPICO VALENTIOR. *Ex.* G . LOOS D . KULLRICH F.   1·67. GILT.

15. [**Christiania.**] **K. Norske Frederiks Universitet.** Medal founded 1872, on the occasion of the celebration of the union of Norway as one Kingdom one thousand years prior. A female figure representing Norway is seated to *l.*, helmeted, hair long : in right hand a spear, the left rests on the Norwegian shield. A mantle fastened at the throat with a brooch is thrown back, disclosing a vest of mail with waistbelt. Alongside the shield a stone, inscribed M[ILLE] ANNI. *Leg.* TEMPORI SVPERSTES. *Ex.* MDCCCLXXII. Below, MIDDELTHUN . INV : CONRADSEN . SCULP.

    Rev. Within an olive wreath, REGNI NORVEGICI ANNVM MILLESIMVM PIA CELEBRAT VNIVERSITAS REGIA FREDERICIANA.   2·08. Æ.

16. ———— ———— **K. Norske Frederiks Universitet.** Medal founded 1873, on the occasion of the crowning of King Oscar II. Busts conjoined, *r.*, of Oscar II. of Sweden and Norway, and Sophia his Queen, both crowned. He wears a mantle fastened with a pin ; she, a necklace. *Leg.* OSCAR II ET SOPHIA NOR. SUEC. REX ET REGINA MDCCCLXXIII. On truncation, G . LOOS D. On the rim, W . KULLRICH F.

    Rev. Clio, seated, holding a scroll and pen. Around, an olive wreath. *Leg.* VETAT MORI. Below, U . R . F . [Universitas Regia Fredericiana.] On the rim, E. WEIGAND FEC. 1·68. Æ.

17. ———— ———— **K. Norske Frederiks Universitet.** Busts conjoined, *r.*, of Charles XV. of Sweden and Norway, and Louisa his Queen, both crowned. He wears a mantle fastened with a pin ; she, a necklace. *Leg.* CAROLUS ET LOUISA NORV. SVEC. REX ET REGINA. Below, G. LOOS DIR. On the rim, SCHNITZSPANN FEC.

    Rev. The goddess Athena, standing to *r.*, reading a scroll ; on her breast the head of Medusa. To the right of the figure an owl flying to front. Inscription, within a border, VOVENS ET MEMOR. UNIVERSITAS REGIA FREDERICIANA.   1·68. Æ.

Clarke, Rev. William Branwhite, F.R.S. *See* Sydney, Royal Society of New South Wales.

18. **Combe, Taylor, F.R.S.** Head of Combe, *l.*, bare, hair short. On truncation, W. J. TAYLOR . F. Below, PISTRUCCI D.

    Rev. Within a laurel wreath the inscription, TAYLOR COMBE M.A. SEC . ROY . SOC . DIRECT . SOC . ANT . KEEPER OF COINS & ANTIQUITIES BRITISH MUSEUM DIED 1826 AGED 52.
    1·78. Æ.

Mr. Combe was Secretary of the Royal Society 1812–24. Pistrucci's original plaster model for this medal was presented to the British Museum by Dr. John Gray, F.R.S.

19. **Conduit, John, F.R.S.** Bust of Conduit, *r.*, hair short, neck bare, in mantle, fastened with brooch on the shoulder. *Leg.* IOHANNES CONDUITT . REI . MONET: PRÆF: Below, TANNER . LONDINI . F.

    Rev. Truth introduces Conduit to Hampden holding a staff surmounted by a cap of Liberty, a stork at his feet, and to Newton, seated, resting his hand on a slab, on which is a diagram of the planetary system. *Leg.* MEMORES FECERE MERENDO. *Ex.* M.DCC.XXXVII 2·26. Æ.

    Conduit succeeded Sir Isaac Newton, who was his uncle by marriage, as Master of the Mint.

20. **Copenhagen. Universitet.** Medal struck in celebration of the 400th anniversary. Busts conjoined, *r.*, of Christian I. (founder) and Christian IX., the one wearing a cap and falling collar, the other bare. *Leg.* CHRISTIANVS I . CHRISTIANVS IX . MDCCCLXXIX. On truncation, H. CONRADSEN.

    Rev. Denmark seated, *l.*, laureate, and clad in loose draperies, clasps the extended hand of the goddess Athena standing, who holds an owl, on her breast the head of Medusa. The left hand of Denmark rests upon the Danish shield (three crowned lions, and nine hearts). Inscription, QVATTVOR EXEGIT SPERAT NOVA SAECVLA VIVAX. *Ex.* VNIVERSITAS HAVNIENSIS. 1·86. Æ.

21. **Copernicus, Nicholas.** Bust of Copernicus, *l.*, hair long, in coat and fur vest. *Leg.* NICOLAUS COPERNICUS. Below, PETIT F.

    Rev. Inscription, spaced on the face, NATUS TORUNII IN PRUSSIA AN.M.CCCC.LXXIII . OBIIT AN.M.D.XLIII. SERIES NUMISMATICA UNIVERSALIS VIRORUM ILLUSTRIUM. M.DCCC.XVIII. DURAND EDIDIT. 1·6. Æ.

    Copley Medal. *See* London, Royal Society.

22. **Czuczor, Gergely,** and **János Fogarasi.** Busts conjoined, *l.*, hair short, both bare. *Leg.* CZUCZOR GERGELY FOGARASI JÁNOS. Below, C. RADNITZKI.

    Rev. Inscription, A MAGYAR NYELV SZÓTÁRA BEFÉJEZÉSÉNEK EMLÉKEÜL A MAGYAR TUDOMÁNYOS AKADEMIA MDCCCLXXIV. 1·68. GILT.

    This medal was struck in commemoration of the completion of their great dictionary of the Hungarian language.

23. **Darwin, Charles, F.R.S.** Medallic Portrait. Cast. Bust of

Darwin, *l.*, hair and beard long, crown of head bare. *Leg.* On sunk band, CHARLES DARWIN 1881. Below, A. L. [A. Legros.]
Rev. Plain. 4·5. Æ.

Darwin Medal. *See* London, Royal Society.

Davy Medal. *See* London, Royal Society.

24. **Descartes, René.** Bust of Descartes, *r.*, hair long, in plain falling collar and closely buttoned doublet. *Leg.* RENE DESCARTES. Below, GALLE F.
Rev. Inscription, spaced on the face, NÉ A LA HEYE EN TOURAINE EN M.D.XCVI. MORT EN M.DC.L. GALERIE METALLIQUE DES GRANDS HOMMES FRANÇAIS. 1819. 1·6. Æ.

25. **Doncaster. Horticultural Society.** Bust of Linnæus, *r.*, hair short, in vest and cravat, with loose mantle. ' On the breast a sprig of *Linnæa borealis. Leg.* DONCASTER HORTICULTURAL SOCIETY, 1835. CAROLUS LINNAEUS. Below bust, J. B.
Rev. Within a wreath of flowers, the arms and crest of Doncaster. 2·1. Æ.

26. **Donders, Franz Cornelis, For. Mem. R.S.** Medal struck in honour of his Jubilee, celebrated at Utrecht in 1888. Head of Donders, *r.*, bare, hair short. *Leg.* FRANCISCVS CORNELIVS DONDERS. D. XXVII MAII A. MDCCCXVIII—MDCCCLXXXVIII. Below truncation, L. JÜNGER. D. J. P. M. MENGER. F.
Rev. Within an olive wreath, PER VARIAS GENTES ILLVSTRIS BATAVI ADMIRATIONE JVNCTI. Inscribed around, IN MEMORIAM DIEI QVO CONDITVM PIVM CORPVS IPSIVS NOMINE INSIGNE. Below, W. SCHAMMER. F. 2·6. Æ.

27. **Edinburgh. Royal Society.** The Keith Prize Medal. Bust of John Napier of Merchiston (the inventor of logarithms), *l.*, hair long, in ruff and close-fitting doublet. *Leg.* IOANNES NEPERUS DE MERCHISTON. Below, C. F. CARTER SCULP.
Rev. Within a laurel wreath, INGENII FELICITER EXCULTI PRÆMIUM KEITHIANUM. *Leg.* SOC. REG : EDIN : ADJUDICAVIT. 1·75. Æ.

Evans, John, F.R.S. *See* London, Numismatic Society.

Fogarasi, J. *See* Czuczor and Fogarasi.

28. **Folkes, Martin, P.R.S.** Bust of Folkes, *r.*, hair short, cap on head, in loose robe. *Leg.* MARTINUS FOLKES ARM^R. Below, JA.. ANT. DASSIER.
Rev. Within an ornamental compartment, SOCIETATIS REGALIS LONDINI SODALIS. M.DCC.XL. 2·15. Æ.

Folkes was President of the Royal Society for 11 years, having been elected in 1741.

29. **Freind, John, F.R.S.** Bust of Freind, *l.*, hair long, no drapery. *Leg.* IOANNES . FREIND . COLL . MED . LOND . ET . REG . S . S . On truncation, S V.
Rev. An ancient and a modern physician meeting and grasping right hands; between them, on the ground, are herbs, book, crucible, &c. *Leg.* MEDICINA . VETVS . ET . NOVA. *Ex.* VNAM FACIMVS VTRAMQVE. SV. 2·26. Æ.

30. **Galileo Galilei.** Bust of Galileo, *r.*, hair short, bearded, wearing ruff and doublet. *Leg.* GALILÆUS GALILÆI. Below, GAYRARD F.
Rev. Inscription, spaced on the field, NATVS PISIS IN ITALIA . AN . M.D.LXIV . OBIIT AN . M.DC.XLII. SERIES NUMISMATICA UNIVERSALIS VIRORUM ILLUSTRIUM. M.DCCC.XVIII. DURAND EDIDT. 1·6. Æ.

31. **Gauss, Carl Friedrich, For. Mem. R.S.** Bust of Gauss, *r.*, bare, hair long. *Leg.* CAROLVS FRIDERICVS GAVSS . NAT . MDCCLXXVII APR . XXX OB . MDCCCLV FEB . XXIII. Below, BREHMER . F.
Rev. Within an ivy wreath, GEORGIVS V REX HANNOVERAE MATHEMATICORVM PRINCIPI. Inscribed around, ACADEMIAE SVAE GEORGIAE AVGVSTAE DECORI AETERNO. Below wreath a star. 2·75. Æ.

32. **[Gauss, Carl Friedrich.]** Another copy. 2·75. Æ.

33. **Glasgow. University.** Bust of Joseph Black, *l.*, hair long, and tied behind, in coat and cravat. *Leg.* JOSEPHUS BLACK MDCCXXIII . MDCCXCIX. On truncation, N. MACPHAIL . SC.
Rev. Inscription, spaced on the field, in ACADEM . GLASGUENS FACULTATE MEDICA DISCIPVLUS INGENIO AC LABORE INSIGNIS PRŒMIUM HOCCE MERITO CONSECUTUS EST. 2·76. Æ.
A medical class medal of the University of Glasgow, where Dr. Black had been a professor.

34. **Gray, John Edward, F.R.S., and Maria E. Gray.** Busts conjoined, *r.*, of Gray and Mrs. Gray. He, bare, hair short; she wears cap and dress with ribbon round the neck. Behind busts, in the field, I . E . ⚭ M . E . GRAY. Below, G. G. ADAMS . SC. 1863.
Rev. Within an olive wreath, TRUST IN THE LORD AND DO GOOD. 2·26. Æ.
The Society possesses two copies of this medal.

35. **Haidinger, Wilhelm, For. Mem. R.S.** Head of Haidinger, *r.*, hair short. *Leg.* WILHELM HAIDINGER. Below, K. LANGE.
Rev. In reilef, the Eastern hemisphere, around which are the signs of the zodiac. *Leg.* Inscribed within a border, NIE ERMÜDET STILLE STEHEN . MDCCCVI. 2·52. Æ.

36. **Halley, Edmund, F.R.S.** Bust of Halley, *r.*, hair long, in loose mantle trimmed with fur. *Leg.* EDMUNDUS HALLEY . A . DASSIER . F.

Rev. Within an ornamental border, at the top part a festoon of flowers under a winged cherub, ASTRONOMUS REGIS MAGNÆ BRITANNIÆ. MDCCXLIV. 2·15. Æ.

Halley was Secretary of the Royal Society, 1713-21.

37. **Hamilton, Sir William, F.R.S.** Bust of Hamilton, *l.*, hair long and tied with ribbon. On coat the decoration of a Knight Commander of the Bath. Inscribed around, GVL . HAMILTON . EQVES . EX . ORD . BALN . SR & AS.

Rev. The representation of a Greek vase in relief. Inscribed around, LUCI . & . LITERIS . RESTITUIT. Cast. 4·25. Æ.

38. **Hansteen, Christopher, For. Mem. R.S.** Bust of Hansteen, *l.*, bare, hair short. *Leg.* CHRISTOPHORO HANSTEEN. Below, B. BERGSLIEN. F.

Rev. Within a wreath of oak and olive, the inscription, SPLENDET IN ORBE DECUS; above, a star. Inscribed around, SOLENNIA SEMISECULARIA GRATULATUR . UNIV : REG : FRED : MDCCCLVI.

1·5. Æ.

39. **Heidelberg. Universität.** Medal in celebration of the 500th anniversary of the University. Bust of Frederick of Baden, Protector of the University, *l.*, bearded, in uniform, with decoration, and loose mantle trimmed with ermine. *Leg.* FRIDERICVS . D . G . BADARVM . M . DVX . RECTOR . HEID . PERP. Below, SCHWENZER.

Rev. The Genius of Heidelberg standing and facing, her hands resting, on either side, on oval panels, bearing, on left, the bust of the Elector Rupert, *r.*, founder of the University, 1356; on right, bust of the Elector Charles Frederick, *l.*, who reconstituted the same in 1803. Jewelled scrolls carried from the base of each panel terminate with a laurel and palm branch. The central figure has long flowing hair, and wears loose drapery which leaves the arms bare; in left hand a laurel branch; her feet in sandals; at the girdle of her waist the arms of Baden. In the distance, in low relief, the Castle of Heidelberg. *Leg.* Inscribed within a border, VNIVERSITAS . HEIDELBERGENSIS . A . RVPERTO . CONDITA . A . CAROLO . FRIDERICO . INSTAVRATA. In the exergue, on a scrolled panel, SAECVLVM . SEXTVM . PIE . AVSPICATVR . A . D . MDCCCLXXXVI. Below, H . GÖTZ INV.; H . SCHWENZER FEC.

2·9. Æ.

40. **Hermite, Charles, For. Mem. R.S.** Bust of Hermite, *r.*, hair

short, in a robe. *Leg.* CHARLES . HERMITE . DE . L'ACADEMIE . DES . SCIENCES. On truncation, J. C. CHAPLAIN.

Rev. Spaced on the field, partly encircled by a myrtle branch, the stem tied with ribbon—A CHARLES . HERMITE M^{BRE} DE . L'INSTITUT PROFESSEUR . D'ALGEBRE SUPERIEURE A . LA . FACULTE . DES . SCIENCES SES ELEVES . SES . ADMIRATEURS SES . AMIS EN . SOUVENIR DE SON . 70ME ANNIVERSAIRE 24 . DECEMBRE . 1892.— SOUSCRIPTION INTERNATIONALE. 2·38 × 1·75. Æ.

41. **Hirn, Gustave Adolphe.** Medal, rectangular, struck in 1890, as a tribute of admiration for M. Hirn and his labours. Bust of Hirn, *r.*, hair long, in coat, collar, and cravat. *Upper leg.* GVSTAVE . ADOLPHE . HIRN. *Lower leg.* SES . COMPATRIOTES . SES . AMIS . SES . ADMIRATEVRS. Behind, NÉ AV . LOGELBACH . XXI . AOVT . MD.CCC.XV. Below, O . ROTY MDCCCLXXXIX.

Rev. Science, seated, *r.*, watches the flames of a fire burning upon an antique and raised altar, symbolical of thermodynamics. Her hair, with bandeau, gathered into a knot behind; she is clad in loose drapery, which leaves the arms bare; in left hand a scroll. At her feet an oak garland and a portfolio, whilst a balance recalls the applications of M. Hirn's researches on vapour. Behind her rise branches of laurel, among which the inscription SCIENTIA, on a band. In the distance the profile of the mountains of Logelbach with the ruins of the "Trois-Châteaux d'Eguisheim;" in the sky are stars, and Saturn. *Leg.* On a panel in the right hand corner, AMICVS . PLATO SED . MAGIS . AMICA VERITAS. Below, O. ROTY. 2·42 × 1·8. Æ.

M. Hirn died Jan. 14, 1890, just before the issue of this medal.

Howard, John, F.R.S. *See* London, Statistical Society.

42. **Hume, Joseph, F.R.S.** Bust of Hume, *l.*, almost facing, hair short, in coat, collar, and cravat. *Leg.* JOS. HUME ESQ. M.P. F.R.S. Below, T.H. F.

Rev. A wreath of oak leaves above, underneath which inscription, OF CIVIL AND RELIGIOUS LIBERTY, THE VIRTUOUS AND ENLIGHTENED FRIEND : OF JUSTICE AND NATIONAL INTEGRITY, THE IMPARTIAL AND UNDAUNTED DEFENDER. 1·52. Æ.

43. **Hunter, John, F.R.S.** Bust of Hunter, *r.*, bare; top of head, bare, hair around, curly. *Leg.* IOHANNES HVNTER. Below, B. WYON.

Rev. Within a laurel wreath, the armorial bearings of Yorkshire College, Leeds; below, on an ornamental scroll the motto ET AVGEBITVR SCIENTIA. Inscribed around, within a border, COLLEGIVM . COMITATVS . EBORACENCIS and SCHOLA MEDICINÆ.

Roses separate the two groups of words. Below the shield, ALLAN WYON SC. 2·2. Æ.

44. **Hunter, William, F.R.S.** Bust of Hunter, *l.*, in tasselled cap, and shirt with collar open. *Leg.* GULIELMUS HUNTER MDCCXVIII. MDCCLXXXIII. On truncation of shoulder, N. MACPHAIL SC.

Rev. Inscription, spaced on the l field, IN ACADEM . GLASGUENS . FACULTATE MEDICA DISCIPULUS INGENIO AC LABORE INSIGNIS PRŒMIUM HOCCE MERITO CONSECUTUS EST. 2·76. Æ.

Keith Medal. *See* Edinburgh, Royal Society.

45. **Lawrence, Sir William, Bart, F.R.S.** Head of Lawrence, *l.* bare. *Leg.* GULIELMUS LAWRENCE, BARONETTUS . NAT : 1783 OB : 1867. Below, A. B. WYON.

Rev. Within an olive wreath, a shield bearing the arms of St. Bartholomew's Hospital. Inscribed around, within a border, S. BARTHOLOMÆI HOSP. ET COLL. INST. 1123. J.S & AB. WYON. 1·52. Æ.

Lee, John, F.R.S. *See* London, Numismatic Society.

46. **Linnæus, Carolus.** Bust of Linnæus, *r.*, hair long, in vest and cravat, with mantle over the shoulders. On the breast of the coat a sprig of *Linnœa borealis*, and his decoration as Knight of the Polar Star. *Leg.* CAROLUS LINNAEUS ARCH . REG . EQV . AURATUS. Below, LIUNGBERGER.

Rev. Cybele standing, murally crowned, with lion crouching by her side; in her left hand a key, the right is upraised; she is surrounded by animals and plants, in the distance are clouds with flying birds. Three small butterflies are represented to the left of the figure. Inscription, DEAM LUCTUS ANGIT AMISSI. *Ex.* POST OBITUM UPSALIAE D . X . JAN . MDCCLXXVIII . REGE JUBENTE. *See* Doncaster, Horticultural Society. 2·1. Æ.

47. **Locke, John.** Bust of Locke, *l.*, hair long, in shirt open at the collar, and loose mantle. *Leg.* JOANNES LOCK. Below, JAC . ROETTIERS.

Rev. Inscription, spaced on the face, MENS HABITAT MOLEM . VIRG . GEOR: M.DCC.LXXIV. 2·1. Æ.

48. **London. Medal struck to commemorate the visit of H.M. Queen Victoria to the Corporation of London, Nov. 9, 1837.** Bust of Queen Victoria, *l.*, bare, wearing a diadem, hair bound with fillet and gathered into a knot behind. *Leg.* VICTORIA REGINA. On truncation, W. WYON . R.A.

Rev. A representation of the frontage of the Guildhall, with the Royal Standard floating above. *Exergual leg.* only, IN HONOUR OF HER MAJESTY'S VISIT TO THE CORPORATION OF LONDON 9TH NOV : 1837. 2·16. Æ.

Catalogue of the Medals.   193

London. British Association. *See* Montreal, McGill University.

49. ———— City and Guilds of London Institute. Siemens Medal. Head of Siemens, *l.*, bare, bearded, crown of head bare. *Leg.* SIR C. WILLIAM SIEMENS . F.R.S. D.C.L. IN MEMORIAM . BORN 1823 . DIED 1883. Below neck, ALLAN WYON.

Rev. Within an ivy wreath, FOR PROFICIENCY IN ELECTRICAL ENGINEERING. Inscribed around, THE CITY AND GUILDS OF LONDON INSTITUTE . CENTRAL INSTITUTION. Below wreath, A. WYON.   2·02. Æ.

50. ———— Geological Society. Bigsby Medal. Bust of Bigsby, bare, *l. Leg.* J. J. BIGSBY M.D. F.R.S. BIENNIAL PRIZE MEDAL FOUNDED 1876. Below, A. B. WYON.

Rev. In the centre, a representation of an extinct species of echinoderm (*Agelacrinites Dicksoni*), and inscribed around, AGELACRINITES DICKSONI. FOUND . 1822 . CANADA. Below, J. S. & A. B. WYON. Beyond, within a border, AWARDED BY THE GEOLOGICAL SOCIETY OF LONDON FOR WORK OF GREAT MERIT.
1·78. Æ.

A gold example of this medal is awarded biennially by the Geological Society of London. The Royal Society possesses another specimen of nearly similar design but larger type; it was struck in bronze, and subsequently discarded for the smaller size in gold.

51. [London.] Geological Society. Bigsby Medal. *See* note above.   2·52. Æ.

52. ———— King's College. Siemens Medal. Head of Siemens, *l.*, bearded. *Leg.* CAR . GUL . SIEMENS PRAEMIUM IN ARTE METALLURGICA D . D . MDCCCLXXXII. Below truncation, J. S. & A. B. WYON.

Rev. The arms, crest, and supporters of King's College, London, with inscription above, COLL : REG : LOND :   In the exergue on scrolls, SANCTE ET SAPIENTER. Below, A . B . WYON . SC.
1·7. Æ.

53. ———— King's College. Todd Medal. Bust of Todd, *l.*, hair long, in coat, collar, and bow tie. *Leg.* ROBERT BENTLEY TODD M.D. F.R.S. DIED 30 JAN. 1860. Below, J. S. WYON SC.

Rev. The arms, crest, and supporters of King's College, London. with inscription, KINGS COLLEGE LONDON . FOR CLINICAL MEDICINE. On scrolls beneath arms, SANCTE ET SAPIENTER. Below, J. S. WYON SC.   3·0. Æ.

54. ———— Numismatic Society. Bust of John Lee, F.R.S. (first President), *r.*, drapery on neck. Below, STOTHARD . F.

O

Rev. Spaced on the field, NUMISMATIC SOCIETY OF LONDON FOUNDED DEC^R. XXII MDCCCXXXVIII. JOHN LEE, LL.D F.R.S : F.S.A : F.R.A.S PRESIDENT. 1·75. Æ.

55. [London.] **Numismatic Society.** Jubilee Medal, 1887. Bust of John Evans, F.R.S., *r.*, hair short, in coat and collar. *Leg.* IOH . EVANS . D.C.L. S.R.S. PRAESIDI. On truncation, PINCHES . F.

Rev. Within an olive wreath, SIC / L / SIC / C Inscribed around, SOCIETAS NVMISM . LOND . ANNOS CONST . LI . MDCCCLXXXVII. 2·26. R.

56. ——— ——— Jubilee Medal. Another copy. 2·26. Æ.

57. ——— **Royal Astronomical Society.** Medal of the Royal Astronomical Society. Bust of Newton, *l.*, bare; behind, NEWTON *Leg.* ROYAL ASTRONOMICAL SOCIETY INST : MDCCCXX. Below, NUBEM PELLENTE MATHESI. On truncation, W. WYON . A R A . MINT.

Rev. Herschel's telescope. *Leg.* QUICQUID NITET NOTANDUM. (In the exergue of this specimen is inscribed, STRUCK BY PERMISSION OF THE COUNCIL FOR THE COLLECTION OF THE REV^D. CHARLES TURNOR . 1840.) 1·9. R.

This medal was ordered to be struck when the Society received its Royal Charter of Incorporation in 1831, it replacing an earlier type. The first impression was issued in 1834. It is struck in gold, and awarded annually or otherwise, as the Council determines.

58. ——— **Royal Exchange.** Medal struck to commemorate the laying of the first stone of the Royal Exchange. Bust of Queen Victoria, *l.*, bare, wearing a diadem, hair bound with fillet, and gathered into a knot behind. *Leg.* VICTORIA D : G : BRITANNIARUM REGINA F : D : On truncation, W WYON . R A.

Rev. Inscription, spaced on the field, IN COMMEMORATION OF LAYING THE FIRST STONE OF THE NEW ROYAL EXCHANGE BY H : R : H : PRINCE ALBERT CONSORT OF H : M : QUEEN VICTORIA 17 JANUARY 1842 IN THE FIFTH YEAR OF HER REIGN.
1·78. Æ.

59. ——— **Royal Society.** Buchanan Medal. Head of Sir George Buchanan, F.R.S., *l.*, bearded, crown of head bare. *Leg.* SIR GEORGE BVCHANAN M·D· F·R·C·P· F·R·S·

Rev. Hygeia, daughter of Æsculapius, and goddess of health, is standing, attended by a maiden, both clad in loose draperies. Behind them a flying figure in cloak and hood carrying a scythe representing the angel of death. Below, the prone figure of a man. *Ex.* The staff of Æsculapius with a serpent entwined and bowl of Hygeia. *Leg.* Inscribed around, IN SALVTEM PVBLICAM AVDACIA ET INDVSTRIA. 2·12. Æ.

The Buchanan Medal was founded in 1894. It is awarded every three or five years in respect of distinguished services to hygienic science or practice, in the direction either of original research or of professional, administrative, or constructive work. It is struck in gold, and is awarded without limit of nationality or sex.

60. [**London.**] **Royal Society.** Copley Medal. Athena, seated amidst emblems of her own attributes, and of the arts and sciences, holds out in the right hand a wreath; in her left arm is the Ephesian Artemis; on her breast the head of Medusa; near her the armorial shield of Sir Godfrey Copley. *Leg.* G . COPLEY BAR^{T.} DIGNISSIMO. Below, T. [John Sigismund Tanner.]

Rev. The armorial shield of the Royal Society, with crest and supporters. *Leg.* SOCIETAS REG . LONDINI. *Ex.* On a band the motto NULLIUS IN VERBA. 1·7. Æ.

On the obverse of this specimen is inscribed, in the exergue, CAROLO LYELL EQ: 1858.

The Copley Medal, founded in 1736 under the will (1709) of Sir Godfrey Copley, Bart., F.R.S., is awarded annually for distinguished philosophical research, and irrespective of nationality. It is struck in gold.

61. —— —— —— —— —— Copley Medal. Another copy, but without exergal inscription. 1·7. Æ.

62. —————— **Royal Society.** Darwin Medal. Bust of Darwin, *l.*, hair and beard long, crown of head bare, in coat and collar. On truncation, ALLAN WYON SC.

Rev. Within a wreath, composed of the leaves and flowers of plants identified with Darwin's researches (*Ampelopsis, Drosera, Primula, Nepenthes, &c.*), the inscription CAROLVS DARWIN between the dates MDCCCIX and MDCCCLXXXII. Below wreath, ALLAN WYON. 2·25. Æ.

The Darwin Medal was founded in 1890, and is awarded biennially for work of distinction in the field in which Mr. Darwin himself laboured. It is struck in silver or bronze. The name of the recipient is engraved around the rim.

63. —————— **Royal Society.** Davy Medal. Bust of Sir Humphry Davy, *r.*, hair short, in coat, collar, and cravat, with frilled shirt. On truncation, A. B. JOY SC. N. MACPHAIL F.

Rev. Inscription, spaced on the face, THE ROYAL SOCIETY TO [recipient's name.] IN ACCORDANCE WITH THE WILL OF HUMPHRY DAVY WHO DEVOTED THE TESTIMONIAL PRESENTED TO HIM BY THE

COALOWNERS OF THE TYNE AND WEAR TO THE ENCOURAGEMENT OF CHEMICAL RESEARCH. Below, under a line, the date. [The date on this medal is 1890.] 2·98. Æ.

The Davy Medal was founded in 1869 under the will of Dr. John Davy, F.R.S., a brother of Sir Humphry Davy, and is awarded annually for the most important discovery in chemistry made in Europe or Anglo-America. It is struck in gold.

64. [**London.**] **Royal Society.** Davy Medal. Another copy, inscribed ROBERT WILHELM BUNSEN : GUSTAV ROBERT KIRCHHOFF. Dated 1877. 2·98. Æ.

65. —— —— **Royal Society.** Royal Medal. Bust of Queen Victoria, *l*., bare, wearing coronet, hair bound with fillet and gathered into a knot behind. *Leg.* VICTORIA REGINA SOC : REG : LOND : PATRONA . MDCCCXXXVIII. On truncation, W. WYON . R.A.

Rev. A representation of the statue of Sir Isaac Newton, by Roubiliac, in the Chapel of Trinity College, Cambridge. On either side of the statue are devices illustrative of Newton's discoveries. The diagram on the right is taken from the sixty-sixth proposition of the "Principia;" that on the left illustrates the solar system. *Leg.* REGINAE MVNIFICENTIA ARBITRIO SOCIETATIS. Below statue, NEWTON. 2·86. Æ.

Two Royal Medals were founded by George IV, and are awarded annually for the two most important contributions to the advancement of Natural Knowledge published originally in the British dominions, within a period of not more than ten and not less than one year of the date of the award. They are struck in gold and in silver.

66. —— —— **Royal Society.** Rumford Medal. A tripod, surmounted by a flame, with inscription around, NOSCERE QUÆ VIS ET CAUSA. Below, J . MILTON F.

Rev. Inscribed within an ornamental border of leaves, PRÆMIUM OPTIME MERENTI EX INSTITUTO BENJ . A RUMFORD S . R . I . COMITIS ADJUDICATUM A REG . SOC . LOND. 3·4. Æ.

The Rumford Medal was founded by Count Rumford in 1796, and is awarded biennially for the most important discoveries in heat or light during the preceding two years. The medal is struck in gold and in silver.

This type was discontinued by order of the Council of the Society, Jan. 15, 1863, and on the recommendation of the Master of the Mint. *See* description below of medal now in use.

67. —— —— —— —— Rumford Medal. Head of Rumford, *l*., bare.

Leg. BENIAMIN AB RVMFORD S . ROM . IMP . COMES INSTITVIT. Below, MDCCXCVI. On truncation, CH . WIENER.

Rev. Within a wreath of oak and laurel leaves bound with ribbons, OPTIME IN LVCIS CALORISQVE NATVRA EXQVIRENDA MERENTI ADIVDICAT SOC : REG : LOND : 3·4. Æ.

68. [London.] **Royal Society.** Rumford Medal. Another copy.
3·4. Æ.

69. **London. St. Thomas's Hospital.** Solly Medal. Head of Solly, *l.*, bare, hair short, crown of head bare. *Leg.* SAMUEL . SOLLY . F.R.S. Below, AFTER E . B . STEPHENS A.R.A. J . S . & A. B . WYON.

Rev. Inscribed around, IN MEMORY . OF . SAMUEL . SOLLY . F . R . S. SURGEON TO S$^{T.}$ THOMAS'S HOSPITAL ✤ FOUNDED . A.D. 1873 ✤ Inside on the face, AWARDED FOR EXCELLENCE OF SURGICAL REPORTS TO [recipient's name]. 2·76. Æ.

70. ——— **Statistical Society.** Howard Medal. Bust of Howard, *l.*, hair long, and tied behind; in coat, collar, and cravat. *Leg.* JOHN HOWARD F.R.S. SHERIFF OF BEDFORD . 1773. Below, A. B. WYON.

Rev. A sheaf of corn, erect, with inscription, HOWARD . PRIZE . FOUNDED . 1873 . WILLIAM A. GUY M.B. F.R.S. PRESIDENT. Inscribed around, within a border, STATISTICAL SOCIETY . ESTABLISHED . 1834. 3·0. Æ.

71. **Marlborough, Charles Spencer, Duke of, F.R.S.** Bust of the Duke, *r.*, in armour and riband across the breast. *Leg.* CAROLUS SPENCER. Below, J. A. DASSIER.

Rev. Inscription, DUX DE MARLBOROUGH. M.DCC.XLII. 2·16. Æ.

72. **Martius, Carl Friedrich Philipp von.** Bust of Martius, *l.*, bare, hair short. *Leg.* CAR . FR . PH . MARTIVS . Below, A. STANGER . F.

Rev. Within a border, spaced on the face, the inscription, VIRO IN BOTANICA PRINCIPI STVDIO FIDE CONSILIO SIBI PROBATISSIMO ACADEMIA R . BOICA D . LVB . MERITO TERTIO KALEND . APRIL M.D.CCC.LXIIII. *Outer leg.*, above, CANDIDE ET FORTITER. Below, RERVM COGNOSCERE CAVSAS. 1·9. Æ.

73. **Milne-Edwards, Henri, For. Mem. R.S.** Bust of Milne-Edwards, *l.*, hair long, in coat, collar, and bow necktie. *Leg.* HENRI MILNE EDWARDS DE L'ACADEMIE DES SCIENCES. Behind bust, ALPHÉE DUBOIS.

Rev. Inscription, spaced on the face, LEÇONS SUR L'ANATOMIE ET LA PHYSIOLOGIE COMPAREES 1857–1880. A. H. MILNE EDWARDS SES DISCIPLES ET SES ADMIRATEURS. 2·65. Æ.

74. **Modena. Società Italiana delle Scienze.** Medal in celebration of the centenary of the Society. An eagle upon her nest,

with wings expanded, the rayed sun above. Below, INSENGA. *Leg.* within a border, SOCIETA' ITALIANA DELLE SCIENZE . FONDATA NEL 1782.

Rev. Within a circle, the inscription, LA SOCIETA' ITALIANA DELLE SCIENZE NELL' AN . 1882 CENTENARIO DELLA FONDAZIONE. Without, a wreath of oak and laurel. 2·22. Æ.

75. **Moivre, Abraham de, F.R.S.** Bust of De Moivre, *r.*, hair long, in coat buttoned in front. *Leg.* ABRAHAMUS DE MOIVRE . Below, I . A. DASSIER .

Rev. Within an ornamental border, UTRIUSQE SOCIETATIS REGALIS . LOND . ET . BEROL . SODALIS . M.DCC.XLI.
2·15. Æ.

76. **Montreal. McGill University.** Head of Sir Isaac Newton, *l.*, bare. *Leg.* SCIENTIIS . MATHEMATICIS . ET . PHYSICIS . FELICITER . EXCULTIS. Behind bust, NEWTON. Below, J. S. & A. B. WYON SC.

Rev. Above, the arms, crest, and motto of the Molson family. Within an olive wreath, ANNA MOLSON DONAVIT 1864. Inscribed around, UNIVERSITAS M^C GILL MONTE REGIO . IN DOMINO CONFIDO. 1·78. Æ.

77. —————— —————— —————— Head of Watt, *r.*, hair short. Behind, in the field, JAMES WATT. *Leg.* PRESENTED AT M^C GILL UNIVERSITY . MONTREAL . PRIZE FOR APPLIED SCIENCES. Below truncation, ALLAN WYON . SC.

Rev. A wreath of maple and rose leaves, with thistles and roses. Inscribed around, IN MEMORY OF THE MEETING OF THE BRITISH ASSOCIATION AT MONTREAL. 1884. Below wreath, A. WYON.
1·78. Æ.

78. **Muratori, Ludovico Antonio.** Bust of Muratori, *r.*, hair long, in the cap and garb of a priest of the Roman Church. *Leg.* LODOVICO ANT . MURATORI. Below, F. SPERANZA.

Rev. Within a laurel wreath, the inscription, AL . PADRE DELLA STORIA . ITALIANA IL . MUNICIPIO DI . MODENA XXI . OCTOBRE MDCCCLXXII. 2·16. Æ.

79. **Newton, Sir Isaac, P.R.S.** Bust of Newton, *l.*, hair short, in shirt with open collar and mantle round the shoulders. *Leg.* ISAACVS . NEWTONVS. Below, I . C .

Rev. Science, with wings on her head, seated, *l.*, leans upon a table, and holds a diagram of the solar system. *Leg.* FELIX . COGNOSCERE . CAVSAS. *Ex.* M.DCC.XXVI. 2·04. Æ.

80. —————— —————— ————— Bust of Newton, three-quarters, *r.*, hair long, in shirt with open collar, and mantle around the

shoulders. *Leg.* ISAACVS NEWTONIUS. Below, I. DASSIER. F.
Rev. A representation of Newton's monument in Westminster Abbey; on the base is inscribed, NAT. 1642. M. 1726.
1·68. Æ.

81. **Newton, Sir Isaac, P.R.S.** Bust of Newton, three-quarters, *l.*, looking *r.*, hair long, in shirt with open collar, and mantle round the shoulders. *Leg.* ISAACUS NEWTONIUS.
Rev. A wreath of flowers enclosing the inscription, EQ. AUR. PHILOSOPHUS. OBIIT 31. MART. 1727. NATUS ANNOS 85.
1·32. Æ.

82. ——— ——— ——— ——— Bust of Newton, *l.*, hair long, in shirt with open collar, and loose mantle. *Leg.* S^R ISAAC NEWTON.
Rev. A device of a caduceus, with cornucopiæ and laurel branch. Inscription, HALFPENNY. 1793. 1·12. Æ.

83. ——— ——— ——— Another copy. Same as preceding, but smaller, and *rev.* without caduceus; the inscription, FARTHING. 1793. 0·88. Æ.

84. ——— ——— ——— ——— Bust of Newton, *l.*, hair long, in cravat and plain coat. *Leg.* ISAACUS NEWTONIUS. Below truncation, PETIT. F.
Rev. Inscription, spaced on the face, NATUS VOLSTROPII IN ANGLIA AN. M.DC.XLII. OBIIT AN. M.DCC.XXVII. *Ex.* SERIES NUMISMATICA UNIVERSALIS VIRORUM ILLUSTRIUM. M.DCCCXIX. DURAND EDIDIT. *See* Nos. 57 and 76. 1·63. Æ.

85. **Nordenskiöld, Adolphus Ericus, Baron.** Bust of Nordenskiöld, *r.*, bare, hair short. *Leg.* ADOLPHUS ERICUS NORDENSKIÖLD. Below, W. RUNEBERG C. JAHN SC.
Rev. The Genius of Science, laureate, standing, *r.*, partially clad in loose drapery. In her right hand she holds aloft a lamp illuminating the north polar region of a globe beneath. Near figure, an anchor, with compass, a ship's log, and other navigational instruments. *Leg.* ASIA CIRCUM = NA = VIGATA *Ex.* IN HONOR. POPULARIS SUI SOC. SCIENT. FENNICA CUD. CUR. Below. AHRENBERG DEL. W. RUNEBERG C. JAHN SC.
This medal was struck by the Société des Sciences de Finlande, in honour of Baron Nordenskiöld, and an example in gold was presented to him January 13, 1881. 2·21. Æ.

86. **Paris. Société d'Encouragement pour l'Industrie Nationale.** Head of Lavoisier, *l.*, hair long and tied with ribbon. Inscribed around, LAURENT LAVOISIER. Below truncation, CAQUÉ. F.

Rev. In the centre, spaced on the field and encircled by a laurel wreath, A WALTER WELDON GRANDE MÉDAILLE DES ARTS CHIMIQUES 15 JUIN 1877. Inscribed outside, SOCIÉTÉ D'ENCOURAGEMENT POUR L'INDUSTRIE NATIONALE. 2. Æ.

87. **Parkes, Edmund Alexander, F.R.S.** Head of Parkes, *l.*, bare, *Leg.* EDMUND ALEXANDER PARKES . B . 1819—D . 1876. Below truncation, J. S. & A. B. WYON.

Rev. Within a laurel wreath, PARKES MEMORIAL MEDAL. Inscribed without, 'Η ΠΕΡΙ ΤΟ ΣΩΜΑ ΚΑΙ ΤΗΝ ΨΥΧΗΝ 'ΥΓΙΕΙΑ. 2·2. Æ.

88. **Philadelphia. Numismatic and Antiquarian Society.** Medal struck to commemorate the 21st anniversary of the foundation of the Society. Bust of Eli K. Price, *l.*, hair long, in coat, collar, and tie. *Leg.* ELI K. PRICE PRESIDENT. Below, 1879. On truncation, W. H. KEY F.

Rev. The arms, crest, and motto (*vestigia rerum sequi*) of the Society. Inscribed within a border, THE NUMISMATIC & ANTIQUARIAN SOCIETY OF PHILADA . FOUNDED JAN. 1. 1858.
1·66. Æ.

Only one copy was struck in silver, which was presented to the President himself; in bronze, 199 were issued.

89. **Presl, Johann Svatopluk, and Karl Bořivoj Presl.** Busts, opposite each other, of K. B. Presl and J. S. Presl. The former in profile, *r.*, hair short, wearing coat, collar, and cravat; the latter, three-quarter face to left, hair parted in middle, wearing coat, collar, and cravat. *Leg.* CAROLVS . BORZVVOJ . PRESL . NATVS . PRAGAE . XVII . FEB . A . MDCCLXXXXIIII . MORTVVS IBIDEM . II . NOV . A . MDCCLII . DR . MED . ET . PHIL . PROF . P . O . VNIV . PRAGENSIS .

JOANNES . SVATOPLVK . PRESL . NATVS . PRAGAE . IIII . SEPTEMB . A . MDCCLXXXXI . MORTVVS . IBIDEM . VI . APRIL . A . MDCCCXXXXVIIII . DR . MED . PROF . P . O . VNIV . PRAGENSIS. Below the busts, IN . MEMORIAM . JOANNIS . ANTE . HOS . CENTVM . ANNOS . NATI.

Rev. A branching tree fern. Inscribed around, FRATERNIS . ET . NATVRAE . ET . DISCIPLINAE . VINCVLIS . CONIVNCTI. 3·4. Æ.

90. **Pulteney, William, Earl of Bath.** Bust of Pulteney, *r.*, hair long, in loose mantle. *Leg.* GUILIELMUS PULTENEY . A DASSIER F.

Rev. Within a wreath of oak, COMES DE BATH . MDCCXLIV.
2·15. Æ.

91. **Purkyně, Johann E., For. Mem. R.S.** Bust, *r.*, hair short in coat, collar, and bow tie. *Leg.* JOANN . EV . PURKYNĚ. Below, SEIDAN.

Rev. Inscription, PHYSIOLOGIAE RECENTIORIS FUNDATORI DECEM ABHINC LUSTRIS UNIVERSITATI CAROLO-FERDINANDEAE ADLECTO FACULTAS MEDICA PRAGENSIS IX . DEC. MDCCCLXVIII.
1·74. Æ.

92. **Quetelet, Lambert Adolphe Jacques, For. Mem. R.S.** Head of Quetelet, *l.* *Leg.* ADOLPHUS QUETELET. Below, BRAEMT F.
Rev. Inscription, spaced on the face, ADOLPHO QUETELET VIRO DE ACADEMIA EGREGIE MERITO QUINQUE LUSTRA IN ACTUARII PERPETUI MUNERE FELICITER PERACTA CONGRATULANTES HUNC NUMMUM PIETATIS ET REVERENTIAE TESTEM CUDENDUM CURAVERUNT ACADEMIAE REGIAE BELGICAE SOCII ANN MDCCCLX. 1·75. R.

93. **Rotterdam. Bataafsch Genootschap der Prœfondervindelijke Wijsbegeerte.** Medal struck in celebration of the Batavian Society's centenary, 1769–1869. *Inner leg.* Within a circle formed by a coiled snake, SOCIETAS PHILOSOPHIAE EXPERIMENTALIS BATAVA ROTERODAMI CENTESIMUM NATALEM CELEBRANS. *Outer leg.* IN MEMORIAM STEPHANI HOOGENDIJK FUNDATORIS; MDCCLXIX–MDCCCLXIX.
Rev. Experience, in loose draperies, standing, looking to left. In her left hand a crowned staff, with scroll entwined, bearing the legend, RERVM MAGISTRA; in right an anchor. Near, a column, on the top of which a pair of scales, on the front the Netherlands arms surmounted by a crown. On the left of the figure an altar, with flames arising, on front the Netherlands lion rampant, on a shield. Inscription, CERTOS FERET EXPERIENTIA FRUCTUS. *Ex.* J. P. MENGER F. 1·59. Æ.

Rumford Medal. See London, Royal Society.

94. **San Francisco. Astronomical Society of the Pacific.** Comet Medal. Across field a comet, in relief, and scattered stars. Inscribed around, ASTRONOMICAL SOCIETY OF THE PACIFIC. Below, A.D.
Rev. Spaced on the field, THIS MEDAL, FOUNDED A.D. MDCCCXC BY JOSEPH A. DONOHOE IS PRESENTED TO [recipient's name] IN COMMEMORATION OF THE DISCOVERY OF A COMET ON 2·37. Æ.

95. **Schemnitz. Königl. Ungarische Berg- und Forst-Akademie.** Medal in celebration of the 100th anniversary of the Academy, 1770–1870. Bust of Maria Theresa, Queen of Hungary, *r.*, wearing bandeau, with falling drapery gathered at the breast. On either side a laurel and palm branch *Leg.* within a border, A . MARIA . THERESIA . HUNG: REGE . METALLICORUM . ACADEMIA. Below, C. RADNITZKY.
Rev. Knowledge, laureate, seated facing, holding lamp and book. In the distance, mountains and town. *Ex.* The arms

of Schemnitz. Inscribed within a border, SCHEMNICII . CONDITA . 1770 . PRIMUM . SECULUM . CELEBRAT . 1870. 2·74. Æ.

Siemens, Sir Charles William, F.R.S. *See* London, City and Guilds Institute, *and* King's College.

96. **Sloane, Sir Hans, Bart., P.R.S.** Bust of Sir Hans Sloane, *l.*, cap on head, in loose robe. *Leg.* HANS SLOANE EQU . BARONETTUS. Below, A. DASSIER . F.
Rev. Inscription, PRÆSES SOCIETATIS REGIÆ LONDINENSIS . MDCCXLIV. Above, festoons of flowers; below, branches of oak. 2·15. R.

97. ——————— ———— ——— ——— Another copy. 2·15. Æ.

98. **Soane, Sir John, F.R.S.** Bust of Soane, *r.*, bare, hair short. *Leg.* JOHN SOANE. Below, W . WYON . A . R . A . MINT.
Rev. A representation of the elevation of the north-west angle of the Bank of England, with inscription, A TRIBUTE OF RESPECT FROM THE BRITISH ARCHITECTS. Below, in exergue, MDCCCXXXIV. 2·26. Æ.

Solly, Samuel, F.R.S. *See* London, St. Thomas's Hospital.

99. **Stas, Jean Servais, For. Mem. R.S.** Head of Stas, *l.*, Below, A . MICHAUX . D'APRES L.W.
Rev. Inscription, spaced on the field, A JEAN-SERVAIS STAS, NÉ A LOUVAIN LE 21 AOUT 1813, ÉLU MEMBRE DE LA CLASSE DES SCIENCES EN 1841 . SOUVENIR JUBILAIRE (5 MAI 1891). Inscribed around, within a border, ACADÉMIE ROYALE DES SCIENCES, DES LETTRES ET DES BEAUX-ARTS DE BELGIQUE.
2·02. R.

100. **Stukeley, William, F.R.S.** Head of Stukeley, *r.*, with wreath of oak leaves. *Leg.* REV . GVL . STVKELEY . M.D . SR & AS. Below, truncation, *æt.* 54.
Rev. Representation of Stonehenge, and below, OB . MAR . 4 . 1765. Æ : 84. Cast. 3·32. Æ.

101. **Sydney. Royal Society of New South Wales.** Bust of Rev. William Branwhite Clarke, F.R.S., *r.*, bearded, wearing academicals. *Leg.* WILLIAM BRANWHITE CLARKE . M.A. F.R.S. 1878. Below, J. S. & A. B. WYON.
Rev. Within a wreath, composed of the palms and flowering plants of Australia, FOR RESEARCHES IN NATURAL SCIENCE. Inscribed around, THE ROYAL SOCIETY OF NEW SOUTH WALES . SYDNEY. Below, J. S. & A. B. WYON. 2·18. Æ.

102. **Sylvester, James Joseph, F.R.S.** Bust, *l.*, hair and beard long, crown of head bare, in coat and collar. Behind, SYLVESTER. Below truncation, C. E. BARBER F.

Rev. Within a wreath of oak leaves, INDE . AB . A.D . MDCCCLXXVI . VSQVE . AD . A.D . MDCCCLXXXIII. Inscribed around within a border, PER . SEPTEM . ANNOS . IN . VNIVERSITATE . AB . IOHNS . HOPKINS . FVNDATA . PROFESSOR. 2·52. Æ.

103. **Thiersch, Frederick von.** Bust of Thiersch, *r.*, hair short, bare. Below, J. RIES.
Rev. Within an ornamental border, FRIDERICVS THIERSCH PHILOLOGVS. Inscribed without, NATVS D . XIV . M . JVNII MDCCLXXXIV . OBIIT D. XXV. M . FEBRVARII MDCCCLX. 1·89. Æ.

104. **Tiedemann, Friedrich, For. Mem. R.S.** Bust of Tiedemann, *r.*, bare. *Leg.* FRIDERICVS TIEDEMANN NAT . D. XXIII AVG . MDCCLXXXI. Below, C. VOIGT.
Rev. A star-fish, with inscription VIRO DE AVGENDA NATVRAE SCIENTIA PER X LVSTRA EGREGIE MERITO SODALES. FRANCOF . A . M . D . X MART . MDCCCLIV. 1·76. Æ.

Todd, Robert Bentley, F.R.S. See London, King's College.

105. **Upsala. Universitet.** Medal struck in celebration of the 400th anniversary of the University. Head of Oscar II of Sweden and Norway, *r.*, bare, hair short. *Leg.* OSCAR II REX SVECIÆ ET NORVEGIÆ. Below, A . LINDBERG.
Rev. The Genius of Upsala, laureate, clad in loose robes, is seated, facing. In her right hand she holds aloft the lamp of knowledge, the left rests upon the triangular crowned shield of Svealand, the head of a crouching lion appearing from behind (in allusion to Götaland). On the left of the figure emblems of the arts; above the pole star casts its rays. In the field a flying bat. Inscription, EX TENEBRIS PER UMBRAS AD LUCEM. *Ex.* PERACTA QUATUOR SECULA CELEBRAVIT UNIVERSITAS UPSALIENSIS MDCCCLXXVII . LINDBERG. 2·22. Æ.

106. **Virchow, Rudolph, For. Mem. R.S.** Medallion cast in honour of Prof. Virchow on the occasion of his 70th birthday. Bust of Virchow, *r.*, bearded, in coat, collar, and cravat, Inscribed around, RVDOLPHVS . VIRCHOW . POMERANVS . CIVIS . BEROLINENSIS; in the field, ÆTAT: LXX. Inscribed below, right and left, *A. Scharff, C. Waschmañ.*
Rev. Anatomy seated, *r.*, near ornamental table, looking left, open book on lap, upon which she rests right hand, the left at arms length holding a human skull. Science, winged, stands near, holding aloft and over Anatomy a flaming torch, the right hand raises drapery from the figure of the Ephesian Diana near, a serpent's head appearing from behind. On

right, a mummy; in foreground and beyond, books, skulls, a microscope, and other emblems of the arts and sciences. Inscribed in exergue, OMNIS . CELLVLA . A . CELLVLA.

Cast. 7 × 7. Æ.

107. **Wales, Frederick, Prince of, F.R.S.** Bust of the Prince, *l.*, hair long, in armour, riband and star of the Garter. *Leg.* FREDERIC . WALLIÆ PRINCEPS. Below, J. A. DASSIER.

Rev. Two genii, among clouds, supporting the Prince's coronet, with plumes and motto. 2·15 Æ.

108. **Watt, James, F.R.S.** Bust of Watt, *r.*, with mantle over the shoulders. Behind, in the field, JAMES WATT 1736–1819. Below, JOSEPH S. WYON S.

Rev. Representation of a steam engine, with sun and planet motion, and inscription below, STEAM ENGINE AS CONSTRUCTED BY JAMES WATT. 1·86. Æ.

109. —— —— —— Head of Watt, *l.*, behind head, I. WATT. On truncation, A. J. STOTHARD.; below, F. L. CHANTREY. R.A. D.

Rev. Clio, looking to *r.*, leans in almost upright position against low pillar, on which rests her left hand, with scroll, bearing legend, TO GREAT MEN; in right hand a pen. Below, PUB^D BY S PARKER LONDON . MDCCCXXVII. Right and left, A. J. STOTHARD F. T. STOTHARD R.A. D. 2·46. Æ

—— —— —— *See* also Montreal, McGill University.

110. **Whitworth, Sir Joseph, Bart., F.R.S.** Bust of Whitworth, *l.*, bearded, hair long, crown of head bare, in collar and coat. *Leg.* SIR JOSEPH WHITWORTH . BART .'. F R S .'. D C L .'. L L D B^N ∴ DEC^R XXI .'. MDCCCIII. On truncation, 18EJP83. Below, ALLAN WYON.

Rev. A representation of Whitworth's measuring machine. Inscription above, A DIFFERENCE OF ONE MILLIONTH OF AN INCH IS MEASVRED BY VSING FOVR TRVE PLANES IN CONCERT; beneath, WHITWORTH SCHOLARSHIPS FOVNDED MDCCCLXVIII; to right, J . S . & A . B . WYON. 2·26. Æ.

111. **Wray, Daniel, F.R.S.** Bust of Wray, *r.*, hair short, in mantle fastened with brooch on the shoulder. *Leg.* DANIEL . WRAY . ANGLVS . AET . XXIV. On truncation, 1726. Below, G . POZZO F.

Rev. Inscription, NIL ACTVM REPVTANS CVM QVID SVPERESSET AGENDVM. 2·7. Æ.

112. **Wren, Sir Christopher, P.R.S.** Bust of Wren, *l.*, hair long, in vest and loose mantle. *Leg.* . CHRISTOP . WREN . EQVES

. AVR & ARCHITECT . Below bust, . OBIIT . A . D . 1723. ÆT. 91 .

Rev. The west front of St. Paul's Cathedral. *Upper leg.* VNVM . PRO . CVNCTIS . FAMA . LOQVATVR . OPVS . *Lower leg.* INCEPT . A.D . 1675 . PERFECT . A.D . 1711. *Ex.* AEDES . S . PAVLI . LOND.; G . D . GAAB . SCVLP. Cast. 3·92. Æ.

PRESIDENTS OF THE ROYAL SOCIETY.

	Date of Election.	Years in Office.
William, Lord Viscount Brouncker	April 22, 1663	14

b. 1620 (?); *d.* April 5, 1684. Adhered to Chas. I, and after the Restoration was appointed by Chas. II Chancellor of the Queen Consort, and Keeper of her Great Seal (1662); one of the Commissioners for executing the office of Lord High Admiral (1664), and Master of St. Catherine's Hospital (1681). Mathematician. The first to introduce continued fractions, and to give a series for the quadrature of a portion of the equilateral hyperbola. For portrait see Plate 1.

Sir Joseph Williamson, Kt.	Nov. 30, 1677	3

Died 1701. M.A. (Oxon.). Secretary of State (1674). For portrait see Plate 1.

Sir Christopher Wren, Kt.	Nov. 30, 1680	2

b. Oct. 20, 1632; *d.* Feb. 25, 1722-3. D.C.L. (Oxon.). Professor of Astronomy at Gresham College (1657). Savilian Professor at Oxford (1660). Architect of St. Paul's Cathedral and many London Churches. For portrait see Plate 1.

Sir John Hoskins, Bart.	Nov. 30, 1682	1

b. July 23, 1634; *d.* Sept. 12, 1705. Master in Chancery. Evelyn describes him as "a most learned virtuoso, as well as lawyer." For portrait see Plate 1.

Sir Cyril Wyche, Kt.	Nov. 30, 1683	1

Died December 29, 1707. M.A., LL.D. (Oxon.). Secretary for Ireland. Lord Justice (1693).

Samuel Pepys	Dec. 1, 1684	2

b. Feb. 23, 1632-3; *d.* May 26, 1703. Author of the celebrated Diary. Clerk of the Acts of the Navy (1660). Master of Trinity House (1676). Secretary to the Admiralty (1680). For portrait see Plate 2.

	Date of Election.	Years in Office.

John, Earl of Carbery (Lord Vaughan) ...... Nov. 30, 1686 — 3

Died Jan. 16, 1712-13. For some years Governor of Jamaica. For portrait see Plate 2.

Thomas, Earl of Pembroke, K.G. .... Nov. 30, 1689 — 1

b. 1656; *d.* Jan. 22, 1732-3. First Lord of the Admiralty (1690). Lord Privy Seal (1692). Lord Lieutenant of Ireland (1707). Lord High Admiral (1708). Mathematician and Antiquary.

Sir Robert Southwell, Kt. .... Dec. 1, 1690 — 5

b. 1635; *d.* 1702. Envoy extraordinary to the Court of Portugal (1672). Appointed by Will. III Principal Secretary of State for Ireland. Contributed papers to the 'Philosophical Transactions,' principally on physiological and chemical subjects.

Charles Montague (afterwards Earl of Halifax, K.G.) .... Nov. 30, 1695 — 3

b. April 16, 1661; *d.* May 19, 1715. Appointed a lord of the Treasury (1692), Chancellor of the Exchequer (1694). Aided by Somers, Locke, Newton, and Halley, he determined to remedy the depreciation of the currency, and succeeded in passing the Re-coinage Bill (1696). First Lord of the Treasury (1697).

John, Lord Somers .... Nov. 30, 1698 — 5

b. 1652; *d.* April 26, 1716. Appointed Solicitor-General upon accession of William and Mary; Attorney-General (1692); Lord Keeper of the Great Seal (1693); Lord Chancellor (1697); Lord President of the Council (1708).

Sir Isaac Newton, Kt. .... Nov. 30, 1703 — 24

b. Dec. 25, 1642; *d.* March 20, 1727. Discovered the Binomial Theorem, in the beginning of 1665; the direct method of Fluxions or elements of the differential calculus, Nov., 1665; the unequal refrangibility of the rays of light, Jan., 1666; the integral calculus, May, 1666. Made his first reflecting telescope, 1668. Lucasian Professor of Mathematics at Cambridge, 1669. In 1686 the MS. of the 'Principia' was presented to the Royal Society, and in 1687 it was published. Warden of the Mint (1695); Master of the Mint (1699). Publication of the "Opticks," 1704. Knighted by Queen Anne, 1705.

Sir Hans Sloane, Bart. .... Nov. 30, 1727 — 14

b. April 16, 1660; *d.* Jan. 11, 1753. Fellow of the Coll. Phys. in 1687. Shortly afterwards accompanied Duke of Albemarle to Jamaica, where he collected natural history specimens for fifteen months. Created a baronet by Geo. I, an honour to which no English physician had before attained. Physician General to the Army (1716). Pres. Coll. Phys. (1727). There are twenty-four papers by Sir Hans Sloane in the 'Philosophical Transactions.'

	Date of Election.	Years in Office.

Martin Folkes .... Nov. 30, 1741   11
    b. Oct. 29, 1690; *d*. June 28, 1754. Appointed Vice-President of the Royal Society by Sir I. Newton (1723). Pres. Soc. of Antiquaries (1750). Contributed ten papers to the 'Philosophical Transactions.'

George, Earl of Macclesfield .... Nov. 30, 1752   12
    b. 1697; *d*. March 17, 1764. Mathematician and Astronomer. In 1739 aided by James Bradley erected an Astronomical Observatory, with the finest instrumental equipment then existing. His series of personal observations extended from June 4, 1740, to his death. He was mainly instrumental in procuring the change of style in 1752, being virtually the author of the "Bill for Regulating the Commencement of the Year," which passed the Peers in 1751. He contributed papers to the 'Philosophical Transactions.'

James, Earl of Morton (Lord Aberdour) ...... Nov. 30, 1764   4
    b. 1702; *d*. Oct. 12, 1768. Astronomer. Instrumental in founding (1739) the Philosophical (afterwards the Royal) Society of Edinburgh. Was one of the Commissioners of Longitude, and took an active part in the preparations for observing the Transit of Venus in 1769. One of the earliest Trustees of the British Museum, and Keeper of the Records of Scotland. Contributed several papers to the 'Philosophical Transactions.'

James (afterwards Sir James) Burrow .... Oct. 27, 1768   —
    b. Nov. 28, 1701; *d*. Nov. 5, 1782. Legal Reporter and Antiquary. Contributed five papers on Earthquakes to the 'Philosophical Transactions.' He was elected to the chair only to serve until the ensuing anniversary.

James West .... Nov. 30, 1768   4
    d. July, 1772. M.A. Balliol Coll., Oxford. M.P. for St. Albans in 1741. Joint Secretary to the Treasury till 1762. A Collector of Manuscripts, Coins, and Medals, and a Fellow of the Society of Antiquaries. "Astronomy is indebted to Mr. West for the preservation of several manuscript volumes and papers of Flamsteed's." (Weld, vol. ii, p. 50.)

James (afterwards Sir James) Burrow .... July 2, 1772   —
    See above. Elected a second time to fill the chair till the following anniversary.

Sir John Pringle, Bart .... Nov. 30, 1772   6
    b. April 10, 1707; *d*. Jan. 18, 1782. Studied medicine at Leyden, and settled as a physician in Edinburgh. Appointed (1734) Joint Professor of Pneumatics [*i.e.*, Metaphysics] and Moral Philosophy in Edinburgh. Physician to the Earl of Stair (1742), and Physician-General to the Forces in Flanders (1744). Afterwards Physician to the Forces ordered to march against the Pretender's

	Date of Election.	Years in Office.

adherents in Scotland. In 1764 Physician in Ordinary to the Queen. In 1774 Physician to the King. Author of medical works, especially on Military Hygiene, and of several papers read before the Royal Society.

Sir Joseph Banks, Bart.................... Nov. 30, 1778   41

    b. Feb. 13, 1743–44; *d.* June 19, 1820. In 1766 accompanied Lieut. Phipps to Newfoundland and Labrador, where he made collections in Natural History. In 1768 joined Captain Cook in his first voyage of discovery. In 1772 fitted out and accompanied a scientific expedition to Iceland, where he made large natural history collections, and purchased numerous Icelandic books and manuscripts, all of which he presented to the British Museum. Baronet, 1781; Privy Councillor, 1797.

William Hyde Wollaston .... June 29, 1820   —

    b. Aug. 6, 1766; *d.* Dec. 22, 1828. Studied for Medicine, and became a Tancred Fellow at Cambridge. In 1789 settled at Bury St. Edmunds as a physician. From 1797 to his death a constant contributor to the 'Philosophical Transactions,' in which appear 39 of his papers in Chemistry, Astronomy, Optics, Mechanics, Acoustics, Mineralogy, Crystallography, Physiology, Pathology, and Botany. He was the discoverer of palladium (1804) and rhodium (1805). In 1828 he described his method for rendering platinum malleable. He established the Donation Fund of the Royal Society (see p. 121).

Sir Humphry Davy, Bart.................... Nov. 30, 1820   7

    b. Dec. 17, 1778; *d.* May 29, 1829. Superintendent of Dr. Beddoes' Pneumatic Institution at Bristol (1798), where he commenced his researches. Director of the Laboratory of the Royal Institution (1801). Invented the Safety-lamp (1815); the first safety-lamp is still in the possession of the Society. In 1823 he communicated to the Royal Society his "Researches on Electro-magnetic Phenomena." He contributed 46 memoirs and lectures to the 'Philosophical Transactions,' and published nine separate works on Science.

Davies Gilbert .... Nov. 6, 1827   3

    b. March 6, 1767; *d.* Nov. 7, 1839. M.P. for Bodmin (1806). "He took a prominent part in parliamentary investigations connected with the arts and sciences" ('Dict. Nat. Biog.'). In 1819 he suggested, with success, the establishment of the Observatory at the Cape of Good Hope. He contributed several papers to the 'Philosophical Transactions.'

H.R.H. The Duke of Sussex................ Nov. 30, 1830   8

    Augustus Frederick, Duke of Sussex, sixth son of George III. *b.* Jan. 27, 1773; *d.* April 21, 1843. During his tenure of office he constantly presided at all meetings of the Council and Society.

Presidents.

	Date of Election.	Years in Office.
The Marquis of Northampton	Nov. 30, 1838	10

b. Jan. 1, 1790: d. Jan. 17, 1851. One of the earliest Presidents of the Geological Society; Pres. Brit. Assoc. 1836 and 1848.

The Earl of Rosse	Nov. 30, 1848	6

b. June 17, 1800: d. Oct. 31, 1867. Astronomer. Construction of great reflecting telescope commenced 1845. Researches on nebulæ and other celestial phenomena in 'Philosophical Transactions,' 1840, '44, '50, '61, and '68. Chancellor of University of Dublin (1862).

Lord Wrottesley	Nov. 30, 1854	4

b. Aug. 5, 1798; d. Oct. 27, 1867. Practical Astronomer, carrying on his observations at two small observatories, one at Blackheath, the other at Wrottesley. Gold Medal of the Astronom. Soc. for a catalogue of Stars (1839). Pres. Astronom. Soc. (1841). Author of two Astronomical Papers in the 'Philosophical Transactions.' Pres. Brit. Assoc. (1860). Specially interested in Government measures for improving the position of Science in this country, and in the introduction of Science as a branch of teaching in Public Schools.

Sir Benjamin Brodie, Bart.	Nov. 30, 1858	3

b. 1783; d. Oct. 21, 1862. Physiologist and Surgeon. For thirty years on the Staff of St. George's Hospital. Medical adviser to three successive Sovereigns. First President of the Medical Council. Author of an important work on the Diseases of the Joints, and of numerous papers in the 'Philosophical Transactions,' and the 'Transactions of the Royal Medical and Chirurgical Society.'

Sir Edward Sabine	Nov. 30, 1861	10

b. Oct. 14, 1788; d. June 26, 1883. K.C.B. (1869); General (1870). On active service 1812-16. Astronomer with Sir John Ross's Expedition in Search of North West Passage (1818). Accompanied Parry's first expedition (1819). Appointed to conduct pendulum experiments in different latitudes (1819), and Joint Commissioner to determine the difference of longitude between the observatories of Paris and Greenwich (1825).

Sir George Airy	Nov. 30, 1871	2

b. June 27, 1801; d. Jan. 2, 1892. Senior Wrangler (1823). Lucasian Professor of Experimental Science (1826). Plumian Professor of Astronomy and Director of Cambridge Observatory (1828). Astronomer Royal (1835). Chairman of the Commission charged with the Construction of Standard Weights and Measures (1834). Pres. Brit. Assoc. (1851). Organised Expedition for Observing Transit of Venus (1874).

210   *Record of the Royal Society.*

	Date of Election.	Years in Office.
Sir Joseph D. Hooker	Nov. 30, 1873	5

    b. June 30, 1817. Botanist to Sir J. C. Ross's voyage ("Erebus" and "Terror"). Botanist to the Geological Survey. Expedition to India and the Himalayas (1848); to Syria (1860). Pres. Brit. Assoc. (1868). Botanical Expedition to Morocco (1871) and across America (1877). Director of Royal Gardens at Kew (1865–85).

William Spottiswoode	Nov. 30, 1878	5

    b. Jan. 11, 1825; *d.* June 27, 1883. Mathematician, Physicist, and Oriental Scholar. Queen's printer. Lecturer in Mathematics at Balliol College. *Meditationes Analyticæ* (1847). Numerous papers on the Polarisation of Light and other physical subjects in the 'Philosophical Transactions,' 'Phil. Mag.,' &c. Pres. Math. Soc. (1871). Pres. Brit. Assoc. (1878).

Thomas Henry Huxley	July 5, 1883	2

    b. May 4, 1825; *d.* June 29, 1895. Lecturer on General Nat. Hist. at the Metropolitan School of Science (1854). Naturalist to the Geological Survey (1855); subsequently Prof. of Biology in the Royal College of Science. Fullerian Professor of Physiology in the Royal Institution (1856–58). Hunterian Professor at the Royal College of Surgeons (1863–70). Pres. Geolog. Society, and of the Brit. Assoc. (1870). Inspector of Fisheries (1881). Trustee of the Brit. Museum. Member of many Royal and other Commissions.

Sir George Gabriel Stokes, Bart.	Nov. 30, 1885	5

    b. Aug. 13, 1819. Senior Wrangler (1841). Lucasian Professor of Mathematics (1849). Lecturer on Physics at the Royal School of Mines (1854–60). Pres. Brit. Assoc. (1869). Author of Burnett Lectures on Light (Aberdeen) and Gifford Lectures on Natural Theology (Edinburgh), and of various mathematical and physical papers in the 'Transactions of the Cambridge Philosophical Society,' the 'Philosophical Transactions,' and other scientific serials.

Lord Kelvin (Sir William Thomson)	Nov. 30, 1890	5

    b. June 26, 1824. Second Wrangler and first Smith's Prizeman at Camb. (1845). Prof. of Nat. Philosophy in Glasgow Univ. (1846). Pres. Brit. Assoc. (1871). Author of numerous papers on heat, electricity, and other physical subjects in the 'Philosophical Transactions,' 'Phil Mag.,' &c. Author of 'Treatise on Natural Philosophy' in conjunction with Professor Tait. Inventor of the mirror galvanometer, siphon recorder, a special form of mariner's compass, and naval sounding machine, and many electrical measuring instruments.

	Date of Election.	Years of Office.

Lord Lister .... Nov. 30, 1895 —
  b. April 5, 1827. Prof. of Surgery in the Univ. of Glasgow (1860–69). Prof. of Clinical Surgery in the Univ. of Edinburgh (1869–77). Pres. Brit. Assoc. (1896). Surgeon Extraord. to the Queen. Emeritus Prof. of Clinical Surgery in King's Coll., Lond., and Consulting Surgeon to King's Coll. Hospital.

TREASURERS OF THE ROYAL SOCIETY.

Date of Election.
April 22, 1663. William Ball.
Nov. 30, 1663. Abraham Hill.
Nov. 30, 1665. Daniel Colwal.
Dec. 1, 1679. Abraham Hill.
Nov. 30, 1700. Alexander Pitfield.
Nov. 30, 1728. Roger Gale.
Nov. 30, 1736. James West.
Nov. 30, 1768. Samuel Wegg.
Nov. 30, 1802. William Marsden.
Nov. 30, 1810. Samuel Lysons.
July 29, 1819. Davies Gilbert.
Nov. 30, 1827. Henry Kater.
Nov. 30, 1830. Sir John William Lubbock, Bart.
Nov. 30, 1835. Francis Baily.
Nov. 30, 1838. Sir John William Lubbock, Bart.
Nov. 30, 1845. George Rennie.
Nov. 30, 1850. Lt.-Col. E. Sabine.
Nov. 30, 1861. Prof. W. A. Miller.
Nov. 30, 1870. Wm. Spottiswoode.
Nov. 30, 1878. Sir John Evans, K.C.B.

SECRETARIES OF THE ROYAL SOCIETY.

Date of Election.
April 22, 1663. John Wilkins, D.D.
April 22, 1663. Henry Oldenburg.
Nov. 30, 1668. Thomas Henshaw.

Date of Election.	
Nov. 30, 1672.	John Evelyn.
Nov. 30, 1673.	Abraham Hill.
Nov. 30, 1675.	Thomas Henshaw.
Nov. 30, 1677.	Nehemiah Grew, M.D.
Nov. 30, 1677.	Robert Hooke.
Nov. 30, 1679.	Thomas Gale, D.D.
Nov. 30, 1681.	Francis Aston.
Nov. 30, 1682.	Robert Plot, LL.D.
Nov. 30, 1684.	William Musgrave.
Nov. 30, 1685.	Tancred Robinson, M.D.
Dec. 16, 1685.	Sir John Hoskyns, Bart.
Dec. 16, 1685.	Thomas Gale, D.D.
Nov. 30, 1687.	Richard Waller.
Nov. 30, 1693.	Hans Sloane, M.D.
Nov. 30, 1709.	John Harris, D.D.
Nov. 30, 1710.	Richard Waller.
Nov. 30, 1713.	Edmund Halley, LL.D.
Jan. 13, 1714.	Brook Taylor, LL.D.
Dec. 1, 1718.	John Machin.
Nov. 30, 1721.	James Jurin, M.D.
Nov. 30, 1727.	William Rutty, M.D.
Nov. 30, 1730.	Cromwell Mortimer, M.D.
Nov. 30, 1747.	Peter Daval.
Nov. 30, 1752.	Thomas Birch, D.D.
Nov. 30, 1759.	Charles Morton, M.D.
Nov. 30, 1765.	Matthew Maty, M.D.
Nov. 30, 1773.	Samuel Horsley, LL.B.
Nov. 30, 1776.	Joseph Planta.
Nov. 30, 1778.	Paul Henry Maty, M.A.
May 5, 1784.	Charles Blagden, M.D.
Nov. 30, 1797.	Edward Whitaker Gray, M.D.
Nov. 30, 1804.	William Hyde Wollaston, M.D.
Jan. 22, 1807.	Sir Humphry Davy, Bart.
Nov. 30, 1812.	Taylor Combe.
Nov. 30, 1816.	William Thomas Brande.
Nov. 30, 1824.	Sir John Frederick William Herschel, Bart., M.A.
Nov. 30, 1826.	John George Children.
Nov. 30, 1827.	Peter Mark Roget, M.D.
Nov. 30, 1827.	Lieut.-Col. Edward Sabine, R.A.
Nov. 30, 1830.	John George Children.
Nov. 30, 1837.	Samuel Hunter Christie, M.A.
Nov. 30, 1848.	Thos. Bell.
Nov. 30, 1853.	Dr. W. Sharpey.

Date of Election.
Nov. 30, 1854.   Prof. George Gabriel Stokes.
Nov. 30, 1872.   Prof. Thomas Henry Huxley.
Nov. 30, 1881.   Prof. Michael Foster.
Nov. 30, 1885.   Lord Rayleigh.
Nov. 30, 1896.   Prof. Arthur William Rücker.

FOREIGN SECRETARIES OF THE ROYAL SOCIETY.

Date of Election.
April 11, 1723.   Philip Henry Zollman.
April 18, 1728.   Dr. Dillenius and Dr. Schuchzer.
Aug. 29, 1748.   Thomas Stack, M.D.
Nov. 20, 1751.   James Parsons, M.D.
Mar. 4, 1762.   Matthew Maty, M.D.
Dec. 11, 1766.   John Bevis, M.D.
Feb. 13, 1772.   Paul Henry Maty.
June 30, 1774.   Joseph Planta.
Jan. 14, 1779.   Charles Hutton.
June 17, 1784.   Charles Peter Layard.
Mar. 22, 1804.   Thomas Young, M.D.
Nov. 30, 1830.   Charles König.
Nov. 30, 1837.   Capt. William Henry Smyth, R.N.
Nov. 30, 1839.   John Frederic Daniell.
Dec. 1, 1845.   Lieut.-Col. E. Sabine, R.A.
Nov. 30, 1850.   Capt. W. H. Smyth.
Nov. 30, 1856.   Prof. W. H. Miller.
Nov. 30, 1873.   Prof. A. W. Williamson.
Nov. 30, 1889.   Sir A. Geikie.
Nov. 30, 1893.   Sir J. Lister, Bart.
Nov. 30, 1895.   Dr. E. Frankland.

NAMES OF PERSONS TO WHOM THE MEDALS OF THE ROYAL SOCIETY HAVE BEEN AWARDED.

COPLEY MEDAL.

1731. Stephen Gray.
1732. Stephen Gray.
1734. John Theophilus Desaguliers.
1736. John Theophilus Desaguliers.
1737. John Belchier.
1738. James Valoue.
1739. Stephen Hales.
1740. Alexander Stuart.
1741. John Theophilus Desaguliers.
1742. Captain Christopher Middleton.
1743. Abraham Trembley.
1744. Henry Baker.
1745. Sir William Watson.
1746. Benjamin Robins.
1747. Gowin Knight.
1748. Rev. James Bradley.
1749. John Harrison.
1750. George Edwards.
1751. John Canton.
1752. Sir John Pringle.
1753. Benjamin Franklin.
1754. William Lewis.
1755. John Huxham.
1757. Lord Charles Cavendish.
1758. John Dollond.
1759. John Smeaton.
1760. Benjamin Wilson.
1764. John Canton.
1766. William Brownrigg.
      Edward Delaval.
      Hon. Henry Cavendish.
1767. John Ellis.
1768. Peter Woulfe.
1769. William Hewson.
1770. Sir William Hamilton.
1771. Matthew Raper.
1772. Joseph Priestley.
1773. John Walsh.
1775. Rev. Nevil Maskelyne.
1776. Captain James Cook.
1777. John Mudge.
1778. Charles Hutton.
1780. Rev. Samuel Vince.
1781. Sir William Herschel.
1782. Richard Kirwan.
1783. John Goodricke.
      Thomas Hutchins.
1784. Edward Waring.
1785. Major-General William Roy.
1787. John Hunter.
1788. Sir Charles Blagden.
1789. William Morgan.
1791. James Rennell.
      John Andrew De Luc.
1792. Benjamin Count Rumford.
1794. Professor Volta.
1795. Jesse Ramsden.
1796. George Attwood.
1798. Sir George Shuckburgh Evelyn.
      Charles Hatchett.
1799. Rev. John Hellins.
1800. Edward Howard.
1801. Sir Astley Paston Cooper.
1802. William Hyde Wollaston.
1803. Richard Chenevix.
1804. Smithson Tennant.
1805. Sir Humphry Davy.
1806. Thomas Andrew Knight.
1807. Sir Everard Home.
1808. William Henry.
1809. Edward Troughton.
1811. Benjamin Collins Brodie.
1813. William Thomas Brande.
1814. James Ivory.
1815. David Brewster.
1817. Captain Henry Kater.
1818. Sir Robert Seppings.
1820. John Christian Oersted.
1821. Captain Edward Sabine.
      John Frederick William Herschel.
1822. Rev. William Buckland.
1823. John Pond.

Recipients of Medals. 215

1824. John Brinkley, Bishop of Cloyne.
1825. François Arago.
       Peter Barlow.
1826. Sir William South.
1827. William Prout.
       Captain Henry Foster.
1831. George Biddell Airy.
1832. Michael Faraday.
       Baron Simeon Denis Poisson.
1834. Giovanni Plana.
1835. William Snow Harris.
1836. Jöns Jacob Berzelius.
       Francis Kiernan.
1837. Antoine C. Becquerel.
1837. John Frederic Daniell.
1838. Karl Friedrich Gauss.
1838. Michael Faraday.
1839. Robert Brown.
1840. Justus Liebig.
       Jacques Charles François Sturm.
1841. George Simon Ohm.
1842. James MacCullagh.
1843. Jean Baptiste Dumas.
1844. Carlo Matteucci.
1845. Theodor Schwann.
1846. Urbain Jean Joseph Le Verrier.
1847. Sir John Frederick William Herschel.
1848. John Couch Adams.
1849. Sir Roderick Impey Murchison.
1850. Peter Andreas Hansen.
1851. Richard Owen.
1852. Baron Alexander von Humboldt.
1853. Heinrich Wilhelm Dove.
1854. Johannes Müller.
1855. Jean Bernard Leon Foucault.
1856. Henry Milne-Edwards.
1857. Michel Eugène Chevreul.
1858. Sir Charles Lyell.
1859. Wilhelm Eduard Weber.
1860. Robert Wilhelm Bunsen.
1861. Louis Agassiz.
1862. Thomas Graham.
1863. Rev. Adam Sedgwick.
1864. Charles Darwin.
1865. Michel Chasles.
1866. Julius Plücker.
1867. Karl Ernst von Baer.
1868. Sir Charles Wheatstone.
1869. Henri Victor Regnault.
1870. James Prescott Joule.
1871. Julius Robert Mayer.
1872. Friedrich Wöhler.
1873. Hermann Ludwig Ferdinand Helmholtz.
1874. Louis Pasteur.
1875. August Wilhelm Hofmann.
1876. Claude Bernard.
1877. James Dwight Dana.
1878. Jean Baptiste Boussingault.
1879. Rudolph J. E. Clausius.
1880. James Joseph Sylvester.
1881. Karl Adolph Würtz.
1882. Arthur Cayley.
1883. Sir William Thomson.
1884. Carl Ludwig.
1885. August Kekulé.
1886. Franz Ernst Neumann.
1887. Sir Joseph Dalton Hooker.
1888. Thomas Henry Huxley.
1889. Rev. George Salmon.
1890. Simon Newcomb.
1891. Stanislao Cannizzaro.
1892. Rudolf Virchow.
1893. Sir George Gabriel Stokes.
1894. Edward Frankland.
1895. Carl Weierstrass.
1896. Carl Gegenbaur.

RUMFORD MEDAL.

1800. Benjamin Count Rumford.
1804. John Leslie.
1806. William Murdock.
1810. Etienne Louis Malus.
1814. William Charles Wells.
1816. Sir Humphry Davy.
1818. David Brewster.
1824. Augustin Jean Fresnel.
1832. John Frederic Daniell.
1834. Macedonio Melloni.
1838. James David Forbes.
1840. Jean Baptiste Biot.
1842. Henry Fox Talbot.
1846. Michael Faraday.
1848. Henri Victor Regnault.
1850. François Jean Dominique Arago.
1852. George Gabriel Stokes.
1854. Neil Arnott.
1856. Louis Pasteur.
1858. Jules Jamin.
1860. James Clerk Maxwell.
1862. Gustav Robert Kirchhoff.
1864. John Tyndall.
1866. Armand Hippolyte Louis Fizeau.
1868. Balfour Stewart.
1870. Alfred Olivier Des Cloizeaux.
1872. Anders Jonas Ångström.
1874. Joseph Norman Lockyer.
1876. Pierre Jules César Janssen.
1878. Alfred Cornu.
1880. William Huggins.
1882. William de W. Abney.
1884. Tobias Robertus Thalén.
1886. Samuel Pierpont Langley.
1888. Pietro Tacchini.
1890. Heinrich Hertz.
1892. Nils C. Dunér.
1894. James Dewar.
1896. Philipp Lenard.
　　　Wilhelm Conrad Röntgen.

ROYAL MEDAL.

1826. John Dalton.
　　　James Ivory.
1827. Sir Humphry Davy.
　　　Friedrich Georg Wilhelm Struve.
1828. Johann Friedrich Encke.
　　　William Hyde Wollaston.
1829. Charles Bell.
　　　Eilhard Mitscherlich.
1830. David Brewster.
　　　Antoine Jerome Balard.
1833. Auguste Pyrame De Candolle.
　　　Sir John Frederick William Herschel.
1834. John William Lubbock.
　　　Charles Lyell.
1835. Michael Faraday.
　　　Sir William Rowan Hamilton.
1836. George Newport.
　　　Sir John F. W. Herschel.
1837. Rev. William Whewell.
1838. Thomas Graham.
　　　Henry Fox Talbot.
1839. James Ivory.
　　　Dr. Martin Barry.
1840. Sir John F. W. Herschel.
　　　Charles Wheatstone.
1841. Robert Kane.
　　　Eaton Hodgkinson.
1842. William Bowman.
　　　John Frederic Daniell.
1843. James David Forbes.
　　　Charles Wheatstone.
1844. Thomas Andrews.
　　　George Boole.
1845. George Biddell Airy.
　　　Thomas Snow Beck.
1846. Michael Faraday.
　　　Richard Owen.
1847. George Fownes.
　　　William Robert Grove.

1848. Thomas Galloway.
Charles James Hargreave.
1849. Colonel Edward Sabine.
Gideon A. Mantell.
1850. Benjamin Collins Brodie.
Thomas Graham.
1851. Earl of Rosse.
George Newport.
1852. James Prescott Joule.
Thomas Henry Huxley.
1853. Charles Darwin.
1854. August Wilhelm Hofmann.
Joseph Dalton Hooker.
1855. John Russel Hind.
John Obadiah Westwood.
1856. Sir John Richardson.
William Thomson.
1857. Edward Frankland.
John Lindley.
1858. Albany Hancock.
William Lassell.
1859. George Bentham.
Arthur Cayley.
1860. William Fairbairn.
Augustus Waller.
1861. William B. Carpenter.
James Joseph Sylvester.
1862. Rev. Thomas Romney Robinson.
Alexander William Williamson.
1863. Rev. Miles J. Berkeley.
John Peter Gassiot.
1864. Jacob Lockhart Clarke.
Warren De La Rue.
1865. Joseph Prestwich.
Archibald Smith.
1866. William Huggins.
William Kitchen Parker.
1867. John Bennet Lawes and Joseph Henry Gilbert.
Sir William Logan.
1868. Alfred Russel Wallace.
Rev. George Salmon.
1869. Sir Thomas Maclear.
Augustus Matthiessen.
1870. William Hallowes Miller.
Thomas Davidson.
1871. John Stenhouse.
George Busk.
1872. Thomas Anderson.

1872. Henry John Carter.
1873. George James Allman.
Henry Enfield Roscoe.
1874. Henry Clifton Sorby.
William Crawford Williamson.
1875. William Crookes.
Thomas Oldham.
1876. William Froude.
Sir C. Wyville Thomson.
1877. Frederick Augustus Abel.
Oswald Heer.
1878. John Allan Broun.
Albert C. L. G. Günther.
1879. William Henry Perkin.
Andrew Crombie Ramsay.
1880. Joseph Lister.
Andrew Noble.
1881. Francis Maitland Balfour.
John Hewitt Jellett.
1882. William Henry Flower.
Lord Rayleigh.
1883. Thomas Archer Hirst.
J. S. Burdon Sanderson.
1884. George Howard Darwin.
Daniel Oliver.
1885. David Edward Hughes.
Edwin Ray Lankester.
1886. Francis Galton.
Peter Guthrie Tait.
1887. Colonel Alexander Ross Clarke.
Henry Nottidge Moseley.
1888. Baron Ferdinand von Mueller.
Osborne Reynolds.
1889. Walter Holbrook Gaskell.
Thomas Edward Thorpe.
1890. David Ferrier.
John Hopkinson.
1891. Charles Lapworth.
Arthur William Rücker.
1892. John Newport Langley.
Rev. Charles Pritchard.
1893. Arthur Schuster.
Harry Marshall Ward.
1894. Victor Alexander Haden Horsley.
Joseph John Thomson.
1895. James Alfred Ewing.
John Murray.
1896. Charles Vernon Boys.
Sir Archibald Geikie.

DAVY MEDAL.

1877. Robert Wilhelm Bunsen.
Gustav Robert Kirchhoff.
1878. Louis Paul Cailletet.
Raoul Pictet.
1879. Paul Emile Lecoq de Boisbaudran.
1880. Charles Friedel.
1881. Adolf Baeyer.
1882. Dimitri Ivanovitch Mendeleeff.
Lothar Meyer.
1883. Marcellin Berthelot.
Julius Thomsen.
1884. Adolph Wilhelm Hermann Kolbe.
1885. Jean Servais Stas.
1886. Jean Charles Galissard de Marignac.
1887. John A. R. Newlands.
1888. William Crookes.
1889. William Henry Perkin.
1890. Emil Fischer.
1891. Victor Meyer.
1892. François Marie Raoult.
1893. J. H. van't Hoff.
J. A. Le Bel.
1894. Per Theodor Cleve.
1895. William Ramsay.
1896. Henri Moissan.

DARWIN MEDAL.

1890. Alfred Russel Wallace.
1892. Sir Joseph Dalton Hooker.
1894. Thomas Henry Huxley.
1896. Giovanni Battista Grassi.

INDEX.

	PAGE
Admission Fee, History of Statutes relating to the	112
Admission Money, original Regulation concerning	7
Admission of Fellows, History of Statutes relating to the	102
Admission of Strangers to Meetings, History of Statutes relating to	113
Airy, Sir George. Biographical Note	209
Amanuensis, Original Office of	6
Anatomical Experiments, the Society's right to demand Bodies of executed Criminals for	13
Annual Contributions, History of Statutes relating to the	112, 113
Apothecaries, Society of, Correspondence of the Royal Society with the, respecting the Botanic Gardens, Chelsea	154
Arms of the Royal Society	14
Arundel House, the Society meets at	13
Assistant Secretary, Office of, created	108, 112
Assistant to the Secretaries, use of the Title	112
Bakerian Lecture Fund, History of the	123
Banks, Sir Joseph. Biographical Note	208
Benefactors of the Society, early Registration of	115
—— List of	115
Bodies of executed Criminals, the Society's right to demand for Dissection	13
Botanic Gardens, Chelsea, History of the	153
—— Relation of the Royal Society to the	153
Brady Library Fund, History of the	131
Brodie, Sir Benjamin. Biographical Note	209
Brouncker, William, Lord Viscount, early connection with the Society	3, 5, 8, 15
—— Biographical Note	205
Buchanan Medal Fund, History of the	131
Burlington House, the Society moves to	13
Burrow, James. Biographical Note	207
Busts in the Apartments of the Society, List of	175
Cambridge University, Professorship at, in the election of which the Society is represented	135
Carbery, John, Earl of. Biographical Note	206
Catalogue of Scientific Papers, History of the	166
Charles II approves the Design of the Society	4
—— becomes a Member of the Society	7
—— grants a Charter of Incorporation	7
—— gives the Society a Mace	14
—— Experiments instituted at the Instigation of	17
—— Reconveyance to, of the three Closes granted by the Third Charter	98

INDEX.

	PAGE
Charter of Incorporation granted by Charles II	7
—— read before the Society	7
—— a second, granted	7
—— a third, granted	7
—— Latin Text of the First	19
—— English Translation of the First	31
—— Latin Text of the Second	44
—— English Translation of the Second	58
—— Latin Text of the Third	73
—— English Translation of the Third	85
—— Note to the Third	98
Charter-book, Contents of the	111
Chelsea Gardens. See Botanic Gardens, Chelsea.	
Clerk, History of the Statutes relating to the	108
—— Office of, abolished	112
Committee of Papers. See Papers.	
Committees, List of, in Special Branches of Science, appointed in 1664	18
—— Sectional, Institution of	114
Composition Fee, History of Statutes relating to the	106, 112
Copley Medal, Names of Persons to whom the, has been awarded	214
—— Fund, History of the	123
Correspondence, Foreign, of the Society in its early days	16
Council. See President and Council.	
—— and Officers, History of Statutes relating to the Election of	103, 111, 112
Crane Court, a House in, purchased for the Society	13
Croonian Lecture Fund, History of the	126
Curators of Experiments	6
—— to the Society, Account of early	17
Darwin Medal, Names of Persons to whom the, has been awarded	218
—— Memorial Fund, History of the	129
Davy, Sir Humphry. Biographical Note	208
—— Medal Fund, History of the	128
—— —— Names of Persons to whom the, has been awarded	218
Donation Fund, History of the	121
Election of Council and Officers, History of Statutes relating to the	103, 112
—— of Fellows, Original Regulations concerning	6
—— of Fellows, History of Statutes relating to the	100, 105, 112, 113
—— of Foreign Members, History of Statutes relating to the	112
Experiments, a feature of the Society's early meetings	16
Fee Reduction Fund, History of the	129
Fellows, Admission of, History of Statutes relating to the	102
Fellows, Election of, History of Statutes relating to the	100, 105, 112, 113
Fellows, Payments by, History of Statutes relating to	105
Folkes, Martin. Biographical note	207
Foreign Members, History of Statutes relating to	106, 111, 112, 113
—— Number of, limited to fifty	111
—— Secretaries of the Society, List of the	213
—— Secretary, History of Statutes relating to the	111

INDEX.

	PAGE
Foundation of the Royal Society, some account of the	1
Functions, Public, performed by the Society	136
Gassiot Trust, History of the	128
Gilbert, Davies. Biographical Note	208
Government Fund of £4,000, History of the	159
—— Grant for Scientific Investigations, History of the	158
—— —— of £1,000, History of the	158
—— —— of £4,000, History of the	161
Greenwich Observatory, Board of Visitors to	137
—— —— Connection of the Royal Society with	136
Gresham College	2, 3, 7
Gunning Fund, History of the	131
Halifax, Earl of. See Montague.	
Handley Fund, History of the	128
Historical Relics in the Possession of the Society	171
History of the Royal Society, Some Account of the Foundation and Early	1
—— of the Statutes, a Note on the	100
Hooke, Robert, an Original Member of the Society	9
—— his 'Micrographia' published	11
—— his 'Philosophical Collections' published	12 and footnote
—— appointed Curator	17
Hooker, Sir Joseph. Biographical Note	210
Hoskins, Sir John, Early Connection with the Society	9
—— Biographical Note	205
House-keeper, History of the Statutes relating to the	108
Howard, Henry. See Norfolk.	
Huxley, Thomas Henry. Biographical Note	210
Institutions upon which the Society is represented	135
Instruments in the Possession of the Society	171
Invisible College, The	3
Jodrell Fund, History of the	129
Joule Memorial Fund, History of the	130
Journal-book of the Society commenced	3
Keck Bequest, History of the	125
—— —— Proceeds of, how applied	111
Keeper of the Repository, History of the Statutes relating to the	108
Kelvin, Lord. Biographical Note	210
Kew Committee, List of the	138
—— Observatory, Connection of the Royal Society with	138
—— —— Description of the	139
—— —— History of the	137
—— —— Relation of the, to the Meteorological Office	139
Lawes Agricultural Trust, History of the	155
—— —— —— Committee, List of the	155

INDEX.

	PAGE
Letter-books of the Society	16
Librarian, History of the Statutes relating to the	108
Library, History of the	168
—— History of Statutes relating to the	110, 112, 113
License for purchasing in Mortmain, Text of the Society's	97
Lister, Lord. Biographical note	211
Macclesfield, George, Earl of. Biographical note	207
Mace of the Royal Society	14
Manuscripts in the possession of the Society	170
Medals in the possession of the Society, Catalogue of the	183
—— of the Royal Society, Names of persons to whom the, have been awarded	214
Meetings of the Society, character of the early, exemplified	15
—— —— where formerly held	1, 3, 7, 13
—— —— when formerly held	18, 109, 112
—— —— History of the Statutes relating to the	109, 112, 114
—— —— History of Statutes relating to hour of	113
—— —— History of Statutes relating to Admission of Strangers to	110
Members of the Society, original, chosen by the Council under the Second Charter	8
Meteorological Council, Connection of the Royal Society with the	136
—— —— List of the	136
—— Office, Relation of the, to Kew Observatory	139
Montague, Charles. Biographical note	206
Mortmain, Text of the Society's License for purchasing in	97
Morton, James, Earl of. Biographical note	207
Newton, Sir Isaac, his 'Principia' published	12 (footnote)
—— President of the Society. Biographical Note	206
—— Gifts from, to the Society	116
—— Relics of, in the possession of the Society	171
Norfolk, Henry Howard, afterwards Duke of, places rooms at the disposal of the Society	13, 14
Northampton, the Marquis of. Biographical note	209
Obligation, original, signed by Members	5
Officers and Council, History of Statutes relating to the election of	103, 111, 112
Officers of the Society, History of Statutes relating to the	108
—— —— Original regulations concerning the	6
Oldenburg, Henry, appointed Secretary	8
—— imprisoned in the Tower	13
Operator, original office of	6
Ordinary Meetings. See Meetings.	
Oxford Meetings for "Philosophical Enquiries"	2
—— the Philosophical Society of	3
—— University, Professorships at, in the election of which the Royal Society is represented	135
Papers, Committee of, History of Regulations for the	104, 110
Payments by Fellows, History of the Statutes relating to	105

INDEX.

	PAGE
Pembroke, Thomas, Earl of. Biographical Note	206
Pepys, Samuel, a Benefactor of the Society	116
—— Biographical Note	205
Philosophical Society of Oxford, the	3
"Philosophical Transactions," History of the	164
—— —— History of Statutes relating to the	103, 110
—— —— origin of the	11
Physick Garden. See Botanic Gardens, Chelsea.	
Portraits and Busts in the Apartments of the Society	175
President, Original Regulations concerning the	6
—— and Council, the list of the, named by the Second Charter	7
—— ——, their constitution under the Charters	10
Presidents of the Society, List of, with Biographical Notes	205
Pringle, Sir John. Biographical Note	207
Privileged Class, History of Statutes relating to the Election of Members of the	113
"Proceedings" of the Society, History of the	165
Public Functions performed by the Royal Society	136
—— Schools, Representatives of the Royal Society upon the Governing Bodies of	135
Publications, early, of the Society	11
—— of the Society, History of the	164
—— —— History of Statutes relating to the	110
Records of the Society, History of Statutes relating to the	110
Referees, History of Regulations relating to	104
Register of Fellows, its contents	111 (footnote)
Registrar, original Office of	6
Relics in the possession of the Society	171
Repository, Office of Keeper of the, established	108
Representatives of the Society upon various Institutions	135
Rosse, Earl of. Biographical Note	209
Rothamsted Experimental Station, History of the	155
Royal Medal, Names of Persons to whom the, has been awarded	216
—— Medals, History of the	132
Royal Observatory, Greenwich, Connection of the Royal Society with the	136
—— —— Board of Visitors to the	137
Royal Society, Arms of the	14
—— —— Benefactors of the	115
—— —— Charters of the	19
—— —— Foreign Secretaries of the	213
—— —— Foundation and Early History of the	1
—— —— Library of the	168
—— —— Medals of the, Names of those who have received	214
—— —— Original Members of the	8
—— —— Presidents of the	205
—— —— Public Functions performed by the	136
—— —— Publications of the	164
—— —— Representatives of the, upon various Institutions	135
—— —— Secretaries of the	211
—— —— Statutes of the, Note on the History of the	100

INDEX.

	PAGE
Royal Society, Treasurers of the	211
—— —— Trusts of the	120
Rumford Fund, History of the	123
—— Medal, Names of Persons to whom the, has been awarded	216
Sabine, Sir Edward. Biographical Note	209
Scientific Relief Fund, History of the	120
Secretaries of the Society, List of the	211
—— Foreign, of the Society, List of the	213
Sectional Committees, Institution of	114
Sloane, Sir Hans. Biographical Note	206
Somers, John, Lord. Biographical Note	206
Somerset House, the Society moves to	13
Southwell, Sir Robert. Biographical Note	206
Spottiswoode, William. Biographical Note	210
Standard Weights and Measures, the Royal Society custodians of	137
Statutes, the original	5
—— History of the, from 1663 to 1752	100
—— —— from 1752 to 1776	105
—— —— from 1776 to 1847	111
Statutes made and changed by the President and Council alone	11
—— of the Society, a Note on the History of the	100
Stokes, Sir G. G. Biographical Note	210
Strangers, History of the Statutes relating to the Admission of, to Meetings	110, 113
Sussex, the Duke of. Biographical Note	208
Treasurer, original Regulations concerning the	6
Treasurers of the Society, List of the	211
Trusts of the Society	120
Universities, Representatives of the Society at the	135
Visitors to the Meetings. See Strangers.	
Wallis, Dr. John, his account of the Foundation of the Royal Society	1
Weights and Measures, Standard, the Royal Society custodians of	137
West, James. Biographical Note	207
Williamson, Sir Joseph, early connection with the Society	10
—— Biographical Note	205
Wintringham Fund, History of the	125
Wollaston, William Hyde. Biographical Note	208
Works, early, published by the Royal Society	11
Wren, Sir Christopher, early connection with the Society	3, 10, 15
—— Biographical Note	205
Wrottesley, Lord. Biographical Note	209
Wyche, Sir Cyril, early connection with the Society	10
—— Biographical Note	205

HARRISON AND SONS, PRINTERS IN ORDINARY TO HER MAJESTY, ST. MARTIN'S LANE.

www.ingramcontent.com/pod-product-compliance
Lightning Source LLC
Chambersburg PA
CBHW021809230426
43669CB00008B/685